T0310009

Advanced Fixed Income Analytics

Wesley Phoa, Ph.D.
Vice President, Research
Capital Management Sciences

With contributions from
Michael Shearer, Ph.D.
Vice President, Quantitative Research
Capital Management Sciences

Published by Frank J. Fabozzi Associates

To Margaret Anne Morgan

ISBN: 1-883249-34-1

Printed in the United States of America

Table of Contents

Preface

This book provides an accessible and practical introduction to a number of advanced topics in fixed income theory. It assumes familiarity with the most basic concepts in bond markets — for example, effective duration and convexity, option pricing with the Black-Scholes model, the concept of option-adjusted spread, and mortgage prepayments — together with some practical experience in analyzing bond portfolios.

It is difficult for practitioners to go beyond these fundamentals. Much of the academic literature is extremely technical, and aimed mainly at specialists; and much of it is, in any case, out of touch with the realities of bond markets. On the other hand, there are many topics of critical importance to practitioners which are largely ignored by academics; and even on more fashionable topics such as term structure theory, there is a dearth of useful empirical research, leaving practitioners unsure as to how the theory is applied in the real world.

The purpose of this book, therefore, is twofold. First, it gives an intuitive account of some quite technical topics, stripping away the mathematics to reveal what I believe are the basic concepts. This should give readers the necessary background to evaluate, in a critical and informed way, the models and research which software vendors, brokers, analysts, and academics promote. The exposition makes use of some very useful rules of thumb which are widely relied upon by practitioners, but not usually considered respectable enough to publish. It also relies a great deal on evidence from the markets.

Second, this book gives an introduction to some advanced topics which have considerable market relevance, but which have not been dealt with adequately in the literature, and which are very often glossed over by the "experts." The main focus here is on the concepts and the empirical data. Here "empirical data" does not mean simply market data such as historical yields and volatilities; it also includes the underlying events which explain the behavior of bond yields and implied volatilities. I hope this will help readers to make a connection between the theoretical topics covered and their own market experience.

I have tried to make the book as practical as possible. A reader who wants to see detailed mathematical derivations, or rigorous economic analysis, must go elsewhere. There is a very brief list of useful references at the end of each chapter. Also, working on the assumption that readers are bond market practitioners rather than academics, I have cited papers published in *The Journal of Fixed Income* where possible, mainly for ease of reference.

There is nothing comprehensive or definitive about this book. It would have been impossible to write something useful about every important subject in the domestic bond markets. Instead, I have structured the book around a selection of related topics, in the hope of conveying a general approach or point of view which will be useful in other situations. There are also quite a few statements which are controversial, or at least personal, and most readers will find plenty of things to disagree with. I would like to think that this book will leave readers unsatisfied, and encourage them to do some experimentation and empirical research of their own.

SUMMARY

Chapter 1 is about the foundations of interest rate risk: the dynamics of the yield curve. We describe the main economic factors that cause shifts in the yield curve, and also presents an important, but sometimes misused, statistical tool for identifying fundamental yield curve shifts — principal component analysis. This analysis has subtle shortcomings, and we therefore supplement it with some additional theoretical and empirical results — in particular, a closer examination of how the short end of the yield curve behaves. The chapter also includes a practical discussion of key rate durations, including a new application.

Chapter 2 discusses term structure models for option valuation, drawing on some of the results in Chapter 1. After reviewing the OTC option market and the information it can provide, we describe the main families of interest rate models. Topics discussed include spot rate versus Heath-Jarrow-Morton models; calibration; normal, lognormal, and square root interest rate processes; and, the volatility smile. We then discuss one-factor versus multi-factor models, with examples. Finally, there is a description of the relative merits of different implementations (e.g. trees, finite differences, and Monte Carlo methods). This is probably the most difficult chapter — even though the mathematical derivations are omitted — but fortunately it is not a prerequisite for the remaining chapters.

Chapter 3 is about inflation-indexed bonds. We begin by investigating the concept of real yield, and explaining why — contrary to some often-repeated claims — real yields are volatile. We also discuss the implications for portfolio risk management, and some subtleties in how to interpret the duration of an inflation-indexed bond. There is a brief sketch of the interaction between inflation risk and tax risk. We also describe some potentially discouraging results about inflation-linked bonds in an asset allocation context. The final topic is more advanced. We show how to use real and nominal bond yields to derive a term structure of implied "market" inflation forecasts as well as a term structure of real yields, and how to compare this to economists' forecasts. The analysis is more delicate than one might expect. This analysis has potential applications to liability management, asset valuation, and project finance.

Chapter 4 discusses some little-known results which affect the analysis of long bonds. First we discuss the convexity bias, which explains the typical downward slope of the yield curve from 20 to 30 years. Some methods are presented for analyzing this convexity bias empirically, with interesting results. Next, we describe some very remarkable theoretical results about very long bond yields due to Dybvig and others. Finally, we present some very long-term historical studies of inflation and real bond returns, together with a theoretical account of very long cycles in capitalist accumulation. This work has important theoretical implications for the performance of century bonds and inflation-linked bonds.

Chapter 5 is about prepayment analysis and model risk. Our first goal is to explain precisely what the objectives of prepayment modeling are, and how one goes about constructing, fitting, and evaluating a prepayment model. There is a surprising amount of confusion on this subject. Then there is a detailed discussion of prepayment model risk, which explains why mortgage-backed securities cannot simply be regarded as interest rate derivatives. We describe how model risk arises and suggest ways to quantify it.

Chapter 6 describes some risk measures which are not related to yield curve risk; it thus complements Chapter 1, and draws on material in Chapter 5. The chapter begins with a review of the concept of option-adjusted spread (OAS), how to interpret it, and why it is problematic. We then discuss various ways to measure spread risk, volatility risk, and prepayment model risk. We also discuss the relationship between OAS and zero volatility spread (ZVO). Some care must be taken in interpreting both of these concepts. A long section describes some applications to risk/return analysis and trading strategies for mortgage-backed securities. Finally, an appendix presents a simple model of default risk and theoretical default spreads, and uses it to draw some interesting conclusions about the theoretical behavior of corporate spreads.

Chapter 7 is much briefer and more discursive than the preceding chapters. It begins with an overview of the problem of portfolio risk management, and attempts to provide a framework within which one can organize the multiplicity of different risk measurement tools which have been proposed. It then discusses performance attribution and its role in the risk management process. We describe how to use the results of a performance attribution system — which is not obvious — and how to compare different performance attribution frameworks.

ACKNOWLEDGMENTS

As well as co-authoring the sections on key rate durations and one-factor versus two-factor models, Mike Shearer at CMS has played an invaluable role in many other ways. My other colleagues at CMS have all made useful contributions. In particular, I have had many fruitful discussions with Terence Nercessian (my regular collaborator on prepayment analysis), Bill Burns (who edits most of my research papers), Brig Belvin, Agnes Green, and Jim Kaplan. I have also benefited from the chance to talk to many BondEdge clients, whom I must thank collectively. The input of our clients and their consultants at CMS has been crucial.

Most of the work in this book was originally reported in an ongoing series of CMS research reports distributed to BondEdge clients, CMS *On The Edge* newsletter columns, talks at various industry conferences, or columns written for *Financial Trader* magazine. I would like to thank Laurie Adami at CMS for initiating and supporting this work.

It is especially important that I acknowledge the influence of Richard Mason, my former mentor at Deutsche Morgan Grenfell, Sydney. Although I have not had access to the theoretical details of his approach to analyzing fixed income markets, his ideas have helped shape this book in many ways. And while I have tried to acknowledge these ideas explicitly wherever they are used — particularly in Chapter 3 and parts of Chapters 1 and 4 — his point of view pervades the whole text.

Any errors in this book are entirely my responsibility. In fact, all the errors were inserted deliberately, so that readers could test their understanding by attempting to detect them.

Chapter 1

An Empirical Analysis of Yield Curve Dynamics

FUNDAMENTAL FACTORS DRIVING THE EVOLUTION OF THE YIELD CURVE

Bond yields do not move around in a completely uncorrelated fashion. If they did, it would be impossible to analyze the interest rate risk of a bond portfolio in any meaningful way; even the notion of portfolio duration would be meaningless. Thus, in order to begin analyzing a bond portfolio, we need to make some assumption about the relationship between shifts in bond yields of different maturities. For example, we might try to identify the most important kinds of yield curve shifts that can occur.

The simplest possible assumption is that all Treasury yields always move in parallel: for example, if the 30-year Treasury yield rises by 10 bp, then the 10-, 5-, and 2-year Treasury yields must also rise by 10 bp. Thus, all Treasury yields are perfectly correlated, and equally volatile. Under this assumption, any two Treasury bond portfolios with the same duration are equivalent. The truth is obviously somewhat more complicated than this: bond yields need not always move in parallel, so there can be a big difference between two portfolios with the same duration. For example, if one has more of a barbell profile than the other, it will outperform if the yield curve flattens. There is more to yield curve risk than duration.

We need to find some way of understanding the yield curve which recognizes that different kinds of yield curve shifts occur, and which fits them into some systematic framework. There are at least four approaches that we could take:

1. We could make some arbitrary set of assumptions based purely on *intuition*; this intuition would presumably be derived from market experience.
2. We could devise a plausible *mathematical* model of the yield curve and derive the possible yield curve shifts that could occur if the model happened to conform to reality.
3. We could carry out an *economic* analysis of how investor expectations about economic fundamentals should drive bond yields and then identify the different kinds of shifts in the yield curve which would result from changes in economic expectations.

4. We could look at historical shifts in Treasury bond yields and apply some *statistical* method to identify the different basic kinds of yield curve shifts that have occurred in the past.

All four methods have pitfalls. Our intuitions might be wrong; there is no guarantee that a mathematical model, no matter how elegant, will be realistic; economic arguments might be fallacious, or might overlook relevant non-economic factors; and statistical methods often give spurious results, or even inconsistent results depending on what data is used.

In the first half of this chapter, we will adopt the following strategy. First, recognizing that investors' economic expectations do play a large part in determining bond yields, we construct an informal economic argument which tells us what the yield curve should look like and what kind of important yield curve shifts should be possible. Next, we carry out a statistical analysis of historical Treasury bond yields, using our economic conclusions to cross-check the results and to help determine which of these results are meaningful. Since we are unlikely to detect all relevant phenomena if we only use a single method of analysis, we will also try to analyze the data in alternative ways. Our results will be useful in Chapter 2, where we examine a variety of mathematical term structure models.

Economic versus Non-Economic Factors in Yield Curve Dynamics

Bond yields are determined by investor expectations. Although Keynes was the first to recognize this fact and fully exploit its consequences, we will see in Chapter 4 that this has been true for centuries. The obvious questions, then, are: What expectations are relevant? What is the precise relationship between these expectations — which are not directly observable — and observed bond yields? And finally, how does this help us understand the dynamics of the yield curve?

Writing during the Depression, Keynes focused on expectations about future economic growth, demand, and output, and also about the desire for liquidity arising from uncertainty about the future — a more subtle form of expectation. Since the 1970s, it has been more fashionable to focus on expectations about future inflation, although the old Keynesian ideas have recently been revived in an attempt to understand the stagnant Japanese economy. Economic fashions change, and it would certainly be dangerous to commit ourselves to any school of economic thought.

We therefore take a straightforward, agnostic approach and simply say that forward interest rates, and thus current bond yields, are broadly determined by investors' expectations about:

1. *real interest rates*, which are determined by expected real returns on capital, and
2. *inflation*, i.e., changes in the "price level" — however one wants to define that term.

Exhibit 1-1: How Expectations Determine Expected Future Interest Rates

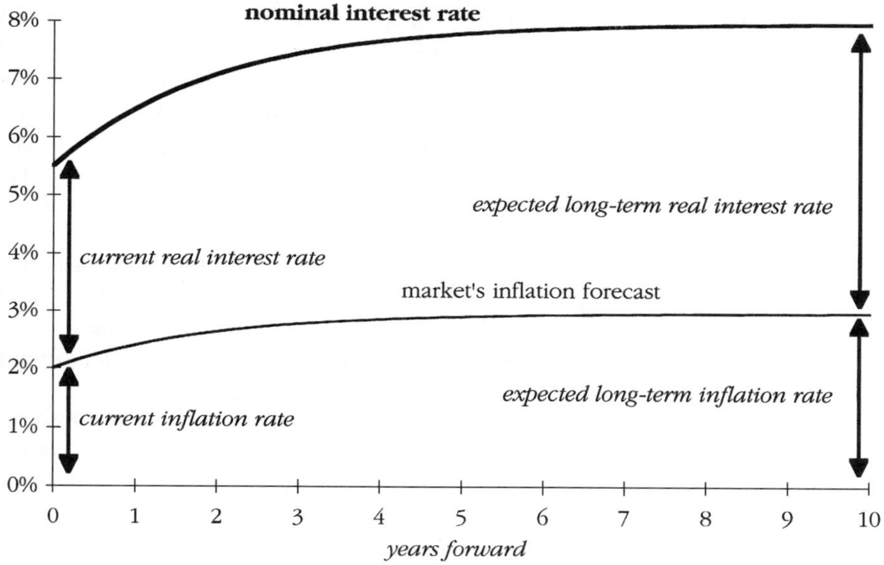

Note that investors would not assume that either the real interest rate or inflation will remain constant; both might be expected to rise or fall over time. However, given the lack of ability to make detailed forecasts more than one or two years forward, investors would probably assume that beyond this time horizon, both real rates and inflation tend to some long-term "equilibrium" levels when forming their expectations. The situation is pictured in Exhibit 1-1.

The concept of the real interest rate, and the various factors that affect real interest rates in practice, are discussed further in Chapter 3; for the moment, we point out that it roughly corresponds to the real growth rate of the economy, or the real growth in output. Also, we have not spelled out the precise relationship between expected future interest rates and current bond yields, but we assume that there is a fixed relationship between expected future interest rates and current forward rates; and of course, knowing the current forward curve is the same as knowing current bond yields. The relationship between expected future rates and forward rates actually depends on expected volatility — i.e., on investor uncertainty — and is discussed more rigorously in Chapters 2 and 4; here, we simply assume that when expected future rates move, forward rates move by the same amount. This turns out to be a reasonable assumption except at extremely long forward dates (see Chapter 4).

An example may help. In our framework, the long bond yield is determined by the expected long-term real interest rate plus the expected long-term inflation rate. In the late 1980s and early 1990s, Australian long bond yields were largely driven by fluctuations in the current account deficit, which affects expectations about real interest rates (see Chapter 3). By contrast, from 1994 onwards, Australian long bond yields have more often been driven by fluctuations in the CPI, which affect investor expectations about inflation.

In the context of the U.S. bond markets, Frankel warned against focusing solely on inflationary expectations and emphasized the fact that — contrary to Fama's assertion in 1975 — real interest rates are not constant: e.g., "when nominal interest rates rose sharply at the beginning of [the 1980s], it was not because expected inflation was rising. Rather contraction of monetary policy had succeeded in raising the real interest rate."

Note that in our framework, the *slope* of the yield curve has a natural interpretation: if investors believe that real interest rates or inflation will rise from their current levels, the curve will slope upwards, while if investors believe that they will fall, it will slope downwards. That is, the yield curve has a slope because the economy is not generally believed to be in static equilibrium.

The other reason that the yield curve might slope upwards is that investors demand a risk premium for holding bonds, which rises with maturity. Empirical studies have shown that, while there does appear to be a risk premium for bonds versus Treasury bills, beyond about two years the risk premium is more or less independent of maturity — i.e., it is a general bond market risk premium or liquidity premium versus the short term money market, rather than a duration risk premium (see Ilmanen or Frankel for an economist's view). Thus, this risk premium mainly affects the slope of the short end of the yield curve.

In fact, at the short end — maturities of less than two years — the behavior of the curve is more complex anyway, since short-term interest rates can depend on more detailed economic forecasts and predictions about monetary policy. We will return to this point later in the chapter.

The Shape of the Yield Curve

Now that we have a picture of what kinds of economic expectations determine bond yields, we can go on to investigate how changes in economic expectations cause shifts in the yield curve. It is convenient to use a simple economic model of the yield curve originally proposed by Frankel.

Let i_0 be the current short-term nominal interest rate, let π^e be the expected long term inflation rate and let r^e be the expected long-term real interest rate; then, by definition, the expected long-term nominal interest rate is $\pi^e + r^e$. It is usually the case that $i_0 \neq \pi^e + r^e$, but it seems reasonable to assume that investors expect the future interest rate i to approach $\pi^e + r^e$ as time passes. In fact, under some realistic economic assumptions, one can show that there is a constant δ such that:

$$\frac{di}{dt} = -\delta(i - \pi^e - r^e)$$

Exhibit 1-2: A Macroeconomic Model of Adjustment in the Price Level and Interest Rates

---

Make the following definitions:

i	short-term nominal interest rate
π^e	expected long-term inflation rate
r^e	expected long-term real interest rate
y	log of output
$\bar{y}$	log of normal or potential output
m	log of the money supply
p	log of the price level
$\gamma, \phi, \lambda, \rho$	constant rate of adjustment/elasticity parameters

The model consists of the following assumptions:

The output gap is related to the current real interest rate through investment demand:

$$y - \bar{y} = -\gamma(i - \pi^e - r^e)$$

Real money demand depends positively on income and negatively on the interest rate:

$$m - p = \phi y - \lambda i$$

Price changes are determined by excess demand and expected long-term inflation:

$$\frac{dp}{dt} = \rho(y - \bar{y}) + \pi^e$$

From these equations, Frankel derived the following formula for the expected rate of change of the interest rate:

$$\frac{di}{dt} = -\delta(i - \pi^e - r^e), \text{ where } \delta = \frac{\rho\gamma}{\phi\gamma + \lambda}$$

The macroeconomic model which Frankel used to derive this relationship is shown in Exhibit 1-2. However, the same relationship appears to hold in a fairly wide variety of models of the economy, including ones which permit random shocks to the level and trend of the money supply. Thus the conclusion is quite general.

The basic intuition is that interest rates take time to adjust to their expected long-term level because prices are sticky. Anyway, given i_0, the current short-term interest rate, it is easy to determine i_t, the expected short-term interest rate at time t:

$$i_t = (1 - \exp(-\delta t))(\pi^e + r^e) + \exp(-\delta t)i_0$$

It is convenient to write this in the form:

$$i_t = (\pi^e + r^e) - \exp(-\delta t)((\pi^e + r^e) - i_0)$$

That is, a rational investor would expect the short-term interest rate to asymptotically approach some long-term equilibrium level $\pi^e + r^e$, and the expected path of future short-term rates can be described by an exponential curve. As we will observe in Chapter 2, there are other ways to arrive at this conclusion.

The economic model need not be "true" for this description of expected interest rates to hold; all we need to assume is that investors implicitly — though perhaps incorrectly — have this kind of economic model in mind when forming expectations about future interest rates. This seems to be a reasonable assumption, given the plausibility of the model and the generality of its assumptions.

The coefficients in this equation are not directly observable, but could be estimated from the current yield curve: the term $\pi^e + r^e$ is the expected long-term nominal interest rate in equilibrium, which will be reflected in current long bond yields, while the term $(\pi^e + r^e) - i_0$ is the spread between current nominal rates and the long-term equilibrium rate, which will be reflected in the slope of the yield curve. For further information on estimating the model, see Chapter 4.

The correct interpretation of the current short term nominal interest rate i_0 is somewhat more subtle than it appears. The model describes an economy which, while not static — adjustment in interest rates takes time because prices are sticky — is moving along an equilibrium path towards a long-term steady state. This is a reasonable way to derive a medium- or long-term economic forecast, say more than two years out. In the near term, however, we know that the economy can behave in a more complex way, and we can make much more detailed forecasts about the economy which do not rely on a simple equilibrium model; the same applies to interest rates in the near term.

Thus it would be incorrect to identify i_0 with an actual current short-term interest rate, e.g., the Fed Funds rate or the 3-month T-bill yield. A more appropriate interpretation, due to Mason, is as follows: i_0 is "extrapolated back" from the medium- to long-term equilibrium interest rate forecasts embodied in the current yield curve; that is, it is what the current short-term interest rate would have to be for the economy to be currently in equilibrium, i.e., to currently conform to the model. In a sense, i_0 is where the bond market thinks short-term interest rates *should* be, based on the economic fundamentals — and this need not coincide with their actual levels, particularly if there is disagreement between the Fed and the markets.

Although the interpretation seems odd at first, it is suggestive. It implies that when attempting to estimate the model, we can and should exclude money market yields from the estimation process and use only bond yields. It also tells us that any information about yield curve shifts that the model gives us will apply to bond yields, not to money market yields.

As there are some practical problems that arise when estimating the model, it is convenient to return to this topic in Chapter 4. For the present we point out that the model predicts three kinds of observable shifts in the yield curve:

1. *level shifts*, which result from changes in the expected long-term rate $\pi^e + r^e$;
2. *slope shifts*, which result from changes in i_0, or rather $(\pi^e + r^e) - i_0$; and,
3. *"curvature shifts,"* which result from changes in δ.

In other words, level shifts arise from changes in long-term expectations; slope shifts arise from changes in expectations about monetary policy in the near term; and "curvature shifts" theoretically occur when investors believe that there has been a secular change in the economy, e.g., which makes prices inherently more sticky. The model implicitly predicts that while level shifts and slope shifts can occur all the time, "curvature shifts" should be much rarer. In fact, in the real world it is unlikely that curvature shifts occur for the economic reasons suggested by the model; non-economic explanations, such as supply/demand imbalances at particular points on the yield curve, are a more plausible explanation for curvature changes. We will discuss curvature shifts further below, but for the moment we concentrate on level shifts and slope shifts.

The idea of focusing on a "long rate" and a "spread" is far from new, and all we have done here is given some theoretical justification for it. Note that so far, we have no reason to assume that level shifts and slope shifts, of the form implied by the model, should be uncorrelated. In fact, the correlation would depend on investors' views about the nature of monetary policy. If the Fed were generally regarded as being slow to move, then a rise in long term inflation or real rate expectations would generally be accompanied by a steepening in the yield curve, while a fall in long bond yields would generally be accompanied by a flattening; thus the correlation would be positive. Exhibit 4-7 shows a graph of actual historical correlations in the U.S. market.

The model makes an interesting prediction about slope shifts. In periods when δ is stable, all slope shifts should follow the same pattern: slope shifts always "look the same," except for a scaling factor. In other words, on different days one might observe slope shifts which look like any of the dotted lines in Exhibit 1-3, but not like the thin solid line. (The latter kind of shift is possible, but would have to be interpreted as a slope shift plus a curvature shift.) This prediction is in fact borne out by the results of the estimation data described in Chapter 4; when δ is stable, which is most of the time, slope shifts do tend to look the same.

A Digression on Expectations Hypotheses

Our next task is to carry out a statistical analysis of historical shifts in bond yields. To do this, we first need to determine whether bond yields are subject to any systematic drift, and if they are, we need to filter out this drift. It turns out that bond yields do tend to drift in the direction implied by their forward yields. To explain the nature of this "drift along the forwards" we describe, briefly, some versions of the expectations hypothesis, and in particular the "local expectations hypothesis," which will turn out to be a useful technical tool in Chapter 2. However, the following discussion is not really necessary for understanding the rest of the chapter, and the casual reader may therefore wish to skip to the next sub-section.

Our starting point is the following question: How does the market *expect* the yield curve to evolve in the future? The key observation that (unless the yield curve is flat), *the market expects some drift in yields: assuming an unchanged yield curve for scenario analysis is not a neutral assumption.*

To see this, consider the solid line in Exhibit 1-4. It shows the 12-month total return from a zero coupon, versus the initial bond maturity, based on U.S. Treasury yields on 9/30/96 and assuming that the yield curve (i.e., CMT yields) remains unchanged for the whole 12-month period.

The graph shows that, assuming an unchanged yield curve, bonds maturing in 10 years or more will outperform shorter bonds by around 100 bp. This will always be the case with an upward-sloping yield curve: if the curve is expected to remain unchanged, the yield on any specific physical bond is expected to fall, resulting in a price effect which is higher for longer bonds. Since long bonds do not in fact systematically outperform shorter bonds, it seems very unlikely that investors expect the yield curve to remain unchanged. The assumption gives rise to an obvious arbitrage.

Exhibit 1-3: Typical Yield Curve Slope Shifts and an Atypical Slope Shift

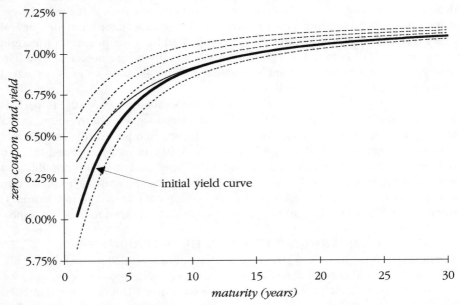

Exhibit 1-4: 12-Month Return from Zero Coupon Bonds if Curve Remains Unchanged

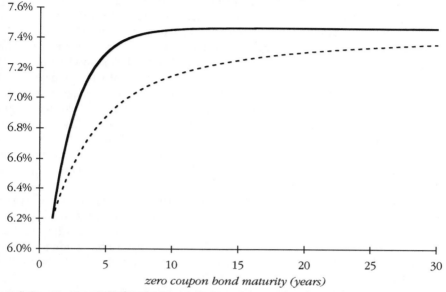

zero coupon bond maturity (years)

What about assuming that the yield on each physical bond remains the same? The dotted line in Exhibit 1-4 shows 12-month returns from zero coupon bonds under this assumption. Again, long bonds outperform short bonds by around 100 bp, although one now has to own 30-year bonds to capture this outperformance. Thus it also seems very unlikely that investors expect yields on physical bonds to remain unchanged.

It is tempting to assume that the expected yield on any bond at some future date is equal to its current forward yield to that date. This is called the *unbiased expectations hypothesis*, or "UEH." Running a 12-month scenario analysis with an assumed future yield curve based on current forward yields, we obviously find that the return on any bond is equal to the 12-month riskless rate used to compute the forward yields. There is no apparent arbitrage, and this makes UEH look plausible.

Unfortunately, if we assume UEH, then long bonds will still tend to outperform shorter bonds. This is because, as random shifts in the yield curve occur, an investor holding long bonds will tend to benefit from their higher convexity. A single scenario analysis does not capture this convexity effect. To take a very simple example, suppose that the yield curve is currently flat, with all bond yields equal to 6%. Exhibit 1-5 shows (a) the 3-month return under a single scenario, where all yields remain at 6%, and (b) the *expected* 3-month return if the yield curve is assumed to remain flat, but its level has a volatility of 75 bp p.a.; note that the expected return is not equal to a single scenario return, but to the probability-weighted average of returns under all possible flat yield curve scenarios. *If we assume that yields may be volatile but that the yield curve remains flat*, long bonds have *expected* returns up to 0.20% higher than those of short bonds.

A concrete example may help us to understand the convexity effect better. We compare a forward rate agreement (IRA) with a Eurodollar future. The former instrument has convexity, since it has a variable basis point value — its payoff is a cashflow occurring at a future date whose present value depends on a discount factor. The latter instrument has no convexity since it has a constant basis point value — profit and loss is realized on an ongoing basis via the margin account, so that no discounting occurs. The impact of convexity is seen by observing what happens when a FRA is hedged using Eurodollar futures. Consider a 3-month out of 5-year FRA on a face value of $200m. For simplicity, assume a flat yield curve with all forward rates equal to 7.50%. How can this long FRA position be hedged using Eurodollar futures?

The duration of a 3-month discount security is 0.245, so a 1 bp shift in the 5-year forward rate changes the expected payoff of the FRA by $200m × 0.245% = $4,900. The effect on the present value of the FRA position is thus $4,900 × (1+ 7.50%/4)^{-20} = $3,379. Eurodollar futures have a basis point value of $25 per $1m face value, so the FRA can be hedged by selling 5-year Eurodollar futures with a face value of 3,379/25 = $135m.

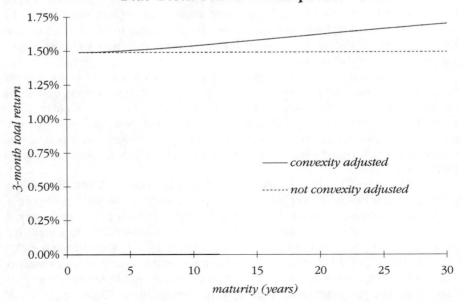

Exhibit 1-5: Expected 3-Month Returns Under Flat Yield Curve Assumption

Now suppose all forward rates rise by 50 bp, to 8.00%. Then the 5-year discount factor is $(1 + 8.00\%/4)^{-20}$ and the P&L value of a 1 bp shift is $3,297, equivalent to $132m of Eurodollar futures. Thus, in order to remain hedged, it is necessary to buy back $3m in futures. This realizes a profit of $3,750. Conversely, suppose forward rates all fall by 50 bp. Then $138m of futures are required to hedge the FRA position; it is necessary to sell a further $3m in futures, and this again realizes a profit of $3,750.

In either case, a 50 bp shift in forward rates results in a profit of $3,750, essentially due to the convexity of the FRA position. The long FRA/short Eurodollar futures position resembles a hedged long option position, where volatility results in profits from rehedging. Thus one would expect the FRA yield to be lower than the futures rate, reflecting the "option cost;" and over time, the FRA yield should converge to the futures rate, reflecting the "option time decay." This is commonly referred to as a "convexity adjustment." Like the price of an option, the size of a convexity adjustment depends on volatility.

We will return to the subject of convexity adjustments in Chapter 4; for the moment, we summarize the conclusion of this discussion. The yield on the 5-year FRA is the forward yield; the yield on a 5-year Eurodollar future is the (market) expected future yield. The latter yield should be higher, since FRAs benefit from convexity and Eurodollar futures do not. *It is implausible that these two yields are equal; that is, UEH is implausible.*

We are thus led to formulate the *local expectations hypothesis* or "LEH:" this asserts that the expected short-term returns on all bonds are equal, where the expectation is not just based on a single "most likely" yield curve scenario, but takes all possible random yield curve shifts into account. If there is no uncertainty in future yields — that is, if we know that they will equal current forward yields — then LEH and UEH are equivalent. If yields are volatile, then they are not equivalent.

For example, suppose the yield curve is currently flat, and that the only *random* yield curve shifts that can occur are parallel shifts. UEH implies that the yield curve must remain flat, while LEH implies that there must be a gradual, systematic steepening in the yield curve (to prevent long bonds from systematically outperforming short bonds). This phenomenon is discussed further in Chapter 2.

It has often been claimed that LEH is the only form of the expectations hypothesis which is economically plausible, i.e., consistent with general equilibrium. This claim, and the fact that LEH is technically very attractive, means that it is common simply to assume that LEH holds and use that as a starting-point in modeling the evolution of interest rates: see Lamberton and Lapeyre for an example of this. However, the claim is not quite true. Borrowing some terminology from the following chapter, McCulloch showed in 1993 how to construct an arbitrage-free model of the term structure satisfying UEH which is consistent with general equilibrium (see also Fisher and Gilles). What one *can* say is that such models are either implausible — the finite-state-variable examples predict that forward rates move around like sine waves, which seems unrealistic — or intractable and hard to visualize, and also prone to generating negative interest rates.

Note that LEH *for bonds of maturities of 2 years or greater* is consistent with the empirical evidence: cf. the work of Ilmanen. Thus it seems reasonable to assume LEH and to work from there, but to keep in mind that it may break down when we deal with the short-term money market.

LEH and UEH make very different predictions about the shape and dynamics of the yield curve, but they make very similar predictions about how yields are expected to change over *short* time horizons. For forward dates less than one year in the future, LEH and UEH say almost the same thing: UEH predicts that the expected future yield on a bond is equal to its current forward yield, while LEH predicts that its expected future yield is equal to its forward yield plus an adjustment (arising from the steepening which was required to compensate for the bond's convexity) which is extremely small for short time horizons.

The main point of this discussion, in the context of the present chapter, is that if we are trying to use historical data to classify random yield curve shifts, we should factor out the non-random drift — the movement along the forwards — predicted by LEH and UEH. Note that both UEH and LEH are consistent with any initial shape for the yield curve, since they only specify how this initial shape is expected to change.

Forward yields are tedious to compute precisely, so it is useful to recall a simple formula that, for near forward dates, is accurate to within a tenth of a basis point. The total return from a bond over a period Δt is, to first order, equal to the yield times Δt plus the change in yield times the duration of the bond:

$$\text{Total return} = y \cdot \Delta t + \Delta y \cdot D$$

The forward yield is the yield on the bond, at a time Δt in the future, which makes the total return equal to $r \cdot \Delta t$ where r is the applicable riskless rate. Solving for Δy gives the following formula for the forward yield:

$$\text{Forward yield} = y + \Delta t \cdot \frac{y - r}{D}$$

This is the forward yield on a physical bond. If we are analyzing CMT data we need to compute forward CMT yields; but the forward T-year CMT yield is, to within a tenth of a basis point, simply the forward yield on a par bond with a current maturity of $T + \Delta t$. We use this formula to calculate drift adjustments for historical yield data.

Using Principal Component Analysis to Identify Yield Curve Shifts

Earlier in this chapter, we used a macroeconomic model of the yield curve to argue that shifts in bond yields should not be totally chaotic but that, since they are driven by changing economic expectations, they should be systematic and classifiable. More specifically, the most important kinds of yield curve shifts should be level shifts and slope shifts. Can we verify this prediction by analyzing random yield curve shifts which have occurred historically? The answer is yes: we can apply a purely statistical analysis to historical bond yields to extract "fundamental yield curve shifts." This was first done by Litterman and Scheinkman, using a very standard method called principal component analysis. Before applying this analysis to bond yields, we briefly describe the intuition behind it by looking at a physical example (taken from Jennings and McKeown). Although there are other ways to motivate principal component analysis, I think the physical analogy is an attractive one.

Consider a 15m plank fixed to a wall, with a bending stiffness of 426×10^6 Nm^2; it has weights attached to it at 5m intervals, which have a mass of 200kg, 400kg and 400kg respectively. In what ways can this cantilever vibrate? It is intuitively clear that it can only vibrate at certain "natural frequencies," or "vibration modes;" that is, any observed vibration is a combination of these vibration modes.

In fact, one can calculate that there are three of these modes, as shown in Exhibit 1-6. Note the scale of each of the diagrams, which indicates the relative importance of each mode: the second mode has less than a twentieth the amplitude of the first mode, and the third mode is ten times smaller again. It would probably not be visible to the naked eye.

Now, suppose that we knew no physics, and wanted to work out what these vibration modes were just by observing the behavior of the plank. It is reasonable to hope that we could carry out the following procedure:

Exhibit 1-6: Vibration Modes of the Cantilever

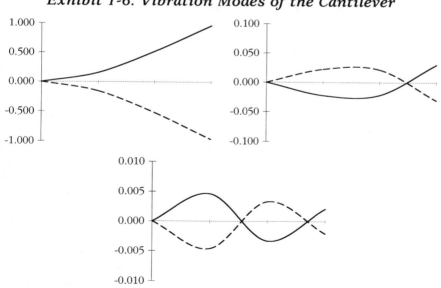

1. Attach sensors 5m, 10m, and 15m along the plank — making the assumption that these are the only points which are relevant.
2. Give the plank a lot of random whacks, and for each whack, measure the amplitude of the observed vibration at each sensor.
3. Work out the 3 × 3 covariance matrix of these amplitudes; the diagonal will show the relative size of the displacements, while the other matrix elements will show whether the sensors tend to move in the same direction; in this case, all the correlations will be strongly positive, but none of them will be equal to one.
4. Extract the vibration modes by somehow "decomposing" this covariance matrix.

It turns out that if **A** is the covariance matrix, then the vibration modes are the eigenvectors of **A**, and the eigenvalues tell us how important each vibration mode is. (Recall that a vector v called an eigenvector of **A**, with associated eigenvalue λ, if it solves the equation $\mathbf{A}v = \lambda v$; there are standard numerical methods for finding all the eigenvectors and eigenvalues of a matrix; also, one can prove that any two eigenvectors are orthogonal, i.e., correspond to uncorrelated modes, and in fact that the eigenvectors form an orthogonal basis.) The required "decomposition" thus amounts to finding the eigenvectors of **A**.

In the above example, the theoretical eigenvectors and their eigenvalues are as follows: the elements of each vector correspond to the 15m, 10m, and 5m points, reading downwards.

$$
\begin{pmatrix} 1 \\ 0.5400 \\ 0.1619 \end{pmatrix}, 849.2; \quad \begin{pmatrix} 1 \\ -0.7061 \\ -0.7333 \end{pmatrix}, 26.83; \quad \begin{pmatrix} 0.4521 \\ -0.7184 \\ 1 \end{pmatrix}, 4.056
$$

Thus, in order to determine the dynamics of the cantilever, it is in principle not necessary to know any physics — only matrix algebra. In practice, of course, things are unlikely to be so easy. Small measurement errors might lead to errors in the covariance matrix, and hence in the numerically computed eigenvectors and eigenvalues. The first vibration mode will be hard to miss, but the second might be difficult to detect. The third is so small, relatively speaking, that any measurement error at all will probably swamp it. Also note that since the eigenvectors are orthogonal by construction, they correspond to uncorrelated or independent vibration modes.

We can apply exactly the same method to analyzing the dynamics of the yield curve: identify some "key points" (bond maturities which represent key liquidity points); look at historical yield shifts at each of these points; compute the covariance matrix of yield shifts; and compute its eigenvectors and eigenvalues. Each eigenvector should correspond to a *fundamental yield curve shift*, and by definition these fundamental shifts are uncorrelated; the eigenvalues are *weights*, which tell us the relative importance of each of these shifts; and the actual yield curve shift on any specific day is a linear combination of fundamental shifts.

Our economic analysis might lead us to expect that the most important fundamental shift will turn out to be a parallel shift, while the second most important will turn out to be a slope shift. But we are not certain that this will be the case — for example, since the parallel and slope shifts predicted by the model are not necessarily uncorrelated, they will both turn out to be linear combinations of the fundamental shifts identified by the statistical analysis, which are by definition uncorrelated. However, since the correlation is low, we might hope that the two most important fundamental shifts would closely resemble a parallel shift and a slope shift.

Note that on its own the economic analysis tells us nothing about the relative importance of these two different kinds of yield curve shift; and we do not know what other kinds of shifts there might be. Here the statistical analysis should yield some valuable insights. However, since the results of this empirical analysis might depend on the dataset used, it is important to test their robustness by running the analysis on a variety of datasets.

The results of a principal component analysis may depend on which bond yields we feed into the analysis. For example, if we include a large number of money market yields, we are more likely to pick up yield curve shifts specifically affecting the money market curve, and we will give a lower weighting to yield curve shifts affecting mid-range bonds, or perhaps fail to detect such shifts at all. Thus, as with any statistical analysis, we must be careful to select the most "relevant" observables. For most bond investors, this means using bond yields in preference to money market yields.

Finally, a technical point: we use the correlation matrix rather than the covariance matrix in our analysis. This corresponds to scaling away differences in yield volatility at different points in the yield curve. Buhler and Zimmermann provide a more detailed discussion of this, and of other statistical points, while Rebonato describes the basis of the analysis on a more fundamental level.

The fundamental yield shifts identified by a principal component analysis of U.S. Treasury yields are shown in Exhibit 1-7, 1-8, and 1-9. One can make the following remarks about these empirically observed fundamental yield curve shifts:

1. The dominant fundamental shift is an empirical *level shift*, a nearly parallel shift in yields across the whole curve. This explains around 90% of observed variation in yields.
2. The next most important fundamental shift is an empirical *slope shift*, in which the yield curve pivots around the 5-year point. This explains around 5% to 7% of observed variation in yields, and seems to have become slightly more important in recent years.
3. The third most important fundamental shift is an empirical *curvature shift* (sometimes called a "butterfly shift"), where 3- to 4-year bond yields move relative to shorter and longer bonds. The precise nature and importance of a curvature shift seems to vary from period to period, and curvature shifts explain less than 2% of observed yield shifts.

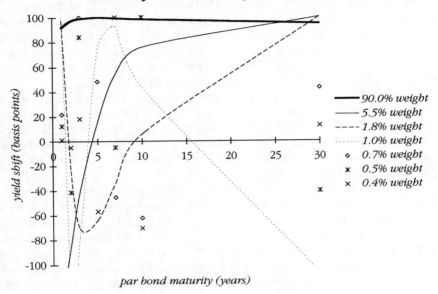

Exhibit 1-7: Principal Component Analysis of U.S. Treasury Yields (Daily Data, 1977-1996)

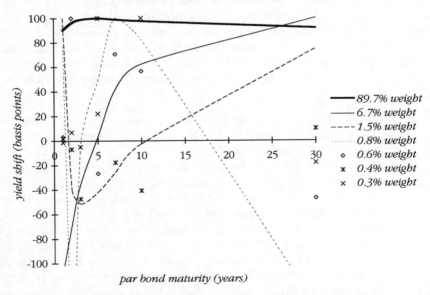

Exhibit 1-8: Principal Component Analysis of U.S. Treasury Yields (Daily Data, 1990-1996)

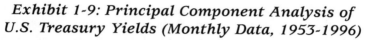

Exhibit 1-9: Principal Component Analysis of
U.S. Treasury Yields (Monthly Data, 1953-1996)

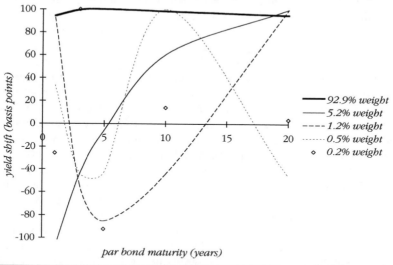

4. The remaining shifts identified by the principal component analysis seem to have no meaningful interpretation, and are probably due to statistical noise; they vary depending on the dataset.

Note that the slope shifts identified by analyzing the 1977-1996 and 1990-1996 datasets look almost identical, but the slope shift from the 1953-1996 dataset looks somewhat different: the yields of mid-range bonds move significantly less. This phenomenon is explained in Chapter 4, where we present a different, cross-sectional analysis of the data, i.e., looking at each observed yield curve individually. It turns out that the 1977-1996 and 1990-1996 slope shifts are more typical, and the 1953-1996 slope shift is distorted by the experience of 1959-1969, when mid-range bonds were "expensive."

It is tempting to conclude that, since parallel shifts account for such a large proportion of variance in Treasury yields, slope shifts and other kinds of shifts are not important. This is incorrect. The reason is that most bond investors are evaluated against a benchmark rather than on the basis of total return. An investor who is tracking benchmark duration closely has, by definition, nearly the same exposure to parallel shifts as the benchmark; but exposure to yield curve slope may be quite different, e.g., if the portfolio has a barbell profile. In this case yield curve slope shifts would play a major role, sometimes the primary role, in determining *relative* performance.

Our analysis so far has focused on the U.S. Treasury market. It is logical to ask whether similar results hold for other bond markets. Since the earlier arguments about how interest rate expectations determine the shape of the yield curve should apply equally to most market economies, one would expect the term structure dynamics in different developed countries to be broadly similar. This turns out to be the case, though there are minor differences which have an interesting interpretation.

Hiraki, Shiraishi, and Takezawa carry out a principal component analysis of shifts in the Japanese Government yield curve from 1987-1995. As with the U.S. Treasury market, the first two principal components dominate, and correspond to a virtually parallel shift and a slope shift. There is also evidence of a third factor which they refer to as a "curvature factor," though in our terminology it corresponds to the formation of a short-end hump at the 9-month part of the yield curve (i.e., it affects the money market curve rather than the bond curve). Note that their analysis uses a relatively large number of short maturity observations, ensuring that it is likely to detect a "hump" factor relevant to the money market, rather than a "curvature" factor relevant to the bond market; cf. Exhibit 1-23 below.

Buhler and Zimmermann carry out a principal component analysis of Swiss and German Treasury yield curve shifts from 1988-1996. Here again, the first two principal components correspond to shifts in the level and slope of the yield curve; they also detect a money market "hump" factor. Interestingly, they observe that the level shifts are not parallel: in the Swiss market, yields at the short end of the curve move nearly twice as much as long bond yields, while in the German market they move about 1.5 times as much: see Exhibit 1-10. Buhler and Zimmermann argue that the non-parallel nature of the empirical level shift is related to monetary uncertainty in each country: inflation was unexpectedly high in Switzerland during most of that period, while Germany was undergoing the effects of reunification.

Exhibit 1-10: Swiss and German First Principal Components (Level Shifts)

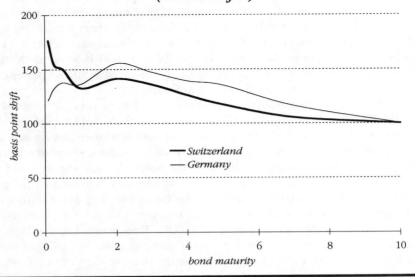

Implications for Portfolio Risk Management

It has been argued that if level shifts are not parallel, then duration is an inappropriate portfolio risk measure. The effective duration of a portfolio measures its sensitivity to a parallel shift in the yield curve; arguably, it should be replaced with a "level duration" which measures its sensitivity to the empirical level shift, which is not perfectly parallel. The natural counter-argument is that duration is more widely understood and easier to calculate; moreover, since a U.S. level shift is approximately parallel, one would get a similar answer anyway. (It is important to note that for maturities of 3 years and greater, even the Swiss level shift looks roughly parallel: it is the 1-month to 6-month part of the curve that moves more violently. Thus, even in this market, a parallel shift is a reasonable proxy for a level shift when one is analyzing portfolios which do not contain many short maturity bonds.)

On a more fundamental level, we argued earlier in this chapter that if we interpret yield curve shifts as arising mostly from changes in economic expectations, it is natural to focus on parallel shifts and slope shifts — where "slope" refers to the spread between the short rate and the long bond yield. We also observed that there was no reason to expect these parallel shifts and slope shifts to be uncorrelated. Now the factors identified by a principal component analysis must, by definition, be uncorrelated; this means that the first two principal components — the empirical level and slope shifts — should be interpreted as certain linear combinations of the economically meaningful parallel and slope shifts. That is, the fact that the empirical factors are forced to be uncorrelated means that they may not be intrinsically meaningful.

This, by the way, may explain the nature of level shifts in the Swiss and German markets. If inflation is unusually volatile and there is a high correlation between rises in inflationary expectations and monetary tightenings — that is, if tightenings tend to occur in response to market perceptions of inflationary pressures, and to overshoot them — the empirical level shift would not look parallel. Thus the nature of the empirical level shift — unlike the economically meaningful parallel and slope shifts — depends on whether unusual economic circumstances may have influenced monetary policy during the period being studied.

When monitoring interest rate risk, it is preferable to focus on economically meaningful parallel shifts and slope shifts, which may have non-zero correlation, rather than the empirical level shifts and slope shifts identified by principal component analysis. That is, rather than constructing new risk measures from the principal components, one should continue to use duration, and supplement it with a "slope duration" derived from the economic analysis. For example, this is essentially the approach adopted by Willner.

Thus, *slope duration* should be calculated as follows: Let a "slope shift" correspond to a yield curve shift as shown in Exhibit 1-3, scaled so that (say) the 6-month yield moves by 100 bp. Given a bond, compute its value after a slope shift has been applied to the current yield curve. The percentage change from the original price is the slope duration of the bond.

Exhibit 1-11: Ordinary Durations and Slope Durations of Non-Callable Treasuries

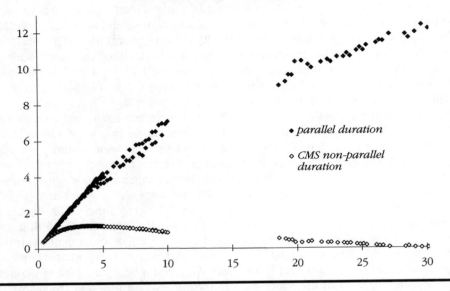

• *parallel duration*

◇ *CMS non-parallel duration*

Note that unlike parallel duration, there is no "standard" definition of slope duration. For example, one could alternatively let a "slope shift" be an empirical slope shift as shown in Exhibits 1-7 and 1-8, but scaled and shifted so that the 6-month yield moves by 100 bp and the 30-year yield remains unchanged: this will give very similar results. The important thing is to apply a consistent definition of slope shift to different bonds, and at different times.

Exhibit 1-11 shows ordinary durations and slope durations for outstanding noncallable Treasury bonds. (The graphs are not smooth curves because of the differing bond coupon rates.) Here the slope duration is the "non-parallel duration" computed by the CMS product BondEdge, which uses an empirically determined slope shift. Note that while parallel duration rises with maturity, slope duration is highest for bonds with a maturity of around 3-5 years. The reason is that the yields of longer bonds are not greatly affected by a yield curve slope shift.

A word on curvature shifts and hump shifts. These crop up persistently in principal component analyses, and thus it is tempting to regard them as "fundamental" factors on a par with level and slope shifts — but which happen to be much less important. This is not quite the case. As we saw earlier in this chapter, level and slope shifts have a natural economic meaning, and the form of a level shift or a slope shift tends to be quite stable over time.

By contrast, a curvature shift or a hump shift generally has no economic interpretation, and the region of the yield curve most affected by such a shift can vary widely. For example, a hump in the money market curve is usually the result of a sophisticated market prediction about future monetary policy, and might center around (say) the 9-month, 12-month, or 18-month part of the yield curve, depending on circumstances Similarly, curvature shifts generally arise because of supply/demand imbalances which affect very particular parts of the yield curve: for example, in late 1995, 3-year Australian Government bond yields were driven down by swap market activity arising from Australian issuance in the Japanese market and from specific deals related to the privatization of the Victorian power industry; 3-year yields were specifically affected because of Japanese retail demand for 3-year investments and because of the nature of the privatization deals being arranged. In different circumstances it might have been the 2-year, or 5-year, part of the curve which was most affected. It was not useful to regard this phenomenon as a "curvature shift" in some generic sense.

The practical conclusion for portfolio risk management is as follows. It makes sense to measure portfolio "level risk" and "slope risk" in a consistent way, as these correspond to fundamental interest rate risk factors: the meaning of a level shift or a slope shift does not change over time. However, it is not advisable to take an equally rigid approach to measuring "curvature risk" or "hump risk," since curvature or hump shifts do not have any fundamental significance, but occur for more specific reasons, and take different forms at different times. Thus, one must adopt a more flexible approach to monitoring this kind of yield curve reshaping risk. We will explore this further later in the chapter.

GOING BEYOND THE FUNDAMENTALS: NUANCES OF THE YIELD CURVE

Empirical Correlations versus Theoretical Correlations

It was suggested that, when monitoring overall portfolio interest rate risk, it is most important to focus on parallel duration and slope duration. For example, these two risk measures capture the effects of long/short duration bets, and of steepening/flattening trades. Since the other principal components have such a low weight, and since we argued that measuring curvature risk and hump risk was problematic, one might think that only parallel and slope risk matter. Unfortunately, this is not quite the case; in practice, these two risk factors are not comprehensive.

First, note that there is a certain kind of risk which is obscured by principal component analysis: the risk that, perhaps for an event-specific reason, a specific part of the yield curve will shift. The behavior of the 3-year part of the Australian yield curve in late 1995, discussed above, is an example. This had a significant impact on bond returns during that period; but if this precise yield curve shift did not happen repeatedly, it would not appear statistically significant when carrying out a principal component analysis using 5 or 10 years of data.

How can we determine what is lost when we focus only on parallel duration and slope duration? To answer this question, Rebonato and Cooper compared:

Exhibit 1-12: Empirical Correlations of Different Treasury Yields

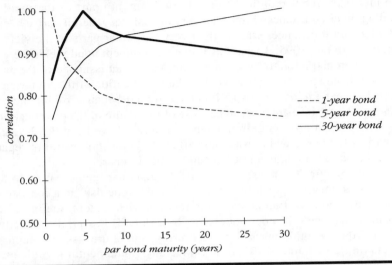

• the empirical correlations of changes in different bond yields; and
• the correlations predicted if only parallel shifts and slope shifts had occurred.

Exhibit 1-12 shows empirical correlations for 1-year, 5-year, or 30-year Treasury yield as a function of the yield to which this is being compared. For example, the 5-year yield has a correlation of around 0.95 with both the 3-year and 7-year yield, but only 0.90 with the 30-year yield and only 0.85 with the 1-year yield. Note that the correlations fall away sharply as we move away from the specified bond.

Exhibit 1-13 shows what these correlations would have been if only parallel shifts and slope shifts had occurred. Note that they fall away much more gradually as we move away from the specified bond. That is, the theoretical correlation between nearby bonds is much higher than the empirical correlation. This shows that focusing only on parallel risk and slope risk understates the basis risk between two nearby bonds; it suggests that (say) the 5-year bond and the 7-year bond should be much closer substitutes than they actually are.

The pattern of gradually declining correlations observed in Exhibit 1-13 is not an accident. Rebonato and Cooper proved mathematically that if you assume only two kinds of yield curve shift, the correlation functions must behave like this.

What is the appropriate way to monitor maturity-specific risks which do not correspond to fundamental yield curve shifts that occur repeatedly? At the moment, the most useful tool seems to be the concept of *key rate duration*, which measures exposure to a yield change at a single point on the yield curve. We briefly review this concept. To compute, for example, a 7-year key rate duration, shift the 7-year point of the zero coupon curve by 100 bp, and recompute the value of the bond. The percentage change from the original price is the key rate duration. Exhibit 1-14 shows the shift in the zero coupon curve, and the corresponding shift in the forward curve, used to compute the 7-year key rate duration.

Exhibit 1-13: Theoretical Correlations of Different Treasury Yields, Two Factor Model

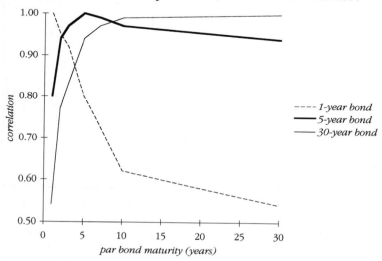

Exhibit 1-14: Yield Curve Shift Used to Compute 7-Year Key Rate Duration

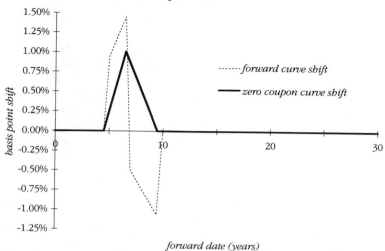

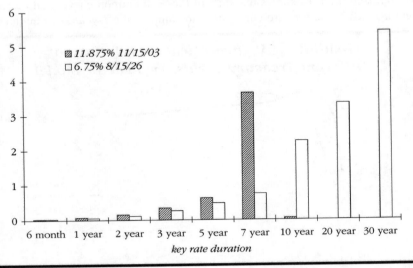

Exhibit 1-15: Key Rate Durations of
Non-Callable Treasury Bonds

There are a number of important observations to make about key rate duration:

- The yield curve shifts used in the definition of key rate duration are not economically meaningful; in fact, they are highly unrealistic. Therefore, single key rate durations do not have any economic interpretation, and are purely tools: "building blocks" of yield curve risk.
- The definition of a specific key rate duration may depend on the set of yield curve grid points chosen. For example, the value and meaning of the 10-year key rate duration will differ depending on whether the adjacent grid points are at 7 and 30 years, or at 7 and 20 years.
- The definition of a specific key rate duration also depends on how zero coupon yields are interpolated between grid points. The above examples assume linear interpolation, but different methods could be used.
- Care must be taken when computing key rate durations for securities with interest-rate sensitive cashflows, particularly ARMs with reset caps or floors. Using 100 bp shifts can give unrealistic results because of the violently sawtoothed displacement to the forward curve, and it may be better to use, say, 10 bp shifts. (For vanilla bonds, using 100 bp shifts and using 10 bp shifts would give almost identical answers.)

These observations partly explain why key rate durations can often look somewhat unintuitive. Parallel and slope durations are easy to interpret, whereas interpreting key rate durations takes some experience. Exhibits 1-15, 1-16, and 1-17 show examples of key rate durations for some different kinds of securities.

Exhibit 1-16: Key Rate Durations of a Callable Treasury Bond

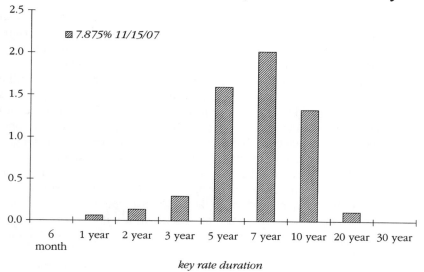

Exhibit 1-17: Key Rate Durations of 30-Year Mortgage Passthroughs

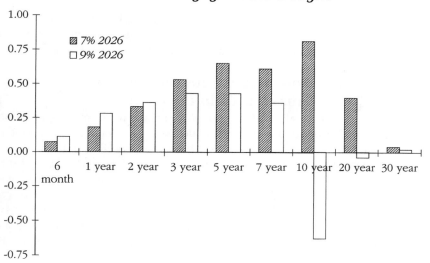

These Exhibits can be interpreted as follows:

- Exhibit 1-15 shows how key rate durations pick up the yield curve exposure arising from a bond's coupon stream as well as its final principal payment. Note that in the case of the 30-year bond, the contribution of the coupon stream to the longer key rate durations is quite significant.
- Exhibit 1-16 shows that for a callable bond, the key rate durations are not concentrated at the maturity date or call date, but are spread out across a range of maturities. The precise pattern of key rate durations depends on the option model used, and on the volatility assumptions used in the option model. But in practice, changing the model or the volatility assumptions usually results in a relatively small change to the key rate durations.
- Exhibit 1-17 shows that key rate durations for mortgage-backed securities are also spread out across a range of maturities. Note that the key rate duration calculation here depends on the prepayment model being used; in this case, the model predicts that prepayments will rise if the 10-year Treasury yield falls. Since it is the 10-year zero coupon rate which has the strongest influence on the 10-year Treasury yield, this explains why the 7% (discount) security has a large positive 10-year key rate duration, and why the 9% (premium) security has a large negative key rate duration. If different Treasury reference yields were used in the prepayment model, the pattern of key rate durations would be different.

Key rate durations permit investors to match yield curve exposures very precisely, and are particularly useful in asset-liability management. However, the precise way in which key rate durations are used will vary from investor to investor.

The Role of Key Rate Durations in Managing Yield Curve Risk

An interesting new application of key rate durations is to compute approximate sensitivities to arbitrary yield curve shifts, such as those identified by a principal component analysis. Various methods have been proposed for computing "yield curve reshaping durations" in specific cases: for example, the approach of Willner represents yield curve displacements using an explicit functional form, following Nelson and Siegel. Implementing this approach on a portfolio level involves considerable additions and modifications to one's existing portfolio analytical system. Also, it is not obvious how to measure exposure to an arbitrary reshaping — for example, different kinds of curvature shift, or the non-parallel level shifts identified in the Swiss and German markets.

There is a more straightforward method for computing the sensitivity of a bond or bond portfolio to an arbitrary yield curve reshaping — more precisely, an arbitrary displacement of the forward curve. For any given reshaping, this exposure is approximately equal to a fixed linear combination of the bond's key rate durations.

This suggests that it may be better to regard key rate durations as providing a general tool for decomposing arbitrary "relevant" or "meaningful" yield curve reshapings.

The idea is that, although the "saw-tooth" forward curve displacement shown in Exhibit 1-14 is not meaningful in itself, the set of all nine key rate saw-tooth functions forms an approximate basis for the set of all possible reshapings of the forward curve, including the meaningful ones. That is, any reshaping of the forward curve can be approximated by a linear sum of the key rate saw-tooth functions. For example, Exhibit 1-18 shows a simple forward curve reshaping — no change up to three years forward and a 100 bp shift at three years and beyond — and its best approximation by a weighted sum of key rate saw-tooth functions. The dotted lines show the individual saw-tooth functions which make up the approximation.

The coefficients of this weighted sum are easy to calculate. One simply picks the coefficients which give the correct sensitivities for the nine on-the-run Treasury bonds corresponding to the key maturities; this can be easily done on a spreadsheet. Thus one is assured of a perfect fit to these nine bonds, which correspond to key liquidity points. Note that this calculation need only be performed once.

The sensitivity of an arbitrary bond or a bond portfolio to the given forward curve reshaping can then be calculated as the given weighted sum of its key rate durations. Thus, any off-the-shelf analytical system which computes key rate durations can be used to calculate approximate sensitivities to yield curve reshapings, which can be specified arbitrarily by each user.

As a practical illustration, consider the curvature shift shown in Exhibit 1-19. The approximation by key rate saw-tooth functions is shown in Exhibit 1-20. This approximation looks reasonably close, except at longer maturities where the widely spaced key rate maturities make it impossible to achieve a close fit.

Exhibit 1-18: Approximating a Forward Curve Shift by Key Rate Sawtooth Functions

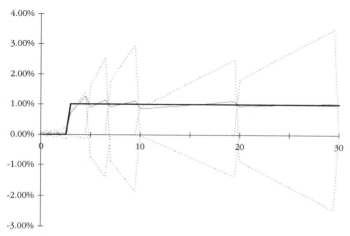

Exhibit 1-19: Sample Curvature Reshaping of the Yield Curve

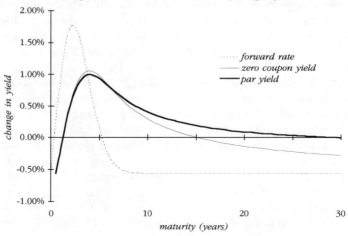

Exhibit 1-20:Approximation of Curvature Reshaping by Key Rate Sawtooth Functions

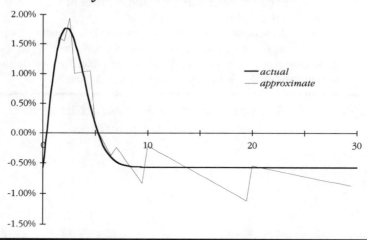

Exhibit 1-21 compares the actual and approximated curvature sensitivity for 4-year, 6-year, 8.5-year, and 15-year Treasury bonds. The accuracy is quite good except for the 15-year bond. To put these results in perspective, it should be remembered that there is no "correct" definition for a curvature reshaping, and thus no "correct" answer to aim for.

In fact, a curvature shift is nearly the worst case; it is possible to approximate slope shifts and hump shifts much more closely. We deliberately chose an example which illustrated both the strengths and the weaknesses of the method. In general, good accuracy is possible provided we are trying to approximate a curve reshaping which is (a) smooth rather than discontinuous, and (b) involves little variation at the longer end of the curve, where the key maturity points are more widely spaced. Using more than nine key rate maturities would improve accuracy, but is not essential.

Idiosyncratic Behavior at the Short End of the Curve

The analysis of correlations showed that there are maturity-specific risks not captured by parallel risk and slope risk. There are two other sources of additional risk: "money market risk" and "long end risk." These arise because both the short and long ends of the curve can move independently of the 2- to 10-year section of the yield curve. Note that idiosyncratic shifts in the short or long end of the curve may not be detected by the principal component analysis unless many observations from the short or long end of the curve are included. For example, we saw earlier that a money market "hump" factor is only detected if we include a larger number of money market yield observations. Similarly, since we only included a single long bond yield observation, a statistically significant "long end" factor is unlikely to be detected.

The behavior of the long end of the yield curve is the subject of Chapter 4; here we concentrate on the short end of the curve. The main facts here are: (a) money market yields are persistently lower than bond yields, i.e., the short end of the curve generally has a positive slope which is not fully explained by expectations that short-term rates will rise; (b) money market yields are more volatile than bond yields; and, (c) money market yields appear to behave idiosyncratically compared to bond yields.

The bias towards an upward-sloping yield curve, at the short end, has been noticed by many authors, and appears to contradict any reasonable expectations hypothesis such as LEH. There are a number of connected reasons why money market yields tend to be lower than bond yields, which are quite unrelated to investors' interest rate expectations:

1. The money market is more liquid than the bond market. It is less complex, has lower transaction costs, and price transparency is generally greater.
2. Some bond investors demand a yield premium (Keynes' "liquidity premium") because they are not guaranteed access at short notice to the full principal amount invested.

Exhibit 1-21: Accuracy of Key Rate Duration Approximation to Curvature Sensitivity

	4-year	6-year	8.5-year	15-year
Actual	3.40	3.87	3.20	1.67
Estimated	3.16	3.87	3.36	2.00
Error	−0.24 (−7%)	0.03 (1%)	0.16 (5%)	0.33 (20%)

3. Bond investors not requiring this kind of liquidity still demand a premium for interest rate risk, since they are attempting to maximize risk-adjusted returns.
4. Capital charges for money market securities are usually lower than those for bonds. Thus lower yields give rise to equivalent returns on risk-adjusted capital.
5. Retail investors demand lower returns from money market funds than from bond funds. Thus money market funds can bid up the prices of money market securities.

The higher volatility of money market yields is also true across different markets. There are a number of reasons why money market yields are more volatile than bond yields in basis point terms:

1. Money market yields are strongly influenced by shifting expectations about near-term monetary policy, whereas this has a more muted impact on bond yields.
2. The very liquidity of the money market means that large transactions are common, and often cause money market yields to fluctuate widely in the short term.
3. Volatility in the bond and equity markets generates volatility in the money market, via repo market activity and cash transfers to meet margin calls.

Note that the precise behavior of money market yields may vary widely from country to country. For example, the monetary authorities in the United States and Australia attempt to make relatively smooth adjustments in monetary policy, thus the very short end of the curve (0-3 months) is often less volatile than longer money market yields (say, 6-18 months). On the other hand, the Reserve Bank of New Zealand has permitted much more volatility in overnight to 3-month yields. The point is that, while the economic factors driving bond yields are generally the same in different countries, the factors driving money market yields are not: they depend on the character of monetary policy in each country.

When attempting to analyze the behavior of money market yields, it is important to take two precautions. First, because rates corresponding to maturities of less than one month have extremely volatile yields, these should usually be excluded from any statistical analysis. Second, because the behavior of the short end of the curve depends on the current character of monetary policy, it does not make sense to use datasets spanning several monetary regimes. Instead, relatively short historical periods should be used.

A detailed analysis of money market curve risk should be carried out in conjunction with an examination of different monetary policy regimes, and there is no room for an extended study here (but see Ciocca and Nardozzi for a brief account which is compatible with our perspective). Purely as an illustration, however, we will look at the behavior of the short end of the curve in the very brief period October 1996-April 1997. Readers will recall that early in this period, monetary policy was very stable; that in November and December 1996 a tightening was expected, but did not occur; that in March 1996 a tightening was expected, and did occur (25 bp on 25 March); and that in April 1996, further tightenings were priced into the yield curve to varying degrees. This should give some idea of the climate of expectations during this period. The dataset included 1-, 2-, 3-, 6-, and 9-month deposit rates and 1-, 2-, and 3-year swap rates. (A more careful analysis might use independent forward rates or Eurodollar futures rates over a somewhat longer period, but the data we use is sufficient to bring out the main points.)

Exhibit 1-22 shows the observed correlations between these different market yields. These correlations are mostly very low, suggesting that there were a large number of idiosyncratic yield shifts; this is a sharp contrast with bond yields, which have a greater tendency to move in step. Again, the correlations drop very sharply as we move away from the specified maturity.

Exhibit 1-23 shows the results of a principal component analysis. The dominant shift is again a level shift, with swap rates moving somewhat less than deposit rates. The second most important shift is a change in the slope of the 0-2 year part of the curve, roughly corresponding to the slope shift we observed when we analyzed bond yields. The third most important shift is the formation of a hump at the 9-month part of the curve, while the fourth most important shift is a change in the 3-month deposit rate. The other shifts are probably statistical noise.

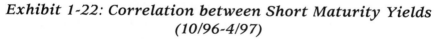

Exhibit 1-22: Correlation between Short Maturity Yields (10/96-4/97)

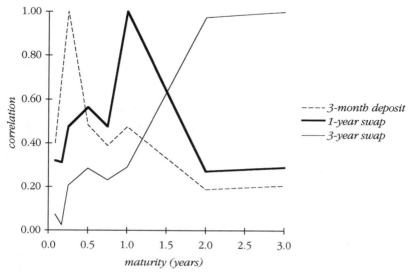

Exhibit 1-23: Principal Component Analysis of Short Maturity Yields (10/96-4/97)

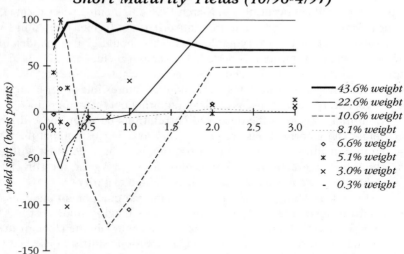

Interestingly, level shifts are less dominant than they were for the bond curve, and slope and hump shifts are relatively more important. This shows that duration is a less important risk measure for money market instruments than it is for bonds, and that it is important to supplement it with non-parallel yield curve risk measures. Furthermore, even level risk and slope risk explain only 66% of variance in yields, so other kinds of curve shifts are extremely important.

It is hard to draw any definitive conclusions about the dynamics of short maturity yields, particularly since a shift in the nature of monetary policy may make any previous conclusions invalid. Probably the best one can do is to monitor carefully chosen key rate durations. In any case, the dollar risk is much lower than for bonds, and investors often have much less flexibility in their money market holdings than in their bond holdings; so in practice there is perhaps more tolerance for error.

As an aside, note that many empirical studies of interest rate dynamics have focused solely on T-bill yields. The above analysis shows that the relevance of such studies to understanding bond yields is dubious. The bond curve must be analyzed separately from the money market curve.

Selected References

Buhler, A. and Zimmermann, H., "A Statistical Analysis of the Term Structure of Interest Rates in Switzerland and Germany," *J. Fixed Income*, December 1996.

Ciocca, P. and Nardozzi, G., *The High Price of Money: An Interpretation of World Interest Rates*, Clarendon Press, Oxford, 1996.

Fisher, M. and Gilles, C., "Around and Around: The Expectations Hypothesis," Federal Reserve Board, May 1996, to appear in *J. Finance*.

Frankel, J. A., *Financial Markets and Monetary Policy*, MIT Press, Cambridge, 1995; see Chapters 8-10.

Hiraki, T., Shiraishi, N. and Takezawa, N., "Cointegration, Common Factors, and the Term Structure of Yen Offshore Interest Rates," *J. Fixed Income*, December 1996.

Ho, T., "Key Rate Durations: Measures of Interest Rate Risk," *J. Fixed Income*, September 1992.

Ilmanen, A., "Does Duration Extension Enhance Long-Term Expected Returns?" *J. Fixed Income*, September 1996.

Ingersoll, J., *Theory of Financial Decision-Making*, Rowman & Littlefield, Savage, 1987; see Chapter 18.

Jennings, A. and McKeown, J., *Matrix Computation (2nd Edition)*, Wiley, Chichester, 1992; see Chapter 6.

Keynes, J. M., *The General Theory of Employment, Interest and Money*, Macmillan, London, 1936.

Lamberton, D. and Lapeyre, B., *Introduction to Stochastic Calculus Applied to Finance*, Chapman & Hall, London, 1996.

Litterman, R., and Scheinkman, J., "Common Factors Affecting Bond Returns," *J. Fixed Income*, June 1991.

Nelson, C. and Siegel, A., "Parsimonious Modeling of Yield Curves," *J. Business*, 60, No. 4, 1987.

Phoa, W., "Can You Derive Market Volatility Forecasts from the Observed Yield Curve Convexity Bias?" *J. Fixed Income*, June 1997.

Rebonato, R., *Interest-Rate Option Models: Understanding, Analyzing and Using Models for Exotic Interest-Rate Options*, Wiley, Chichester, 1996.

Rebonato, R., and Cooper, I., "The Limitations of Simple Two-Factor Interest Rate Models," *J. Financial Engineering*, March 1996.

Willner, R., "A New Tool for Portfolio Managers: Level, Slope and Curvature Durations," *J. Fixed Income*, June 1996.

Chapter 2

Term Structure Models: A Portfolio Manager's Guide

SETTING THE SCENE

This chapter will not tell you how to build your own term structure model. For most investors, this would be a waste of time — it is usually more efficient to rely on "off-the-shelf" models available from software vendors. However, it is dangerous to regard a model simply as a black box. First, one needs to be able to make an informed choice between using different models. Second, every model has shortcomings as well as advantages, and it is important to understand the consequences of relying on a particular model. Third, broker research will often be based on a model different from the one the investor is using; if the implications of this are not recognized, it is easy to misinterpret the research. Thus it is essential to be familiar with the basic issues that arise when building a term structure model.

At present, there is no term structure model which is clearly superior to all others for every purpose. Nor are there universally applicable criteria for determining whether one model is better than another. It depends on the securities being analyzed: for example, an investment bank managing a highly leveraged book of exotic yield curve options, all expiring within the next two years, will have very different requirements from an investor managing a portfolio of 20-year callable bonds. It is therefore critical to focus on precisely how the model will be used.

Since the various models all have their pros and cons, it may make sense for an investment bank to use a wide variety of models, perhaps even incompatible ones, to manage the overall risk of different derivative products; one might choose the "best" model for each product. Portfolio managers are in a different situation. In order to manage the risk of the portfolio, they need to compare the durations of different bonds; and in order to assess relative value, they need to compare the option-adjusted spreads of different bonds. If durations and option-adjusted spreads are computed using different models then, as we shall see below, they may not be comparable — they may be measuring different things. Thus, despite the fact that no single model is "best," *there is a strong argument for using a single term structure model to manage all the bonds in the portfolio*, although in special cases it may be useful to supplement this with further analysis using other models.

There is another important issue to which we have already alluded. Bond investors are primarily concerned with long-dated options, which may be "alive" for the next 20 years. By contrasts, much of the literature has focused on short-

35

dated options, which expire within the next two years or even within the next six months. Long-dated and short-dated options can behave in quite different ways. Thus, a great deal of the literature on interest rate derivatives is not very relevant to bond investors.

Testing a Model Against Historical Yield Data

Some remarks on empirical testing are in order. A lot of past work on term structure models was done in isolation from the real world. In many cases the main criterion was mathematical elegance, or consistency with abstract economic theory. In recent years there has been a greater focus on empirical data, and a great deal of interesting work has been done. The main approach has been time series analysis, and researchers have relied heavily on statistical and econometric tools (the paper of Andersen and Lund is a typical example).

However, time series analysis has some shortcomings. Many methods make a priori assumptions about the nature of the time series — for example, they may assume stationarity, or constant volatility. If these assumptions are incorrect, the results will be meaningless. On the other hand, methods which make fewer assumptions typically require a lot more data to yield statistically significant results, and there may not be enough data available.

One must also note that it may be dangerous to use whole time series to derive single estimates (e.g., of drift, volatility or mean reversion coefficients). One reason is that there is usually no *a priori* reason to expect that these should not vary over time. Another reason is that there may have been a structural change in the market during the period in question. A general example was the deregulation of financial markets around 1980; a more specific example was the legalization of short selling in the Japanese bond market in 1991. In each case, bond yields behaved in quite different ways before and after the break. These were obvious examples, but there are more subtle kinds of structural breaks. Moreover, a break may affect the results of one kind of analysis but not another.

Thus it is often useful to take a cross-sectional approach to analyzing data, as well as a time series approach. For example, one might generate daily parameter estimates rather than just a single parameter estimate for the whole period. This is not always possible, but where it is, the results are nearly always informative.

A particularly useful source of cross-sectional data is the options market. The prices of traded options potentially contain an enormous amount of useful information about market participants' assumptions about the dynamics of interest rates. It would be foolish to ignore this information when trying to evaluate a term structure model. Unfortunately, reported option prices often need to be taken with a grain of salt. Option markets are less liquid, less efficient, and less complete than physical bond markets. This is particularly the case for the market in long-dated options. There are extremely active markets in short-dated options, both exchange-traded and OTC; but as we remarked, the behavior of short-dated options is of limited relevance to most bond investors.

The Raw Data: Caps, Floors, Swaptions and the Black 76 Option Pricing Model

The most relevant option markets are the cap/floor and swaption markets. These give us information about market volatility expectations and distributional assumptions out to at least five years; market data for longer-dated caps can be unreliable owing to illiquidity. This is far shorter than the maturity of many callable bonds, but still long enough to tell us something about the expected long-run behavior of interest rates. We will focus on the cap/floor market, which we now briefly review.

A *caplet* is an option on some floating reference rate: it compensates the buyer if the reference rate is above a specified strike rate K on the expiry date. A *cap* consists of a series of one more caplets: for example, a 2-year cap on 3-month LIBOR consists of a series of 8 caplets, expiring at 3-month intervals. Floorlets and floors are defined similarly. Caps and floors are typically valued by breaking them down into their component caplets or floorlets.

The market convention for translating back and forth between quoted implied volatilities and cap/floor prices is the *Black 76* model. This assumes that:

- the forward value of the reference rate F follows a lognormal process, i.e., follows geometric Brownian motion with constant known volatility σ (the "Black volatility"); and,
- the discount rate to the expiry date is a known, constant rate.

Thus, since the reference rate is assumed to be independent of the discount rate, the forward value of a caplet is given by the Black-Scholes formula:

$$FN(d_1) - KN(d_2)$$

where

$$d_1 = \frac{\log(F/K)}{\sigma\sqrt{t}} + \frac{\sigma\sqrt{t}}{2}, \quad d_2 = \frac{\log(F/K)}{\sigma\sqrt{t}} - \frac{\sigma\sqrt{t}}{2}$$

and the premium in today's money is computed by discounting the forward value at the given discount rate.

It is important to realize that the Black 76 model is simply a market convention. The actual observed cap/floor prices are determined by market participants based on:

- their own proprietary term structure models, which are based on their own assumptions about the nature of the interest rate process;
- their own expectations about the volatility of interest rates, i.e., the probability distribution of interest rates at various times in the future; and,
- market supply/demand or liquidity factors, such as a party attempting to execute an unusually large transaction.

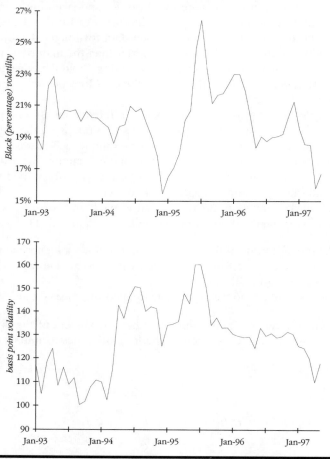

Exhibit 2–1: 5-Year Cap Implied Volatility: Black (Percentage) and Absolute (Basis Point)

The purpose of the convention is simply to provide a common basis for providing quotations. It is also common to provide cap/floor quotations in price terms (i.e., as a percentage of principal), but quoting implied "Black" volatilities is more convenient since this avoids the need to revise quotations after every small shift in the yield curve. Thus if a dealer says that the bid on a 3-year at-the-money cap is based on an implied Black volatility of 19%, everyone knows what this means — which would not be the case if everyone were only using their proprietary models. If the yield curve shifts, anyone can compute the dealer's new price. To give an idea of how implied volatilities have behaved over time, Exhibit 2–1 shows historical implied volatilities for 5-year at-the-money caps, and also translates these volatilities into basis point terms.

Exhibit 2-2: Implied Cap/Floor Volatility Since Late 1996

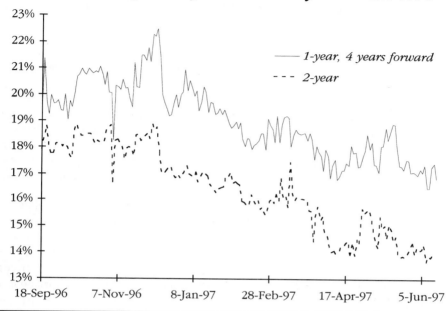

Implied volatility has itself been quite volatile, with Black volatilities ranging from 16% to 26% over the past four years. However, note that when expressed in basis point terms, volatility looks more stable: it fluctuated in the range 100–120 bp p.a. before the bond market crash of 1994 and 120–150 bp p.a. from then until the end of 1996.

In fact, since actual cap/floor prices are determined by many different factors, dealers will generally quote different Black volatilities for different cap/floor transactions depending on the strike rate and tenor. Exhibit 2–2 shows cap/floor implied volatilities since September 1996, for short-dated caps (expiring in 0–2 years) and longer-dated caps (expiring in 4–5 years). Since Fed policy was perceived as stable during this period, short-dated caps traded at lower implied volatilities than longer-dated caps. Note that short-dated and longer-dated implied volatilities are highly, although not perfectly, correlated.

Exhibit 2–3 shows how the quoted volatilities for individual caplets can vary depending on strike rate and expiry (expiry falling in 0–2 years, 2–3 years, 3–4 years or 4–5 years); this exhibit is based on observed cap/floor prices on 2/5/1997. For example, if there is currently high demand for deep out-of-the-money caps, a 7.50% 2-year cap may trade at a higher implied volatility than a 6.50% 2-year cap (although the actual cap price would be much lower).

Exhibit 2–3 shows that market cap/floor prices contradict the assumptions of the Black 76 model. Excluding transitory supply/demand factors, the model assumptions would imply that the implied volatility for all caplets and floorlets with the same expiry should be the same, regardless of the strike rate. This is clearly not the case; instead, we observe:

- a *skew*: Black volatilities are lower for higher strike rates and
- a *smile*: for short expiries (within two years), Black volatilities are lower for at-the-money caps/floors.

Since the skew and the smile tend to persist over time, they are not caused by transitory supply/demand factors. Instead, they probably exist because the market's assumptions about the nature of the interest rate process are not consistent with the assumptions made in the Black 76 model. Later in this chapter, we will try to determine what the skew and the smile can tell us about the market's assumptions.

This is the first important reason to look at market option prices: they can allow us to infer something about what kinds of interest rate models other market participants are using (either implicitly or explicitly). The second reason is that they suggest what volatility parameters we should use as inputs into our own models: we should try to calibrate our models to give the same cap/floor prices, for example, as those we observe in the market. As we shall see, this turns out to be more difficult than we might hope.

Exhibit 2–3: Caplet/Floorlet Implied Volatilities on 2/5/1997

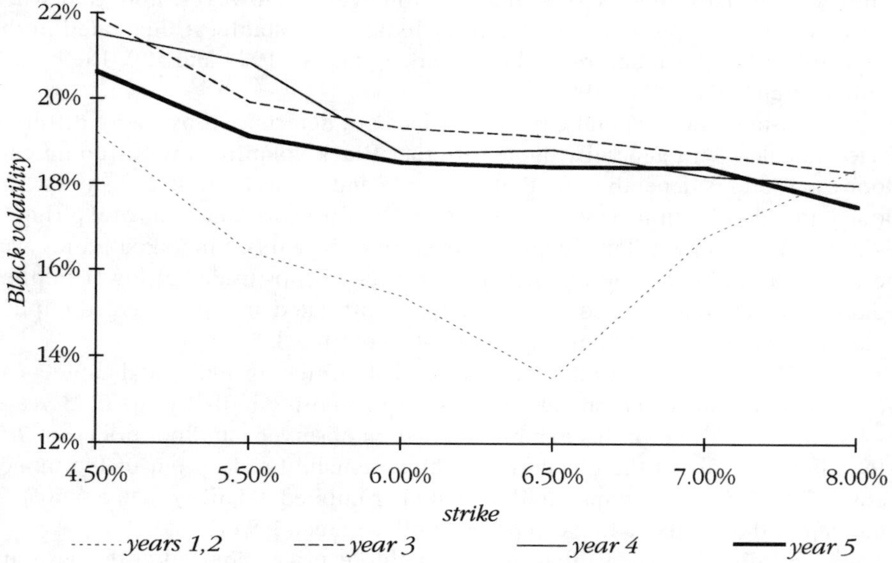

Legend: ······ years 1,2   ---- year 3   —— year 4   ━━ year 5

Axes: Black volatility (y-axis), strike (x-axis)

Cap/floor prices tell us about the expected volatility of 3-month LIBOR and more generally about the random process which money market rates are expected to follow. What about bond yields? We saw in Chapter 1 that, although money market and bond yields are closely linked, they do move independently. It would therefore be useful to analyze implied volatilities for bond options as well as caps and floors.

As mentioned earlier, data on short-dated bond and bond futures options is not very relevant to an investor attempting to value long-dated callable bonds and MBS. Instead, one should look at data from the swaption market — which is unfortunately a great deal less liquid and less transparent.

A swaption is an option to enter into an interest rate swap, on pre-specified terms, at some future date, the expiry date. For example, it might give one the right to enter into a 3-year, 7% fixed-for-floating swap (receiving fixed), exercisable in 2 years' time. Since receiving fixed in a swap is economically identical to purchasing a fixed-rate bond, this swaption can be analyzed as an option to purchase a 3-year 7% coupon bond for $100, expiring in 2 years. Thus swaptions are directly comparable to the options embedded in corporate bonds, except that swaptions are only actively traded out to about 10 years (swap tenor plus expiry).

The Black 76 model has been adapted for swaption pricing, and implied volatilities are quoted by dealers in a similar way. Similarly to the cap/floor market, these vary according to:

- the length of the underlying swap;
- the swap rate of the underlying swap; and,
- the time to expiry of the swaption.

However, swaption data is harder to obtain on a regular basis, particularly for a range of different strike yields. Since it is the ability to observe the skew and smile across a range of strikes which gives us insight into the interest rate process, we will rely mainly on cap/floor data in this chapter.

BASIC CONCEPTS OF INTEREST RATE OPTION MODELS

Review of Notation for Stochastic Processes

Although this chapter focuses on empirical observations and practical experience rather than mathematics, we will sometimes need a little mathematical notation for describing random processes. Since most introductory books on option pricing contain a more detailed description of stochastic processes, we only give a very brief review.

If X is some random process which we are trying to model, we often write X_t for its value at time t, which is random. For example, the Black-Scholes model assumes that an asset price X follows a *lognormal* process, i.e., a process of the form:

$$dX_t = \mu X_t dt + \sigma X_t dB_t$$

That is, the changes in the asset price are proportional to the price itself, and the change in price over a short period of time dt consists of a deterministic drift component $\mu X_t dt$ (where μ is the expected growth rate of the stock price) and a random component $\sigma X_t dB_t$ (where σ is the volatility of the stock price and B_t is a standard Brownian motion, so that dB_t is a normally distributed infinitesimal random motion). For example, if X is the price of a commodity future, then it is reasonable to assume that $\mu=0$ but that $\sigma\neq0$: that is, futures prices will fluctuate randomly, but if they drift up or down systematically, there would be an arbitrage opportunity.

The reason the Black-Scholes model is referred to as a lognormal model is that the random price at some future time has a lognormal distribution: i.e., $\log X$ is normally distributed. Bachelier's original model of stock prices was a *normal* or *Gaussian* model, where changes in the stock price are not proportional to the stock price, but have an absolute scale:

$$dX_t = \mu dt + \sigma dB_t$$

The model implies that the future stock price X at any given time is normally distributed. In particular, the model has the disadvantage that it allows the stock price to become negative and should therefore not be used to price stock options. However, Gaussian models are very useful in other situations.

There is no reason why μ or σ must be constant; they might depend on t or on X. For example, a very useful Gaussian process is the *mean reverting Gaussian* or *Ornstein-Uhlenbeck* process, which in its simplest form has constant σ but non-constant μ:

$$dX_t = -\kappa X_t dt + \sigma dB_t$$

Here X is a random variable which can be either positive or negative. But X cannot wander around freely at random: when it gets positive, the drift term $-\kappa X$ is negative, so it tends to be pulled back down to zero; and when it gets negative, the drift term $-\kappa X$ is positive, so it tends to be pulled back up to zero. Thus, in the long run, it fluctuates around zero. The constant κ measures the strength of the "pull" back towards zero.

More generally, we can describe a Gaussian process which is mean reverting to some average level $\overline{X}$ which is different from zero:

$$dX_t = \kappa(\overline{X} - X_t)dt + \sigma dB_t$$

In this case X tends to fluctuate around $\overline{X}$ rather than zero. We could also describe mean reverting lognormal processes, and so on.

Short Rate Models

Recall LEH, the local expectations hypothesis, which postulated that the expected short-term rate of return on all Treasury bonds was the same; call this rate r. Then

r can be regarded as the theoretical cost of funding a bond position. This theoretical rate r is clearly not constant, or even deterministic; rather, it is a random process, often called the *short rate process*. A *short rate model* is an explicit description of the random short rate process.

What has a short rate model got to do with the dynamics of bond yields? To explain why a short rate model gives rise to a model of the entire yield curve, we need to show how it can be used to price bonds of arbitrary maturity. Let $P_t(T)$ be the price at time t of a zero coupon bond with maturity date T; then $P_t(T)$ is also a random process, although we know what the price must be on the maturity date: $P_T(T) = 1$. Now, suppose an investor is holding this zero coupon bond on a funded basis, i.e., owns the bond and has a short cash position, initially of size $-C_0 = -P_0(T)$. At any future time t, the value of this short cash position must be $C_t = -P_t(T)$, or else there would be an obvious arbitrage. But, by definition, r is the (randomly varying) rate at which the short cash position is growing: that is, $dC_t/dt = r_t C_t$.

Integrating this gives

$$C_t = C_0 \cdot \exp\left(\int_0^t r_s \, ds\right)$$

and a bit of manipulation gives the equation

$$P_0(T)/P_t(T) = \exp\left(-\int_0^t r_s \, ds\right)$$

i.e., the random processes described by the left and right hand sides are the same. Thus their expected values are the same:

$$\mathbf{E}(P_0(T)/P_t(T)) = \mathbf{E}\left[\exp\left(-\int_0^t r_s \, ds\right)\right]$$

When $t = T$, $P_T(T) = 1$, and therefore this gives us a formula for the zero coupon bond price at time $t = 0$:

$$P_0(T) = \mathbf{E}\left[\exp\left(-\int_0^T r_s \, ds\right)\right]$$

More generally, the same argument can be used to prove that the zero coupon bond price at an arbitrary future time t is:

$$P_t(T) = \mathbf{E}_t\left[\exp\left(-\int_t^T r_s \, ds\right)\right]$$

where the expectation is now computed as at time t.

In other words, once we have a full description of the random behavior of r, we can compute the price (and thus the yield) of any zero coupon bond at any time, by computing this expected value. That is, specifying the process r_t determines the behavior of the entire yield curve (although it may be far from obvious just how shifts in r_t affect the yield curve as a whole). Thus, in building a term structure model, we can focus on specifying the process r_t.

For example, consider the so-called *Vasicek model*, which specifies that:

$$dr_t = \kappa(\bar{r} - r_t)dt + \sigma dB_t$$

This model, originally proposed by Merton in 1971 and first analyzed in detail by Vasicek, assumes that the short rate is a Gaussian process which mean reverts to some "long-term average interest rate" $\bar{r}$. One can derive a formula for the expected short rate at time t:

$$\mathbf{E}[r_t] = \bar{r} - \exp(-\kappa t)(\bar{r} - r_t)$$

That is, the Vasicek model forecasts that the expected future path of interest rates has the same mathematical form as that implied by the economic model of the yield curve presented in Chapter 1, provided we identify the "short rate" in the Vasicek model with the "short term nominal interest rate" in the economic model. Of course, the actual future path of interest rates in the Vasicek model is still random. In fact, the short rate can even become negative, although the presence of mean reversion makes this very improbable.

In this simple model, the above formula for zero coupon bond prices (where the price is an expected value of an integral) can be evaluated explicitly: Vasicek found a relatively simple formula for the zero coupon bond yield $y_t(T)$, of the form:

$$y_t(T) = M(T - t) + N(T - t)r_t$$

Here $M(T–t)$, $N(T–t)$ are certain functions of the bond's time to maturity $T–t$, which can both be written as closed form expressions involving the model parameters $\bar{r}$, σ, κ. That is, zero coupon bond yields are affine functions of the short rate.

Of course, there is no reason why one should be able to find constant parameters $\bar{r}$, σ, κ which ensure that the zero coupon bond yields predicted by the model at time $t=0$ should coincide precisely with observed market yields. This leads us to define the *extended Vasicek model*, where the short rate process is specified as follows:

$$dr_t = \kappa(t)(\bar{r}(t) - r_t)dt + \sigma(t)dB_t$$

Useful versions of this model have been popularized by Hull and White. The model takes the expected long-term average interest rate, volatility, and mean reversion strength to be, not constants, but time-dependent functions. It is then possible to derive more complicated explicit formulas for zero coupon bond yields, of the same form as shown above. One can then choose appropriate functions $\bar{r}(t)$, $\sigma(t)$, $\kappa(t)$ to ensure a perfect fit with the initial yield curve — in fact, there are many possible ways to do this. This process is called *calibration* and is usually quite difficult.

What does the Vasicek model say about the dynamics of the yield curve? Well, it only allows changes in the short rate r, not in the long-term average rate $\bar{r}$. In other words — recalling the relationship between the Vasicek model and the economic model of the yield curve presented in the previous chapter — the random shifts in r correspond to the slope shifts described there. The underlying reason is that it is κ which determines the shape of the yield curve.

Exhibit 2–4: Typical Yield Curve Shifts in the Vasicek and Extended Vasicek Models

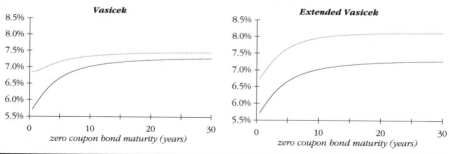

What about the extended Vasicek model? The answer is somewhat unexpected. If we estimate the Vasicek model parameters, we usually get a value for κ of around 0.5. By contrast, many common methods of calibrating the extended Vasicek model give a value for κ of around 0.01–0.05; in other words, they predict very weak mean reversion. This is because in this case it is $\bar{r}(t)$, not κ, which determines the shape of the yield curve. In this case, the random shifts in r correspond to shifts in the yield curve which are nearly parallel.

The situation is pictured in Exhibit 2–4. The solid lines show an initial yield curve, while the dotted lines show typical random yield curve shifts which can occur in each model.

That is, the Vasicek model generates slope shifts, while many versions of the extended Vasicek model generate nearly parallel yield curve shifts. We have learned an important lesson: in order to tell what assumptions a model is making about the dynamics of the yield curve, it is not enough to look at its abstract specification — we must also look at how the model parameters are derived, i.e., at how the model is calibrated.

There are many other short rate models, mostly more complex than the relatively simple Vasicek model. We will have more to say about other short rate models, and about the calibration process, later in this chapter.

Digression: Real World versus Risk-Neutral

A key idea behind the derivation of the standard Black-Scholes formula for stock options is that although the specification of the price process $dX_t = \mu X_t dt + \sigma X_t dB_t$ involves the expected growth rate μ of the stock price — which is unknown — the final pricing formula does not involve μ and only uses the riskless rate r.

From a technical point of view, this has the following interpretation. Intuitively, the value of the option equals its expected payoff at the expiry date, discounted to the present. The idea behind risk-neutral pricing is that if one uses "risk-neutral" rather than "real world" probabilities to compute this expectation, one can discount using the known riskless rate r rather than the unknown growth rate μ. The risk-neutral probabilities are the probabilities of each scenario in a world where the expected rate of return on all assets is r.

Now, LEH already assumes that the expected rate of return on all Treasury bonds is the (random) short rate r_t; in effect, it assumes that the real world and the risk-neutral world are the same, and that discounting in the real world is done using the short rate r_t.

It is not necessary to assume that LEH is true in order to price options. However, one can show the following: in general — i.e., not assuming LEH — if P is the price of a Treasury bond (which varies randomly over time), then the expected rate of return from the bond must be:

$$r_t + \lambda \sigma(r, t) \frac{dP/dr}{P}$$

where $\sigma(r, t)$ is the bond's price volatility at time t and short rate level r and λ is a *market price of risk parameter* which is applicable to all Treasury bonds. This formula has a natural interpretation:

$$\frac{dP/dr}{P}$$

measures how the bond price responds to a change in the short rate r, and can be interpreted as a kind of "effective duration;" thus,

$$\sigma(r, t) \frac{dP/dr}{P}$$

is the price volatility of the bond, and the formula says that every bond must, in expectation, earn a risk premium proportional to its price volatility.

(This is a slightly loose usage of the term "effective duration," for the following reason. Recall that the effective duration of a bond is the percentage change in price resulting from a parallel shift in the yield curve. This will not be equal to

$$\frac{dP/dr}{P}$$

unless, according to the model, a change in the short rate causes a parallel shift in the yield curve. For example, in models with mean reversion, a shift in r_t induces a non-parallel shift in the yield curve — long bond yields move less than short bond yields — so

$$\frac{dP/dr}{P}$$

will not be precisely equal to the bond's effective duration, although if the mean reversion parameter κ is small then it will be very close to the effective duration.)

LEH says that $\lambda=0$, i.e., that investors are risk-neutral. If $\lambda \neq 0$ (i.e., LEH is false), then under suitable assumptions one may be able to eliminate λ from all pricing formulas in the same way as in the classical Black-Scholes analysis: one computes expectations, not in the real world, but in a risk-neutral world where $\lambda=0$, i.e., where LEH holds and where one is allowed to discount using r_t. The problem is to prove that an equivalent risk-neutral world exists and to find an explicit description of the risk-neutral probabilities that allows one to compute expectations. An alternative approach is to derive pricing formulas involving λ and to attempt to estimate λ using current bond prices. One is allowed to assume that λ is time-dependent.

Similar results hold for multi-factor models. In this case, there is more than one source of risk — i.e., more than one underlying random process — thus there is a separate market price of risk corresponding to each source of risk, and for each bond, one must compute a separate price volatility corresponding to each source of risk.

For simplicity, we assume LEH in the rest of the chapter. This frees us from the need to talk about risk-neutral probabilities as distinct from real-world probabilities. However, all the issues we discuss are still relevant if we drop the assumption and are forced to work with risk-neutral probabilities.

Pricing Option-Embedded Bonds Using a Short Rate Model

Once we have a description of the interest rate process, how can we use it to price bonds with embedded options? Intuitively, the bond price should be equal to the expected value of its discounted cashflows; in computing this expectation we should take all possible interest rate paths into account and determine the bond's contingent cashflows under all these paths.

More precisely, if C_t is the cashflow at time t along a given interest rate path $(r_t)_{t \geq 0}$, then the theoretical bond price is:

$$E\left[\int_{t=0}^{T} C_t PV(t) dt\right]$$

where T is the bond's maturity and

$$PV(t) = \exp\left(\int_0^t r_s ds\right)$$

This expectation can be approximated by simulating a large number of random interest rate paths, e.g., via the Monte Carlo method, as discussed later in this chapter.

Actually, this pricing formula is not quite right. LEH is an assumption about Treasury bond returns, and it is not perfectly correct to assume that LEH applies to a corporate bond or an MBS: the expected return should not be equal to r_t, but to r_t plus some spread which compensates the investor for holding a corporate bond or MBS rather than a Treasury bond. This is the *option-adjusted spread*, and one can take it into account in the pricing formula by defining

$$PV(t) = \exp\left(-\int_0^t (r_s + OAS) ds\right)$$

In practice, unless the bond is very illiquid, one does not make an *a priori* assumption about what the OAS should be; instead, one finds the OAS from the market price of the bond, by determining what OAS gives a theoretical price equal to the market price. Intuitively, the OAS is compensation for all risks which are not built into the model, i.e., risks which the model does not tell us how to hedge. We discuss this further in Chapter 6.

Monte Carlo or related methods are required to value mortgage-backed securities, but other methods are required for corporate bonds with calls or puts. The value of such a bond is *non-path-dependent*: it depends only on the current interest rate environment, not on what interest rates have done in the past. By contrast, a security such as a CMO is *path-dependent*, since its value depends on how the various tranches have paid down, which in turn depends on the history of prepayments and thus of interest rates.

The key to valuing a non-path-dependent security efficiently is to notice that its price satisfies a certain partial differential equation. Thus, the valuation problem reduces to solving this PDE, and there are highly efficient methods for doing so. We will sketch the derivation of the PDE — focusing on the intuition, rather than attempting to be rigorous — and show how the notion of OAS fits into this context. Solution methods for PDEs will be discussed later in the chapter.

The return on a bond is its income return plus its price return. Over a short period of time dt, we can write this as:

$$(\text{coupon} + \text{amortization}) \cdot dt + \text{duration} \cdot dy + \tfrac{1}{2} \text{ convexity} \cdot (dy)^2$$

where dy is the change in yield and where we are referring to effective duration and convexity. Now, in the context of the interest rate model, observe that:

- $\dfrac{dP/dt}{P}$ is the rate of amortization if the bond ages but r_t remains unchanged,

- $\dfrac{dP/dr}{P}$ can be regarded as an "effective duration" measure, and

- $\dfrac{d^2P/dr^2}{P}$ can be regarded as a "convexity" measure.

Also, by LEH, the *expected* short-term rate of return from the bond should be r_t+OAS: that is, coupon return plus expected price return equals r_t+OAS. Putting all this together and multiplying everything by P gives us the formula:

$$\left(\text{cpn}(t) + \frac{dP}{dt} \right)dt + \mathbf{E}\left(\frac{dP}{dr}dr_t + \frac{1}{2}\frac{d^2P}{dr^2}(dr_t)^2 \right) = (r_t + \text{OAS}) \cdot P\,dt$$

where $\text{cpn}(t)$ is the coupon yield at time t.

If we have defined a short rate process $dr_t = \mu dt + \sigma dB_t$, we can compute the expectation on the left hand side. Recall that a Brownian motion B_t is a continuous random walk, where each random step dB_t is normally distributed with mean 0 and variance dt. Thus $\mathbf{E}[dt] = \mu dt$, and expanding $(dr_t)^2$ we get:

$$\mathbf{E}[(dr_t)^2] = \mathbf{E}(\sigma^2(dB_t)^2 + \text{lower order terms which go away}) = \sigma^2 dt$$

Substituting into the previous formula and dividing by dt, we get the following PDE, which must be satisfied by the bond price P:

$$\left(\text{cpn}(t) + \frac{dP}{dt}\right) + \mu\frac{dP}{dr} + \frac{1}{2}\sigma^2\frac{d^2P}{dr^2} = (r_t + \text{OAS}) \cdot P$$

Thus, the PDE approach to valuing option-embedded bonds has a natural interpretation in terms of effective duration and convexity, and the option-adjusted spread shows up very naturally in the PDE as a risk premium over the short rate. It also has a clear interpretation. In deriving the PDE, we took duration and convexity risk (as defined by the model) into account; the OAS is the remaining risk premium, compensating the investor for other risks. Note that concepts such as option-adjusted yield do not appear naturally.

RELATIVE MERITS OF
DIFFERENT TERM STRUCTURE MODELS

Whole Yield Curve Models

Short rate models have two important drawbacks, to which we have already alluded:

1. Although the behavior of r_t in principle determines the behavior of the whole yield curve, in practice it can be quite inefficient to compute other bond yields: depending on the model, one may need to use a very complex closed-form formula, or one may even be forced to compute yields numerically. As a consequence, for many short rate models, it is hard to visualize precisely how the yield curve is moving around; there is no obvious way to make the model implement a predetermined kind of yield curve shift. Thus the model may be inefficient to implement and it may be hard to tell whether the model is realistic or to force the model to be realistic.

2. There is no easy way to calibrate the model to the observed yield curve. Models with constant parameters cannot be calibrated, and the best we can to is to look for "best fit" parameters. Models with time-dependent parameters can be calibrated but this may be computationally intensive and there are some pitfalls involved, as discussed below.

Instead of modeling the dynamics of the short rate and then deriving the behavior of the yield curve, why not construct a *whole yield curve model* which models the dynamics of the whole yield curve at once? Then one could simply feed in the initial yield curve directly, and hopefully one could specify directly — and with complete freedom — the kinds of random shifts it could undergo. One could pick a single kind of yield curve shift and get a one-factor model, or one could pick several different kinds of yield curve shift — for example, the major fundamental shifts identified by a principal component analysis — and get a multi-factor model.

The simplest kind of whole yield curve model is the Ho-Lee model, which only allows random parallel shifts in the yield curve. The fully general whole yield curve approach was first developed by Heath, Jarrow, and Morton, and independently by Babbs; they showed how to implement it in considerable generality. However, it is notoriously difficult to implement HJM models efficiently.

As the mathematical details are quite complex, we will present only an elegant special case: the term structure model used at CMS, originally discovered independently by Ritchken and Sankarasubramanian, by El Karoui and Lacoste, and by Cheyette at CMS. This is not very general — it is a one-factor model, it only allows a particular kind of yield curve shift — but it is very efficient and turns out to be quite realistic, at least when used to price most option-embedded bonds.

We would like to model the behavior of the whole forward curve; in other words, the behavior of the forward short rates $f(T)$ for all forward dates T. In other words, we want to specify the random process $f_t(T)$ for all forward dates T. Note that once this is done, it is easy to recover the T-maturity zero coupon yield $y_t(T)$ at any time t; it is simply the average of the forward rates at time t on all the forward dates s between t and T:

$$y_t(T) = \frac{1}{T-t}\int_t^T f_t(s)\,ds$$

What we need to do is specify a drift and volatility for $f_t(T)$, for each T. The problem is to do this in a consistent way. Recall that, while UEH implies that forward rates had no drift, LEH — which is the usual assumption — implies that they must have a gradual upward drift which depends on volatility. For example, the (continuous version of the) *Ho-Lee model* specifies that:

$$df_t(T) = \sigma^2 T dt + \sigma dB_t$$

That is, it is a Gaussian model — random shifts in forward rates are normally distributed — and any given forward rate drifts upward at a rate proportional to the initial time to the forward date. The Ho-Lee model says that the yield curve undergoes random parallel shifts and steepens over time, although this steepening is only gradual because σ^2 is a very small number: see the solid line in Exhibit 2–5. If this steepening were left out, long bonds would tend to outperform shorter bonds because of their greater convexity, contradicting LEH.

Note that in the Ho-Lee model, we have the following relationship between the initial forward rates and expected future short rates, which will reappear in Chapter 4:

$$E[r_t] = f_0(t) + \frac{\sigma^2 t^2}{2}$$

Exhibit 2-5: Drift in Yields in the Ho-Lee and CMS Models, Showing Steepening

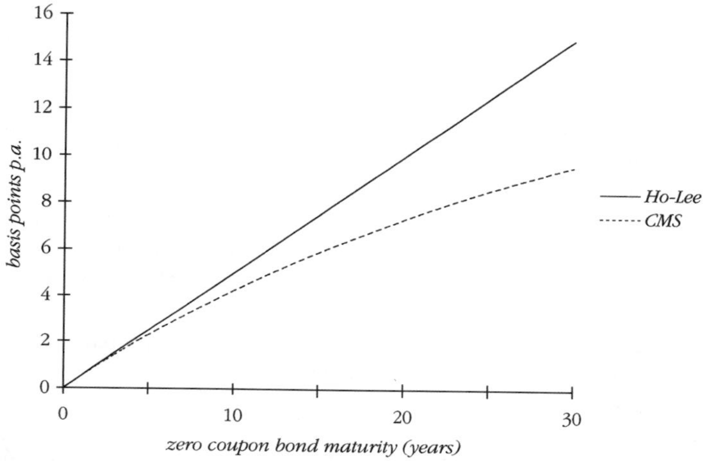

One can prove that the Ho-Lee model is consistent with LEH. The main problems with the Ho-Lee model, in this form, are that negative interest rates are quite likely, the degree of steepening in the yield curve over long time horizons is somewhat unrealistic, and the volatilities of different bond yields implied by the model are unrealistic (this is discussed later, in the section on calibration). The Ho-Lee model with constant volatility assigns unrealistically high values to caps, and can assign unrealistically low values to long-dated call options, causing it to overvalue callable bonds.

Incorporating mean reversion cures all of these problems. This approach leads to the *CMS model*, which is the simplest and most robust version of the class of models discovered by Ritchken and Sankarasubramanian/Cheyette. The CMS model resembles a short rate model, since it describes the behavior of the short rate directly: i.e., it specifies what kind of random shocks the short rate can undergo. What makes it a whole yield curve model is that — unlike most short rate models — one can write down an explicit formula which says how a shock to the short rate affects all the forward rates. Thus, one can start with the initial forward curve as a direct input, and at any point one knows what is happening to the whole forward curve.

More formally, let $\Delta_t = r_t - f_0(t)$ be the difference between what the future short rate turns out to be at time t, and the initial t-forward short rate (i.e., based on the initial forward curve, which can be arbitrary). Δ_t is a random process, although $\mathbf{E}[\Delta_t] > 0$ since we know, by LEH, that the expected short rate at time t is higher than the initial t-forward rate.

The CMS model assumes that Δ_t is a Gaussian process which mean reverts to zero, but that it also has a gradual upward drift $v^2(t)$:

$$d\Delta_t = (v^2(t) - \kappa\Delta_t)dt + \sigma dB_t$$

where

$$v^2(t) = \sigma^2\frac{1 - \exp(-2\kappa t)}{2\kappa}$$

Intuitively, $v^2(t)$ is the "cumulative volatility" which has been experienced up to time t; because of the mean reversion, the cumulative volatility does not keep growing, but approaches a limit of $\sigma^2/2\kappa$ in the long run. The term $v^2(t)$ may be regarded as a convexity adjustment, and the formula for it has been chosen to eliminate arbitrage between forwards and Eurodollar futures.

Then it is possible to derive following formula telling you what any T-forward rate is at time t, provided you know the initial T-forward rate and also Δ_t. The intuition behind this formula is that a shock to the short rate propagates to all the forward rates, but with exponentially decaying amplitude:

$$f_t(T) = f_0(T) + \exp(-\kappa(T-t))\left(\Delta_t + \frac{1 - \exp(-\kappa(T-t))}{\kappa}v^2(t)\right)$$

Like the Ho-Lee model, the CMS model predicts that the yield curve will gradually steepen over time. However, because of the mean reversion, bond yields in the CMS model tend to fluctuate over a narrower range in the long run than in the Ho-Lee model. Thus convexity confers less of a benefit, and less steepening is required to ensure that longer bonds are not expected to outperform shorter bonds. To be more precise, while the Ho-Lee model predicts that the yield curve grows steeper along its entire length, the CMS model predicts that the short end of the curve steepens more rapidly than the long end: see the dotted line in Exhibit 2–5.

The CMS whole yield curve model is in some ways formally similar to the Vasicek short rate model. In fact there is a formula expressing the time t zero coupon yield in terms of the initial zero coupon yield and Δ_t that generalizes the corresponding formula in the Vasicek model.

Letting $\kappa\rightarrow 0$ in the CMS model, we recover the constant volatility Ho-Lee model: this shows that the two are related. These models are both efficient and easy to implement partly because, in their simplest form, they assume that the volatility function is constant — this allows us to derive various explicit formulas and other simplifications. Note that in the Ho-Lee model, a constant volatility function implies that the term structure of volatility should be flat. This is not the case for the CMS model: because of mean reversion, the CMS model predicts a declining term structure of volatility.

General HJM models are significantly more complicated than either the Ho-Lee model or the CMS model. There is one important technical difference which also makes them very inefficient to implement. The Ho-Lee and CMS models, like most popular short rate models, are *non-path-dependent*: this means that the behavior of the yield curve only depends on its current state (which includes the cumulative volatility). In a more general HJM model, the behavior of the yield curve is *path-dependent*, i.e., the drift and volatility of the forward rates depend on the history of the yield curve up to that point. Non-path-dependent models can be implemented much more efficiently than path-dependent models: for example, one can implement a non-path-dependent model using a recombining tree, whereas one may be forced to use a Monte Carlo method to implement a path-dependent model.

Incidentally, the distinction between path-dependent and non-path-dependent *term structure models* should not be confused with the distinction between path-dependent and non-path-dependent *bonds*. The two distinctions are quite different.

Equilibrium Models Versus No-Arbitrage Models

An *equilibrium model* of the term structure is a model which is derived from, or consistent with, some general equilibrium model of the economy — the Vasicek model is an example. Cox, Ingersoll, and Ross studied such models in considerable detail. Equilibrium models tend to use constant parameters, such as constant volatilities, and these are often estimated from historical time series. However, when using such models in practice, it is preferable to estimate parameters using cross-sectional data: today's yield curve and implied volatilities. That is, one aims for a best fit to observed market prices.

An *arbitrage-free model* of the term structure is a model which can be made exactly consistent with the observed initial yield curve; that is, the current bond yields predicted by the model are equal to the market yields. In fact, the terminology can be a bit confusing. Arbitrage is impossible in any sensible term structure model, provided bonds trade at the yields predicted by the model; that is, all models are arbitrage-free in an internal sense. An "arbitrage-free model" is a model which is arbitrage-free when compared with the market.

("Arbitrage-free" is often used in a more restrictive sense, to mean consistency with observed option prices as well as observed Treasury yields. As we shall see in the section on calibration, this requirement is too strong. Incidentally, this is a good example of an area where the requirements of exotic option traders and bond investors diverge markedly.)

An equilibrium model, estimated using today's yield curve, can fail to be arbitrage-free in two ways: it can show small, unbiased errors at particular points on the yield curve, or it can exhibit a large, systematic error over a whole region of the yield curve. For example, fitting parameters to the Vasicek model tends to lead to small random errors in the yields of bonds with maturities of two years or more, but large, systematic errors at the short end of the yield curve. This is related to our observation, in Chapter 1, that current monetary policy and the current economy are rarely regarded as being in equilibrium, and therefore that the "short-term interest rate" in the economic model — which is where the markets think interest rates should be — cannot be identified with an observed money market yield.

It is often said that any equilibrium model can be converted into an arbitrage-free model by making the parameters time-dependent and calibrating them. The story is not so simple; as we have seen with the extended Vasicek model, if we are not careful then this may change the whole nature of the model. In this connection, note that an arbitrage-free need not be realistic. In fact, the calibration process may produce a model that is totally unrealistic; many common calibration methods do just that. We will return to this point in the section on calibration.

For obvious reasons, it is nearly always preferable to use a well-understood arbitrage-free model rather than an equilibrium model. There are two situations in which one might use an equilibrium model. One is where a good arbitrage-free model is not available. For example, it is much easier to specify and implement a realistic equilibrium two-factor model than an realistic arbitrage-free two-factor model.

The other situation is where reliable market data does not exist. This might apply in countries where the bond market is known to be highly inefficient; it may also apply when valuing securities which are longer than 30 years, so that no Treasury yields are available to construct an initial yield curve. In this case one would use an equilibrium model to extrapolate the observed Treasury curve in a consistent fashion. The problem of valuing very long bonds is discussed in more detail in Chapter 4.

Interest Rate Processes: Normal, Lognormal, and Square Root

A further distinction between different term structure models is the kind of process which interest rates follow. For simplicity we will focus on constant parameter short rate models. The question here is: How does the short rate behave? Does it follow a Gaussian process, or a lognormal process, or something other kind of process? The three most popular kinds of process are:

1. Gaussian or normal: the basis point volatility is independent of the current interest rate, so the volatility term has the form σdB_t. A typical example is the Vasicek model.
2. Square root or squared Gaussian: the basis point volatility is proportional to the square root of the current interest rate, so the volatility term has the form $\sigma r^{1/2} dB_t$. A typical example is the Cox-Ingersoll-Ross model.
3. Lognormal: the basis point volatility is proportional to the current interest rate, so the volatility term has the form $\sigma r\, dB_t$. A typical example is the Black-Derman-Toy model.

For example, suppose the short rate is currently 6% and is assumed to have a volatility of 100 bp p.a., and consider an interest rate scenario where the short rate moves to 3% at some future date; what does the model assume about its volatility on that date? A Gaussian model would continue to assume that it had a volatility of 100 bp, a lognormal model would assume that it had a volatility of 50 bp, and a square root model would assume that it had a volatility of 71 bp.

Exhibit 2-6: Distribution of Future Interest Rates Implied by Different Processes

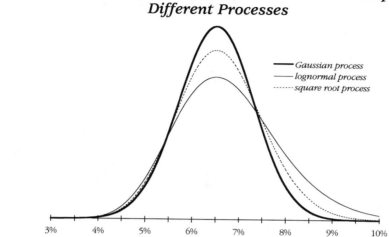

Normal models are easy to implement and highly efficient. Square root models are somewhat harder to implement, but still very efficient, since (as with normal models) one can usually derive explicit formulas for zero coupon bond yields rather than being forced to price these bonds numerically. Lognormal models are the least efficient, since explicit formulas do not exist; however, with some effort it is possible to build quite efficient implementations which run reasonably quickly on modern computers.

The process we choose will affect the statistical distribution of future interest rates predicted by the model. For example, Exhibit 2-6 show normal, square root and lognormal distributions calibrated to give the same option value for a 6.5% coupon 10-year bond callable in one year. The three distributions can give rise to quite different option values: see Exhibits 2-7 and 2-8.

Low interest rate scenarios are more likely using a Gaussian model, whereas very high interest rate scenarios are more likely using a square root or (especially) a lognormal model. From a bond investor's point of view, the practical implications of this are:

- normal models tend to assign higher values to call options, and thus give lower valuations for callable corporate bonds and most mortgage-backed securities (or if valuations are known, lower OAS figures);
- square root and lognormal models tend to assign higher values to put options, and thus give higher valuations (or higher OAS figures) for corporate bonds with investor put options;
- square root and lognormal models tend to assign higher value to caps, and thus give lower valuations (or lower OAS figures) for ARMs and capped FRNs.

Exhibit 2-7: Callable Bond Price versus Yield Using Different Interest Rate Processes

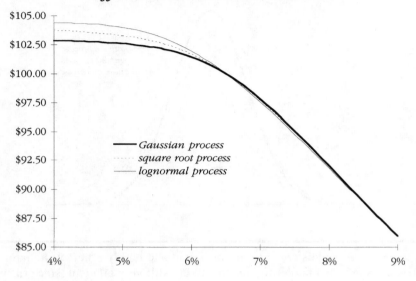

Exhibit 2-8: Put Bond Price versus Yield Using Different Interest Rate Processes

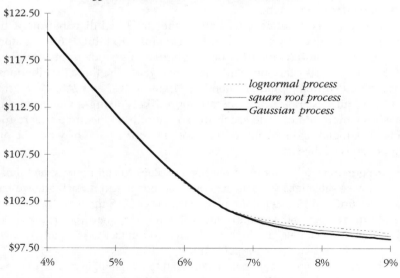

These tendencies become more obvious when using the models for stress testing. Thus Gaussian models are in some sense more "conservative" than square root or lognormal models, except perhaps for ARMs and capped FRNs.

It is natural to ask which of these three models is the most realistic — or indeed, whether any of them are realistic. Unfortunately, this question does not have a simple answer. For example, one might try to make the question more precise by assuming that the random term in the interest rate process has the form $\sigma r^\gamma dB_t$, and then trying to estimate the rate process exponent γ from empirical data. We would then pick a normal, square root or lognormal model, depending on whether our estimate of γ was closest to 0, ½, or 1.

What empirical data should we use? A common approach (e.g., Andersen and Lund) is to use time series of historical money market or bond yields. The results are not entirely consistent but seem to suggest that $\gamma \approx ½$. Unfortunately, this approach has some problems. Firstly, it estimates a single value of γ from the whole of the data, and we therefore run the risk of ignoring a structural shift (γ may be different in different regimes). Secondly, it makes some fixed assumption about the form of the random term in the interest rate process, and if this assumption is not valid for the whole of the sample period then the results are meaningless. Finally, most statistical methods require that we make some a priori assumptions about the statistical properties of the data — for example, that the interest rate is a stationary process, or that σ is constant throughout the sample period — and if these assumptions are false, the results are meaningless. On the other hand, as we mentioned earlier in the chapter, there may not be enough data to let us employ methods which require fewer assumptions and still get statistically significant results.

An alternative is to use, not time series data, but cross-sectional data: option prices. The idea is that the pattern of implied volatilities tells us something about what the market thinks the statistical distribution of future interest rates should be. For example, on any given day one could estimate the rate process exponent γ which gave theoretical option values most consistent with market option prices. That is, we find the value of γ which best models the observed skew in implied volatilities across strikes (e.g., if there were no skew, this would imply $\gamma = 1$, i.e., a lognormal distribution).

The results are show in Exhibit 2–9. An estimate value for γ of between 0.5 and 1.0 is typical, although there is not much consistency either over time or between different option expiries. This would seem to favor using a square root or lognormal process.

However, this is not the end of the story. We have only analyzed cap/floor implied volatilities in the current interest rate environment (USD, late 1996–early 1997). In very low or very high interest rate environments, the story may be different. For example, as interest rates rallied in 1992–93, cap/floor Black volatilities in the U.S. and Australian market rose: this suggests that dealers were abandoning the lognormal rate process assumption, which (if Black volatilities had been stable) would have implied very low basis point volatilities.

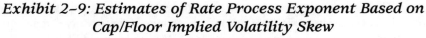

Exhibit 2–9: Estimates of Rate Process Exponent Based on Cap/Floor Implied Volatility Skew

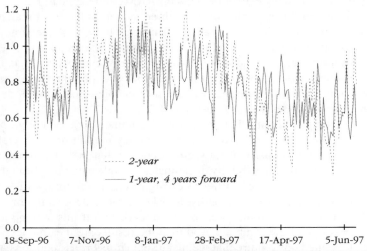

The Japanese and Swiss markets provide more recent examples. Exhibit 2–10 shows the basis point volatilities (not Black volatilities) implied by JPY cap/floor prices on 3/17/1997, at a time when the forward curve sloped up from 0.50% to 4.50%. Quoted Black volatilities sloped down from 65% to 25%, but the corresponding basis point volatilities decline much more gently. The graph strongly suggests that dealers were using a broadly constant basis point volatility assumption regardless of the level of the forward curve at different expiries — rather than assuming that the basis point volatility was proportional to the interest rate. In fact, the cap/floor prices are consistent with a Gaussian model with mild mean reversion (and thus slightly lower volatilities for longer expiries).

The pattern was similar in the Swiss market, where cap/floor Black volatilities declined from 55% to 20% as the level of the forward curve rose, again giving consistent basis point volatilities for different expiries. Though it is hard to be precise, we can summarize our conclusions as follows:

- When interest rates are low (less than 4%), the rate process looks Gaussian.
- When interest rates are high (over 9%), the rate process looks lognormal.
- For intermediate interest rate levels, something in between looks reasonable.

Note that this is the other way round from what one might assume, if one believed that interest rates tend to avoid zero. However, here is a plausible economic explanation for our observations. Recall from Chapter 1 that the interest rate has a real rate component and an inflation component. Thus interest rate volatility arises from real rate volatility and price volatility. Then:

Exhibit 2–10: Basis Point Volatilities Implied by JPY Cap/Floor Prices, 3/17/1997

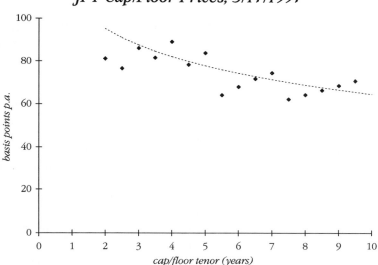

- When interest rates are low, the inflation component is negligible, and it is real rate volatility that matters; but as real rates are linked to growth, which can be either positive or negative, it is reasonable to assume that they are approximately normally distributed. (Indeed, in Israel, real yields on inflation-linked bonds have at times been negative.)
- When interest rates are high, the inflation component dominates, and it is price volatility that matters; but there are good economic arguments supporting the standard assumption that the nominal prices of traded goods are lognormally distributed.
- For intermediate interest rate levels, something in between looks reasonable.

The situation is a little inconvenient in one way. As mentioned above, a common criticism of Gaussian models is that they permit negative interest rates. In practice, the probability of negative interest rates is extremely low, unless interest rates are currently very low; but as we have just seen, this is exactly the situation where we want to use a Gaussian model. Incidentally, it is useful to recall that historical short-term interest rates have in fact been negative, for brief periods, in Hong Kong, New Zealand, and Switzerland; so a model which permits negative interest rates is not necessarily unrealistic provided one assumes that future restrictions on cross-border capital flows are possible.

Note that in a model with mean reversion, bond yields will be positive even when the short rate is slightly negative. It can be shown that problems only arise when pricing extremely long-dated options, i.e., when looking at time horizons of over 30 years. In this case, other factors come into play, which are more problematic than the choice of interest rate process: see Chapter 4.

Probability Distributions and the Volatility Smile

Gaussian, square root and lognormal models all assume that the interest rate process is derived from a Brownian motion — that is, that the expected probability distribution of future interest rates is derived from a normal distribution. How accurate is this assumption?

The existence of the volatility smile suggests that the assumption is not quite right. The smile says that deep out-of-the-money options are worth more than a normal distribution would imply; that is, that extreme interest rate scenarios are more likely than a normal distribution would predict. Thus, the implied volatility smile suggests that in pricing options, dealers are assuming that future interest rates have a "fat-tailed" distribution: see Exhibit 2–11. Under a fat-tailed distribution, both extreme scenarios and "boring" scenarios are more likely than under a normal distribution with the same variance.

There are a number of ways to model the volatility smile mathematically, but none of them are really satisfactory. A popular approach is to assume that volatility itself is not constant, but random, and to model it using a separate random process (there is a graphical example of such a model in Kloeden et al.). This yields fat-tailed distributions for future interest rates: extreme interest rate scenarios are more likely to arise because volatility can become more volatile. However, as pointed out by Bates, stochastic volatility does not explain the observed smile unless we assume that the volatility of volatility is implausibly high.

Exhibit 2–11: Normal Distribution and Fat-Tailed Distribution with Same Variance

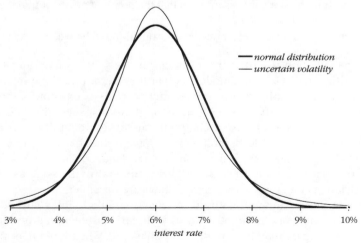

normal distribution
uncertain volatility

3%   4%   5%   6%   7%   8%   9%   10%

interest rate

Exhibit 2-12: Recent History of the Cap/Floor Volatility Smile

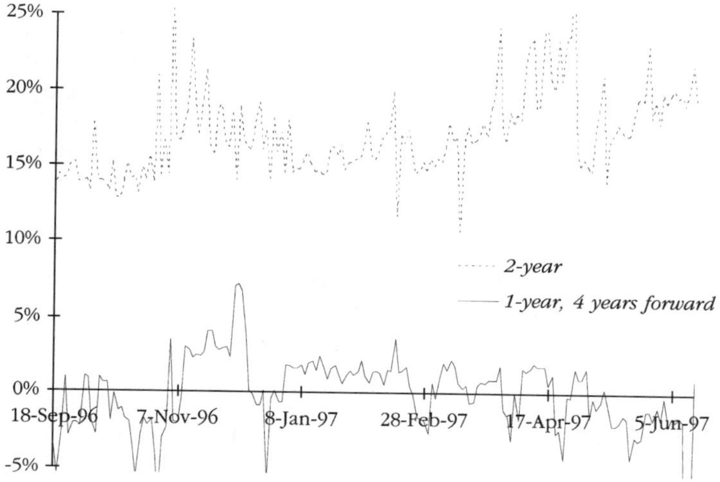

Another way of obtaining a fat-tailed distribution is to replace Brownian motion, which is continuous, with a process with jumps: i.e., a Poisson process. This amounts to assuming that interest rates do not continuously experience small random shocks, but instead tend to "gap" up or down at longer intervals. A Poisson process with the same volatility as a Gaussian process (Brownian motion) will give rise to fatter-tailed distributions: the fact that it is driven by large jumps makes extreme scenarios more likely.

Both these explanations suggest that the smile should be consistent from day to day. In fact, it tends to vary. Exhibit 2–12 shows the historical behavior of the cap/floor volatility smile, measured as the percentage difference in implied volatility between an at-the-money option and a ±100 bp out-of-the-money option.

Option traders have a variety of explanations for the behavior of the smile. For example, in early 1997, implied volatilities were low and the smile was subdued, whereas after the Fed tightened on March 25, implied volatilities were low (see Exhibit 2–2) and the smile was more pronounced. Intuitively, in early 1997 the market expected interest rates to remain low and stable, while after the tightening the market expected interest rates to follow a predictable upward path. The more pronounced smile arose because, while overall volatility expectations remained relatively unchanged, the market gave greater weight to the worst case scenarios in which the Fed would "get it wrong," triggering more extreme interest rate environments.

The real question, however, is whether the volatility smile is relevant to bond investors. Observe from Exhibit 2–3 that the smile is really only evident for relatively short-dated options: it is important for caplets with expiries up to 2 years, but more or less negligible for longer-dated caplets. One-year implied volatilities two years and three years forward show similar behavior, i.e., no consistent smile.

There are plausible reasons why the smile vanishes for longer-dated options. Under the stochastic volatility explanation, long-dated options will exhibit no smile provided we make the plausible assumption that volatility is mean-reverting to some long-run average volatility level. Under the jump process explanation, the smile vanishes because — looked at over long time periods — a Poisson process starts to resemble Brownian motion and the probability distributions converge to normal distributions: this is just the Central Limit Theorem.

In any case, it is clear that the smile is not an important factor over long time horizons; thus it is irrelevant to pricing almost all corporate bonds and MBS. That is, although the smile is very important to an OTC options trader, most bond investors can probably ignore it. Actually, it is very fortunate that bond investors can use models which do not take account of the volatility smile. Building a model which is plausible, stable, and can be calibrated to the smile is difficult, and calibration itself is slow and unstable.

Multi-Factor Term Structure Models

All the models we have considered so far are one-factor models which only permit one kind of shift in the yield curve. We saw in Chapter 2 that many kinds of yield curve shifts could occur — e.g., parallel, slope, and curvature shifts — and thus various multi-factor term structure models have been proposed which permit different kinds of random shifts. Later in this chapter, we will discuss how well multi-factor models perform, in practice, compared to one-factor models. For the moment we simply list a few of them and discuss some of the theoretical difficulties that arise.

The earliest two-factor model to be studied in detail was the *Brennan-Schwartz model*, which described the dynamics of the short rate r and the long yield L (consol yield). Since the model allows these to move independently, both parallel and slope shifts can occur. The original model had some technical defects which made it unrealistic — Hogan showed that the long yield can explode in a finite time — but these can be repaired. For example, Rebonato and Cooper consider a modified version of the Brennan-Schwartz model in which the state variables are the consol price $C=1/L$ and the spread between the long yield and the short rate, $S=L-r$. These are assumed to be random processes of the following form:

$$dC = \mu_C C dt + \sigma_C C dB_t^{(1)}$$

$$dS = \mu_S dt + \sigma_S dB_t^{(2)}$$

where $\mathbf{E}[dB_t^{(1)} dB_t^{(2)}] = p dt$, some assumed correlation, and μ_C and μ_S are chosen to preclude arbitrage between bonds of different maturities. That is, the consol price is a lognormal process (like a stock price) while the spread is a Gaussian process: thus the spread can be either positive or negative, allowing for both positive and inverse yield curves.

Note that the short rate can be recovered as $r_t=(1/C)-S_t$. In this setting, changes in L correspond to parallel shifts while changes in S correspond to yield curve slope shifts; thus any bond has both a "parallel duration"

$$\frac{dP/dL}{P}$$

and a "slope duration"

$$\frac{dP/dS}{P}$$

In practice, models like the modified Brennan-Schwartz model seem to be quite useful; this is because they imply a realistic dynamics for the yield curve, they can be implemented fairly easily, and one can devise fairly easy and robust procedures for estimating the model parameters.

There is a fairly recent method, due to Duffie and Kan, for building very efficient multi-factor models in which the underlying factors can be bond yields: for example, the 2-year and 30-year CMT yields. These "yield factors" are specified to follow either Gaussian or square root processes. Arbitrary bond yields then turn out to be affine functions of the "yield factors," and can thus be computed quite efficiently. While these so-called *affine yield factor models* seem very appealing, they have not yet been widely adopted in the industry — partly because implementing them is technically quite complex, because the coefficients in the discount bond pricing formulas must be derived numerically, by solving a Ricatti differential equation.

Heath, Jarrow, and Morton developed a very general approach for implementing multi-factor whole yield curve models, in which one can use totally arbitrary yield curve shifts (e.g., those identified by principal component analysis) as the "factors." However, these so-called *Heath-Jarrow-Morton* models must in general be implemented using Monte Carlo methods, which make them very slow to run and, especially, to calibrate. For a typical bond investor who needs to analyze portfolios of hundreds of securities, the computation time involved is probably unacceptably long.

The reader should be warned that there are many two-factor models which should not be used. For example, Canabarro has shown that a common two-factor Cox-Ingersoll-Ross model does not specify a realistic dynamics for the yield curve; while the well-known Longstaff-Schwartz two-factor model is difficult to calibrate and plausible-looking parameter sets can give rise to very unrealistic behavior. Again, mathematical elegance and flexibility do not ensure that a model will be useful in practice.

When dealing with very long maturity bonds, such as century bonds, novel issues arise. These are discussed in Chapter 4.

OPTION MODELS IN PRACTICE

Calibration to the Observed Yield Curve and Market Implied Volatilities

There are at least three possible meanings of the word "calibration:"

1. We could calibrate to the initial yield curve, but use predetermined volatility parameters; that is, we would not use market option prices in the calibration process. The risk here is that, if we happen to choose poor volatilities, we may misprice options.
2. We could calibrate to the initial yield curve and to observed market option prices; that is, we would try to choose volatility parameters to match market option prices precisely. This is always time-consuming and unstable, and is often impossible.
3. We could calibrate to the initial yield curve and choose volatility parameters which were consistent with observed OTC option prices to within an acceptable tolerance. This approach is efficient and stable and, in favorable circumstances, gives plausible and stable option values.

For some kinds of research, and for risk management or regulatory applications which do not require a high degree of precision, type 1 calibration is sufficient.

Investment banks, who aim for very high precision when managing highly leveraged option products — and who often have access to a wide range of models, tailor-made for each product, which allow this kind of precision — generally aim for type 2 calibration. However, even with these resources, the results are often very poor. In fact, within most derivatives operations there is a vigorous debate about the precise degree of calibration which is desirable. One problem is that the OTC option market can be inefficient, particularly the market for longer-dated options, and sometimes options are simply mispriced; feeding bad prices into a calibration process almost always creates severe instability.

Bond investors, who are trying to value and manage their portfolio using a single consistent modeling approach, should generally aim for type 3 calibration. They should also separately monitor market implied volatilities in more detail, in case they reveal any relevant information or sources for concern: cf. the above discussion of the smile.

Note that, in many cases, type 2 calibration is not meaningful. For example, if we wanted to use a model to value a 20-year callable corporate, we would need market implied volatilities out to 20 years, and the relevant OTC option prices are simply not available. It is not desirable to derive implied volatilities from the prices of callable bonds, since this involves making arbitrary assumptions about their option-adjusted spreads (which is questionable even for callable Treasuries; we discuss this further in Chapter 6).

A problem with type 2 or even type 3 calibration is that if the model itself is unrealistic, forcing it to match observed option prices can have bad consequences. For example, consider the Ho-Lee model. It is a whole yield curve model, so type 1 calibration is automatic: the initial yield curve is a direct input.

The Ho-Lee model assumes parallel yield curve shifts so, if we use a constant volatility parameter, it implies that all implied volatilities should be the same. However, recall that long bond yields are less volatile than short bond yields: for example, on 3/5/1997, the 1-year volatility of the 4-year swap rate was 19%, while the 1-year volatility of the 9-year swap rate was 16%. Furthermore, long-dated volatilities tend to be lower than short-dated volatilities: the implied volatility on 3-year caps was 21%, but on 10-year caps it was only 18%.

Thus, in order to calibrate the Ho-Lee model, volatility must be made time-dependent, and one has to assume that it declines rather drastically as we move into the future. In fact, the required decline in volatility turns out to be totally unrealistic. Similar problems arise with the Black, Derman, and Toy model. For example, calibrating either of these models to implied volatilities out to 10 years can lead to unrealistically low option values for 20-year (non-call IO) callable bonds — i.e., unrealistically high bond values — because the 10–20 year part of the volatility function has been set to an artificially low level. Similar problems arise when valuing mortgages.

By contrast, models with mean reversion allow more realistic volatility parameters, since it is the mean reversion which makes long bond yield volatilities and long-dated option volatilities lower. This shows that, before attempting type 3 calibration, one should ensure that one is using a model, such as the CMS model, for which the results will be sensible.

Some subtle problems can arise even with type 1 calibration. For example, recall the extended Vasicek model:

$$dr_t = \kappa(t)(\bar{r}(t) - r_t)dt + \sigma(t)dB_t$$

There are various ways of calibrating this to the observed yield curve. To give the three simplest examples of a type 1 calibration:

- We could keep $\bar{r}$, κ constant and calibrate $\sigma(t)$. This corresponds to starting with the economic model of the yield curve described in Chapter 1, adjusting the volatility function to create drift adjustments, and moving this curve into line with the observed yield curve. Since these drift adjustments scale like σ^2, large fluctuations in volatility are required, and we end up with a very unrealistic volatility function. This is a bad way to calibrate.
- We could keep $\bar{r}$, σ constant and calibrate $\kappa(t)$. This corresponds to starting with the economic model of the yield curve described in Chapter 1 and adjusting the mean reversion rate to move this curve into line with the observed yield curve. Problems may arise at the short end of the curve, where the model errors may be large, and at the long end of the curve, where a very large adjustment in $\kappa(t)$ is required to make much difference, but it is sometimes still possible to get reasonable results. Note that we are

relying on the initial short rate plus mean reversion to model the slope of the yield curve; in most cases, $\kappa(t)$ will tend to fluctuate around 0.5, and the typical model yield curve shift looks like a slope shift. Unfortunately, mean reversion this strong tends to result in unrealistically low volatilities for long bond yields. Therefore this method is mainly useful if we are only interested in the short end of the curve — but this is exactly where we can run into problems.

- We could keep σ, κ constant and calibrate $\bar{r}(t)$. This is the most stable of the three calibration methods, hence the most common. The result looks nothing like the economic model of the yield curve: the function $\bar{r}(t)$ will end up resembling the initial forward curve and, since the burden of reproducing the yield curve slope and shape falls entirely on $\bar{r}(t)$, we will tend to get a very small value for κ, generally around 0.01–0.05. The typical model yield curve shift thus looks like a parallel shift. This is the most common approach to type 1 calibration.

Of course, the problems multiply when one is trying to carry out type 2 or even just type 3 calibration, and not just type 1 calibration: in this case one needs at least two time-dependent parameters, and not just one. For example, one would calibrate $\bar{r}(t)$ to the observed term structure and $\sigma(t)$ to observed implied volatilities. In this more complex situation, other problems can arise: for example, mindlessly calibrating $\sigma(t)$ to observed option prices can lead to an implausible, sawtoothed volatility function. Also, it must be remembered that changing $\sigma(t)$ also changes predicted bond yields, so one must calibrate simultaneously to the term structure and implied volatilities. This is usually very slow and unstable.

Thus, to repeat a point made earlier, when trying to understand what a model is doing, one must look not just at its formal specification, but at how it is calibrated; it often takes a lot of effort to understand what is going on. It is unsafe to assume that because calibration is yielding a good fit to the data, everything is okay.

One-Factor Models versus Multi-Factor Models

It is often asserted that two-factor models are "better" than one-factor models. Setting aside the fact that even a two-factor model does not capture the full dynamics of the term structure (cf. Chapter 1), it is reasonable to ask whether this assertion is really true.

A term structure model values securities by generating random interest rate paths. These paths are used in two quite separate ways: to generate the security cashflows and to discount them. It turns out that, for most bonds, a properly calibrated one-factor model can generate very realistic security cashflows and will discount them using acceptably realistic discount rates. Thus a one-factor model performs as well as a two-factor model for most bonds — that is, it computes equally reliable effective durations and convexities, and is equally suitable for stress testing.

The reasons for this are as follows. Whether a callable bond is called on a given date depends only on its price at that date. Thus, when generating the cashflows of a callable bond, it is only necessary to know the bond price at any given date. This is, by definition, a one-factor process (although it may be derivable from a multi-factor term structure process). If we were only interested in a single bond, we could specify this process directly as:

$$dP = \mu_P P dt + \sigma_P P dz$$

For example, this is essentially what happens when the standard Black-Scholes formula is used to find the forward value of a short-dated bond option. Note that this approach does not tell us how to discount the forward value of the option. This requires a further assumption: e.g., using a single fixed discount rate, or a discount rate perfectly correlated with the bond yield.

The alternative approach described in this chapter is to derive the bond price process from a term structure model: this is more consistent and more convenient when dealing with large numbers of securities. In generating the cash-flows of the callable bond, the (possibly multi-factor) term structure process is mapped to the one-factor process P. In this approach, both the bond cashflow scenarios and the discount rates are read off the random interest rate paths, as assumed in section 1. But note that in option valuation, generating accurate contingent cashflow scenarios is much more important than generating accurate discount rates. For a callable bond, the valuation error introduced by applying the wrong discount rate to the bond cashflows is roughly:

option value × (time to expiry × error in discount rate)

For example, if a bond is callable in 10 years and the option value is around $2.50, a 10 bp error in the discount rate leads to an error of around $0.025 in the bond value. By contrast, the valuation error introduced by using the wrong future bond yield to generate the contingent cashflows is roughly:

(option delta × bond forward duration) × error in future bond yield

For example, if a bond will have a duration of 5.0 on the call date and if the option is at-the-money with a delta of around 0.5, then a 10 bp error in the future bond yield leads to an error of around $0.25 in the bond value. These are highly approximate rules of thumb, but they do help to determine the relative magnitude of the errors that arise in option valuation. *Errors in discount rates are about an order of magnitude less important than errors in bond yields, except perhaps for very long-dated options.* In this light, the key observations regarding one-factor models are:

    a) Since a bond price or yield is itself only a one-factor process, a properly calibrated one-factor model can generate accurate cashflow scenarios.

    b) Since a one-factor model assumes bond yields and discount rates are perfectly correlated, it will not generate all relevant discount rate paths. However, since parallel yield curve shifts dominate, the empirical correlation is high, so the resulting error is small.

To expand on b): for short-dated bond options, the empirical correlation is about 0.6–0.7, but the resulting basis point error translates into a small dollar error; for long-dated options, the empirical correlation is about 0.8–0.9, so the basis point error is small.

To expand on a): What does it mean for a model to accurately reflect the random evolution of a bond price P? Assuming that the model is calibrated to the current term structure and correctly predicts the yield curve roll effect and convexity adjustment, the key requirement is that the actual current *and forward* market yield volatilities of the bond are consistent with those implied by the model. If they are, the model will generate the right contingent cashflow scenarios with the right probabilities (and it does not matter that the dynamics of the whole yield curve may be oversimplified in the model). A good one-factor model will satisfy this requirement for nearly all option-embedded bonds.

As a concrete illustration, Exhibit 2–13 compares numerical results from a one-factor model and a two-factor model. The one-factor model is the CMS model — a Gaussian process with mild mean reversion — while the two-factor model incorporates Gaussian parallel shifts with no mean reversion and Gaussian slope shifts with strong mean reversion. The bond is a 10-year bond, currently trading at $100.15, and callable at $100 on any coupon date starting from the next one (in 6 months' time). Both models have been calibrated to the current bond value and to comparable volatilities.

The one-factor and two-factor models give very close bond values, option values, and effective durations under a wide range of parallel scenarios; somewhat surprisingly, they also agree closely under a relatively wide range of yield curve slope scenarios. Both models generate broadly similar convexities: in our example, the convexities generated by the two-factor model are affected by numerical error in the computational lattice used, while the one-factor model uses a finite difference implementation which is more numerically stable (see below).

The overall conclusions are as follows. A good one-factor model can generate reliable valuations and effective durations for most option-embedded bonds. Therefore, a two-factor model should only be used when a one-factor model is inappropriate: see below for examples.

The main disadvantage of two-factor models is speed. A finite difference implementation of a one-factor model might use 50 grid points, while a two-factor model might require 50×50=2500 points, increasing computation time by potentially a factor of 50. Thus naive implementations of two-factor models are almost always too slow to be practicable. More sophisticated numerical schemes, which may exploit the structure of the underlying stochastic differential equations, can lead to dramatic increases in computational efficiency. Nonetheless, a two-factor model will always be significantly slower than a one-factor model, and thus should only be used when necessary. It should also be noted that a poorly chosen two-factor model may well be less realistic than a one-factor model.

Exhibit 2–13: One-Factor versus Two-Factor Model, 10-Year Bond Callable from 6 Months

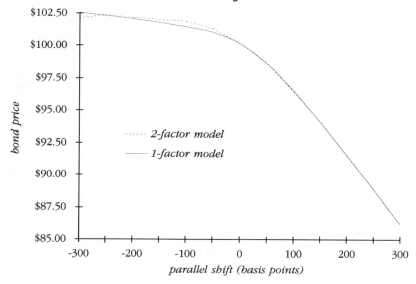

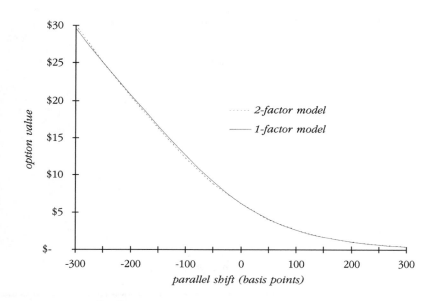

Exhibit 2-13 (Continued)

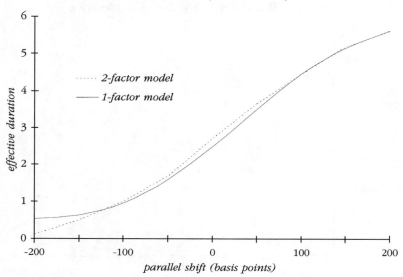

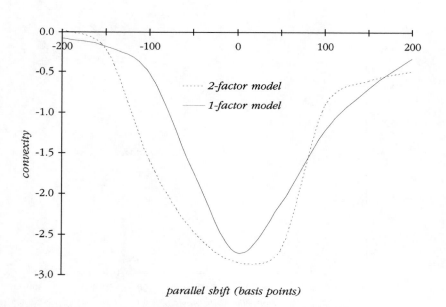

Exhibit 2-13 (Continued)

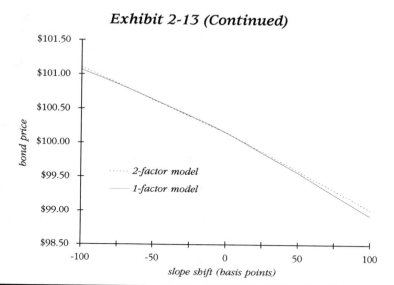

A one-factor model will be inadequate if:

1. It cannot accurately compute certain long dated option risk measures such as option rho, because it does not accurately generate all possible discount rate paths.
2. It cannot value options linked to two separate interest rates, e.g., one whose payoff explicitly depends on the spread between two interest rates. Here, a slope factor is relevant.
3. It may not accurately value positions which are highly sensitive to the implied volatility smile. Here, a stochastic volatility factor appears to be relevant.
4. It may not accurately value securities if their cashflows depend on the slope of the yield curve; e.g., prepayments on mortgage-backed securities are often said to be sensitive to the yield curve slope because of the existence of different mortgage products priced off different parts of the curve. This issue is discussed further in Chapter 5.

It is clear that two-factor models do not provide a universal panacea; rather, the right approach is to identify the key features of each specific situation and how they can be modeled accurately and efficiently.

Implementing a Term Structure Model: Non-Path-Dependent Securities

Recall that the best way to value a corporate bond with embedded options was to observed that its price satisfies a certain PDE. To obtain the bond value, all we have to do is solve this PDE numerically. There are many different ways to do this, but most commercial systems use either binomial or trinomial trees or finite differences.

A finite difference scheme focuses on a finite, regular grid of (t, r_t)-values as shown in Exhibit 2–14, and numerically computes the value of the option at each grid point. Binomial or trinomial trees can be regarded as special kinds of finite difference schemes: as shown in Exhibit 2–14, they pick out a triangular slice of the finite difference grid. (Some of the more sophisticated tree constructions correspond to using less regular grids, where the spacing varies from place to place and is determined on the fly).

The idea behind the finite difference algorithm is as follows. We obviously know what the bond is worth at maturity, i.e., along the rightmost grid line; we would like to be able to time-step backwards along the grid, computing the bond values along each vertical grid line in turn. The derivatives appearing in the PDE can all be approximated by expressions which only involve the bond values at the grid points. For example, we can make the approximations:

$$\frac{dP}{dt} \approx \frac{P(t + \Delta t, r) - P(t, r)}{\Delta t},$$

$$\frac{d^2 P}{dr^2} \approx \frac{P(t + \Delta t, r + \Delta r) - 2P(t + \Delta t, r) + P(t + \Delta t, r - \Delta r)}{(\Delta r)^2}$$

If we substitute these approximations into the PDE and rearrange terms, we can come up with a formula of the following form:

(some linear combination of bond values at time t grid points)
= (some linear combination of bond values at time $t+\Delta t$ grid points)

Exhibit 2–14: Finite Difference Grid and Binomial Tree

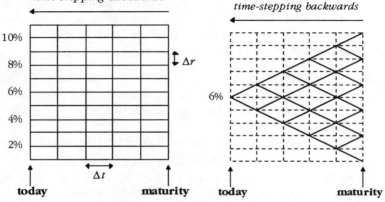

This gives us a recipe for time-stepping backwards. For example, if we take the simplified PDE

$$\frac{dP}{dt} = -\frac{d^2P}{dr^2}$$

and substitute the above approximations, we obtain the following formula:

$$P(t, r) \approx \frac{\Delta t}{(\Delta r)^2}P(t + \Delta t, r + \Delta r) + \left(1 - 2\frac{\Delta t}{(\Delta r)^2}\right)P(t + \Delta t, r)$$

$$+ \frac{\Delta t}{(\Delta r)^2}P(t + \Delta t, r - \Delta r)$$

This is called an *explicit* scheme because we get an explicit formula for each bond value $P(t,r)$ at time t in terms of a few of the bond values at time $t+\Delta t$. Binomial and trinomial trees can be regarded as special examples of explicit schemes. Thus, in the above formula, we could regard the numbers

$$\frac{\Delta t}{(\Delta r)^2}, 1 - 2\frac{\Delta t}{(\Delta r)^2}, \frac{\Delta t}{(\Delta r)^2}$$

as probabilities, making the connection with trinomial trees obvious: $P(t,r)$ is a probability-weighted average of $P(t+\Delta t, r+\Delta r)$, $P(t +\Delta t, r)$, and $P(t+\Delta t, r-\Delta r)$.

(As an aside, note that this probabilistic interpretation only makes sense if $1-2\Delta t/(\Delta r)^2 \geq 0$; but in fact, one can show that if $1-2\Delta t/(\Delta r)^2 < 0$ then the explicit scheme is unstable and cannot be used to solve the PDE numerically. Also, note that if $(\Delta r)^2 = 2\Delta t$ then we have a standard binomial tree with a probability of 0.5 for each branch.)

This is not the only kind of finite difference scheme. For example, suppose we used the alternative approximations:

$$\frac{dP}{dt} \approx \frac{P(t + \Delta t, r) - P(t, r)}{\Delta t}, \frac{d^2P}{dr^2} \approx \frac{P(t, r + \Delta r) - 2P(t, r) + P(t, r - \Delta r)}{(\Delta r)^2}$$

Then this gives us the formula:

$$\frac{\Delta t}{(\Delta r)^2}P(t, r + \Delta r) + \left(1 - 2\frac{\Delta t}{(\Delta r)^2}\right)P(t, r) + \frac{\Delta t}{(\Delta r)^2}P(t, r - \Delta r) \approx P(t + \Delta t, r)$$

This is called an *implicit* scheme because it does not tell us how to calculate $P(t,r)$ directly. However, note that if we know all the bond values at time $t+\Delta t$, then this formula (repeated many times) gives us a simple system of linear equations for all the bond values at time t. Thus we can time-step backwards, obtaining all the bond values $P(t,r)$ at time t from all the values $P(t+\Delta t, r)$ at time $t+\Delta t$, by solving this system of linear equations. This is obviously more complicated than an explicit scheme, but can still be done extremely efficiently.

Note that in solving the system of linear equations we are, in effect, expressing each $P(t,r)$ as a linear combination of *all* the bond values at time $t+\Delta t$, not just two or three of them. That is, there is a relation of the form:

$$P(t, r) = \ldots + p_{r-2\Delta r}P(t + \Delta t, r - 2\Delta r) + p_{r-\Delta r}P(t + \Delta t, r - \Delta r)$$

$$+ p_r P(t + \Delta t, r) + p_{r+\Delta r}P(t + \Delta t, r + \Delta r) + p_{r+2\Delta r}P(t + \Delta t, r + 2\Delta r)$$

$$+ p_{r+3\Delta r}P(t + \Delta t, r + 3\Delta r) + \ldots$$

where $\ldots, p_{r-\Delta r},\, p_r,\, p_{r+\Delta r},\, p_{r+2\Delta r} \ldots$ are coefficients which we could in principle write down explicitly. Interpreting these coefficients as probabilities, we can see that an implicit scheme in effect expresses each bond value $P(t,r)$ as a probability-weighted sum of *all* the bond values at time $t+\Delta t$, not just two or three of them. This is illustrated schematically in Exhibit 2–15.

This strongly suggests that implicit schemes should be more stable and accurate than explicit schemes, and this can be shown to be true. This makes implicit finite difference schemes preferable when implementing whole yield curve models such as the CMS model, for which calibration to the initial yield curve is automatic.

Tree implementations can sometimes offer technical advantages for short rate models which have to be calibrated. Methods which adjust the grid spacing on the fly, as part of the calibration process, can make calibration much easier and more efficient than if we were using a regular finite difference grid. We trade off some efficiency in bond valuation, but since calibration is a major task for these models, the trade-off is usually worthwhile. For whole yield curve models, which do not need to be calibrated to the initial yield curve, trees offer no advantage.

Exhibit 2–15: Option Pricing with Trees versus Implicit Finite Differences

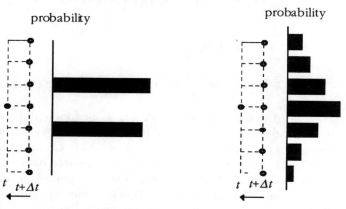

There are certain kinds of options for which both trees and implicit finite difference methods work very poorly — options with discontinuous payoffs, such as certain barrier options, are a notorious example. However, these kinds of options are mostly confined to the OTC option market and are very seldom encountered in option-embedded bonds.

Implementing a Term Structure Model: Path-Dependent Securities

In general, the cashflows from a mortgage-backed security are path-dependent. Thus, except in special cases, it is not possible to value MBS using tree or implicit finite difference methods. In order to value an MBS, we have to simulate random interest rate paths directly, value the security along each interest rate path, and take the probability-weighted average. For example, if we choose the paths at random, this is the *Monte Carlo* method.

A full discussion of the Monte Carlo method and its rivals would take a book, or several books, and would be of interest mainly to specialists. Here we will concentrate on some more fundamental issues which are often taken for granted in the financial literature, but which deserve a closer look. The mathematics is by now fairly standard: a useful reference is Kloeden et al.

Considering a one-factor short rate model for the moment, we have to generate random interest rate paths $(r_t)_{t \geq 0}$ consistent with the assumed interest rate process

$$dr = \mu(r, t)dt + \sigma(r, t)dB_t$$

To generate a random path up to some future time T, we first need to divide time into a series of discrete intervals: that is, we pick some relevant times $0 = t_1 < t_2 < ... < t_N = T$ and simulate r_{t_n} for each n. For example, the *strong Euler approximation* for $\Delta r_n = r_{n+1} - r_n$ is:

$$\Delta r_n = \mu(r_{t_n}, t_n)\Delta t_n + \sigma(r_{t_n}, t_n)\Delta B_n$$

where

$$\Delta t_n = t_{n+1} - t_n$$

and

$$\Delta B_n = B_{t_{n+1}} - B_{t_n}$$

(where B_t is standard Brownian motion). Since ΔB_n is a normally distributed random number with mean 0 and standard deviation

$$\sqrt{\Delta t_n}$$

Exhibit 2–16: Strong Euler Approximation to a Random Interest Rate Path

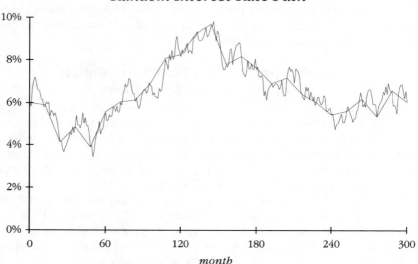

and all the ΔB_n are independent (by the definition of Brownian motion), this gives us an explicit algorithm for generating approximations to the Brownian random paths. Exhibit 2–16 shows the strong Euler approximation to a random interest rate path using uniform 12-month time steps; the model here is Gaussian and mean reverting.

This procedure is not very efficient and virtually all commercial implementations use a more efficient method. However, it is very important to ensure that any improved algorithm is appropriate to the problem we are trying to solve. To illustrate, we will give some examples of techniques that have been devised to make the Monte Carlo method more efficient and discuss why they work.

The first observation is that there is no reason why the time steps must all be the same length. Since the near-term behavior of interest rates is relatively more important than their long-term behavior, it would make sense to use a longer time step as one moved further into the future. Exhibit 2–17 shows how this idea can be used to reduce the number of time steps from 25 to 4, thus reducing computation time, while still staying reasonably close to the "true" random path.

The second idea is a little more subtle. One of the computational burdens of creating a random path using the strong Euler approximation is generating the normally distributed random number ΔB_n. We can save a significant amount of time by replacing the strong Euler approximation with a so-called *weak Euler approximation*:

$$\Delta r_n = \mu(r_{t_n}, t_n)\Delta t_n + \sigma(r_{t_n}, t_n)\Delta \hat{B}_n$$

Exhibit 2-17: Strong Euler Approximation with Increasing Time Step

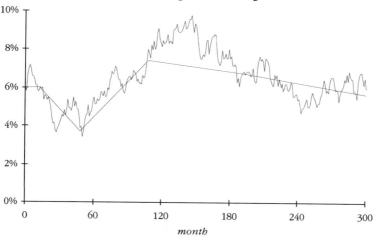

where the random number $\Delta \hat{B}_n$ is no longer normally distributed, but can only take on the values ± 1, each with probability 0.5. This kind of random number is much easier to generate. The result of using a weak Euler approximation, with 12-month time steps, is shown in Exhibit 2–18.

This does not look like a very good approximation to the "true" random interest rate path, and using it requires some justification. The point is that there are two broad kinds of problems that one may be trying to solve: problems which involve the behavior of interest rates along each specific path and problems which only involve taking an average along all possible paths. For the former, "strong approximations" are required; for the latter, "weak approximations" suffice. The idea is that, while a weak approximation to a specific interest rate path may be biased — cf. Exhibit 2–18 — if we are only interested in an average over a large number of paths, the biases cancel each other out. Again, one can refer back to the Central Limit Theorem: intuitively, even though the individual random numbers $\Delta \hat{B}_n$ are not normally distributed, when taken *en masse* they behave as if they were.

Most fixed income applications — including the calculation of effective duration, convexity, OAS, and various other risk measures — only require weak approximations. Situations where strong rather than weak approximations are preferred include:

- cashflow forecasting applications, such as solvency testing;
- the valuation of reset caps and floors in ARMs;
- certain complex CMO tranches with many possible patterns of cashflows; and,
- simulating the performance of trading strategies.

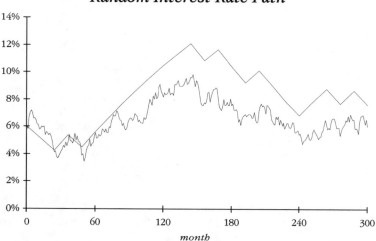

Exhibit 2–18: Weak Euler Approximation to a Random Interest Rate Path

month

There are various other tricks which can be used to make Monte Carlo methods more efficient, including a range of variance reduction methods. For example, a simple but very effective technique is *antithetic sampling*: this simply says that whenever you generate an interest rate path using a sequence of random numbers (ΔB_n), you should also generate another one using the "opposite" sequence $(-\Delta B_n)$. This method helps eliminate random bias.

One can also use more accurate approximations to the "true" random paths (i.e., more accurate discretizations) than the simple Euler approximation. However, these tend to be considerably more complicated to implement: see Kloeden et al.

A little extra accuracy can also be obtained in other ways. For instance, in all the above examples we linearly interpolated interest rates between the times t_n. This is not actually the optimal way to interpolate: one should actually use the "most likely path" as defined by Stroock. For mean reverting Gaussian models this optimization can be done quite easily, but for square root and lognormal models it does not seem to be feasible.

Many interest rate simulation methods do not use random numbers, but generate interest rate paths in a non-random way. In the simplest case, combining weak approximation with uneven time steps drastically reduces the number of possible paths and can sometimes make it feasible to generate every possible path, which is obviously impracticable with the naive Monte Carlo method.

The *representative path* algorithm developed at CMS combines most of the techniques described above to achieve high accuracy with a very low number of paths. It is at least an order of magnitude more efficient than naive Monte Carlo. Exhibit 2–19 shows how rapidly this algorithm converges for a typical pass-through MBS, while Exhibit 2–20 shows how rapidly it converges for some selected CMO tranches.

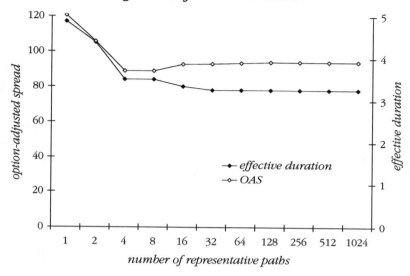

Exhibit 2-19: Convergence of CMS Representative Path Algorithm for 8% FNMA 30

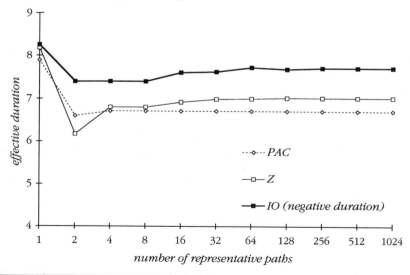

Exhibit 2-20: Convergence of CMS Representative Path Algorithm for Selected CMOs

A so-called *quasi-Monte Carlo* method does not generate every possible path, but uses a number-theoretic algorithm to generate a series of paths which — hopefully — covers all possibilities in a more "uniform" way than purely random paths, thus ensuring more rapid convergence. Although they are theoretically very attractive, it is quite difficult to get quasi-Monte Carlo methods to work well in practice. However, one advantage of quasi-Monte Carlo path generation is that, unlike the Representative Path method, it is suitable for generating strong approximations to random interest rate paths, and thus gives better values for (e.g.) reset caps on ARMs.

The final comment to make about implementing term structure models for MBS is that the results you get are only as good as the prepayment model you are using. In particular, making extra refinements to the implementation is usually less important than checking and improving the prepayment model. We will revisit this issue in Chapter 5.

Selected References

Andersen, T. and Lund, J, "The Short Rate Diffusion Revisited: A Tour Guided by the Efficient Method of Moments," First Annual Computational Finance Conference, 1996.

Bates, D., *Testing Option Pricing Models*, NBER Working Paper #5129, 1995.

Brown, R. and Schaefer, S., "Interest Rate Volatility and the Shape of the Term Structure," in Howison, S. D., Kelly, F. P. and Wilmott, P. (eds.), Mathematical Models in Finance, Chapman & Hall, 1995.

Duffie, D., *Dynamic Asset Pricing Theory* (2nd ed.), Princeton University Press, Princeton, 1996.

Duffie, D. and Kan, R., "A Yield-Factor Model of Interest Rates," *Mathematical Finance*, Vol. 64, 4 (1996).

Fisher, M. and Gilles, C., "Around and Around: The Expectations Hypothesis," *Federal Reserve Board*, May 1996.

Hughston, L. (ed.), *Vasicek and Beyond: Approaches to Building and Applying Interest Rate Models*, Risk Publications, London, 1996.

Kloeden, P. and Platen, E., *Numerical Solution of SDE through Computer Experiments*, Springer, Heidelberg, 1994.

Morton, K. and Mayers, D., *Numerical Solution of Partial Differential Equations*, Cambridge University Press, Cambridge, 1994.

Rebonato, R., *Interest-Rate Option Models: Understanding, Analyzing and Using Models for Exotic Interest-Rate Options*, Wiley, Chichester, 1996.

Rebonato, R. and Cooper, I., "The Limitations of Simple Two-Factor Interest Rate Models," *J. Financial Engineering*, March 1996.

Rogers, L., "Which Model for Term-structure of Interest Rates Should One Use?" in Davis, M., Duffie, D., Fleming, W. and Shreve, S., *Mathematical Finance*, Springer, Heidelberg, 1995.

Stroock, D., *Lectures on Topics in Stochastic Differential Equations*, Tata Institute of Fundamental Research, Bombay, 1982; see Chapter II, §5.

Uhrig, M. and Walter, U., "A New Numerical Approach for Fitting the Initial Yield Curve," *J. Fixed Income*, March 1996.

Chapter 3

Quantitative Approaches to Inflation-Indexed Bonds

INFLATION-INDEXED BONDS AND REAL YIELDS

Bond Structures and the Concept of Real Yield

Inflation-indexed bonds, as a way of financing Government debt, were proposed by Marshall, Keynes, and others in the late 1920s. Inflation-indexed bonds exist in Australia, Canada, Israel, the Netherlands, New Zealand, Sweden, the United Kingdom, and the United States. In Israel, they have been issued since the 1950s, and have often dominated the bond market there. There are significant differences between these markets: a wide variety of bond structures and tax regimes exist, issuance volumes and the breadth of the investor base vary widely from country to country, and liquidity varies from tolerable to nonexistent.

There has been some disagreement about the degree to which inflation-indexed bonds are "risk-free" and the role which they should play in a portfolio. In particular, it has not been universally appreciated that these bonds can have volatile mark-to-market returns. This chapter examines the factors which determine returns on these bonds, hopefully clearing up some misconceptions, and draws some conclusions about portfolio risk management and asset allocation. It also explains how market real yields can be used to derive implied market inflation forecasts (i.e., a term structure of inflation expectations); this makes them an interesting policy tool, and also has implications for macroeconomic portfolio strategy. The analysis, which is a little more subtle than one might expect, also has potential practical applications for liability management and the valuation of revenue streams in, e.g., project finance. As we shall see, it is also useful for forecasting after-tax real returns.

U.S. Government inflation-indexed bonds — called "Treasury inflation-indexed securities," or "TIPS" — are quite new to the U.S. bond markets. Since many investors may still be unfamiliar with how these bonds work, we quickly review the structure in Exhibit 3–1.

For example, in order to determine the purchase price of the 3.375% 1/15/2007 TIPS at the original auction, for settlement on 2/6/1997, one had to carry out the following calculations.

- the Reference CPI for 1/1/1997 was 158.3 (the CPI-U for 10/96);
- the Reference CPI for 2/1/1997 was 158.6 (the CPI-U for 11/96);

83

Exhibit 3–1: TIPS Bond Structure

TIPS pay interest semiannually. Interest payments are based on a fixed coupon rate. However, the underlying principal amount of the bonds is indexed to inflation; this inflation-adjusted principal amount is used to calculate the coupon payments, which therefore also rise with inflation. At maturity, the redemption value of the bonds is equal to their inflation-adjusted principal amount, rather than their original par amount.

The inflation-adjusted principal amount is equal to the original par amount multiplied by an Index Ratio, which is based on inflation and which is recalculated every day. The Index Ratio is simply the Reference CPI on the relevant date divided by the Reference CPI on the issue date.

The Reference CPI for the first day of any month is defined to be the non-seasonally adjusted CPI-U for the third preceding calendar month, while the Reference CPI for any subsequent day in that month is determined by linearly interpolating the Reference CPI for the first of the month and the Reference CPI for the first day of the next month.

Price-yield calculations are as follows. Compute the "real price" of the bond from the quoted real yield via the standard bond pricing formula, using an actual/actual day count basis, round to 3 decimal places (in $100); then multiply the real price by the Index Ratio to obtain the inflation-adjusted price. Accrued interest is computed in exactly the same way, except that no rounding is carried out.

- the Reference CPI for 1/15/1997 was $158.3 + (158.6 - 158.3)^{14/31} = 158.43548$;
- the Reference CPI for 2/6/1997 was 158.6 (since the CPI-U for 12/96 was 158.6);
- the Index Ratio for 2/6/1997 was $\dfrac{158.6}{158.43548} = 1.00104$;
- for a real yield of 3.449%, the real price of the bond was $99.378686; and,
- the inflation-adjusted price was $99.379 \times 1.00104 = \$99.482354$.

An attractive feature of the TIPS structure is that inflation indexation occurs with no substantial lag. In the U.K., there is an eight month lag in the inflation adjustment of index-linked gilts; in Australia and New Zealand, there is a three to six month lag. The lag means that real returns from these inflation-indexed bonds are subject to short-term inflation risk, and considerably complicates the analysis of the bonds.

The obvious question, of course, is: Where does the real yield come from, and how much can it change? To investors used to thinking of bond yields as being driven by inflation expectations, it is not obvious that real yields should be volatile at all — except perhaps because of temporary imbalances in supply and demand, or changes in liquidity. After all, there are respectable economic theories which suggest that real interest rates should be constant. But in practice, there are various economic reasons why real yields do in fact fluctuate. The following discussion of risk factors expands on the account given by Carmody and Mason.

Causes of Real Yield Volatility

The real yield may be defined as the long-term cost of risk-free capital (net of inflation). That is, since TIPS are competing with other investments, real yields on TIPS will move with the cost of capital in the economy as a whole. Of course, other factors affect real yields: for example, index-linked gilts in the U.K. have had artificially low real yields because of their favorable tax treatment. However, in this chapter we will focus on economic and market factors. Broadly speaking, the two main economic factors which affect real yields are:

1. *Long-term expected growth in real GDP:* Strong growth generally drives up real interest rates, since the demand for capital tends to rise, and borrowers — expecting higher real returns — are prepared to shoulder higher real borrowing costs.

2. *Long-term expected changes in the current account deficit:* Demand for capital is by definition higher in countries with a large current account deficit, driving up domestic interest rates in order to attract required international investment.

Note that short-term trends in real GDP and the current account deficit can have a strong influence on real yields, because they tend to influence the long-term expectations of investors: cf. Chapter 12 of Keynes' *General Theory.* (Roll has also argued, based on an analysis of tax effects, that real yields should also rise when expected inflation rises; this argument is outlined later in the chapter. For the moment we ignore tax effects.)

Real yields on inflation-linked bonds are also influenced by relative demand for these bonds, when compared with competing investments which may offer investors some protection — albeit imperfect — against inflation. The balance between competing investments constantly shifts, depending on subjective factors such as investor aversion to different kinds of risk. Relevant investments include:

1. *Money market investments:* If investors are confident that short-term interest rates will move broadly in line with inflation — which has been the case for monetary policy since the early 1980s, but not before then — then real returns on money market instruments will be relatively stable over the long term.

2. *Equities:* When profit margins are stable, corporate profits, and hence dividends and dividend growth rates, tend to rise with the price level; thus, it is reasonable to regard equities as an inflation hedge in the long

term (remembering that equity investors are exposed to additional risks in comparison to holders of inflation-indexed bonds). Therefore when the equity market is strong, real yields will tend to be high, while a weakening in the equity market will tend to trigger a fall in real yields.

3. *Corporate bonds:* As with equities, corporate bonds performance is partly linked to inflation: rising price levels drive up corporate revenues and reduce the real value of existing fixed-rate debt, and both these factors can cause yield spreads to tighten.

4. *Commodities:* A basket of commodities also provides a partial hedge against inflation, but in practice this investment alternative is not as important as the previous three.

To summarize: real yields are far from stable and the behavior of real yields is just as complex as the behavior of nominal yields. Real yields are influenced by both economic fundamentals and market supply/demand factors across asset classes. It is not at all obvious that inflation-linked bonds should be "among the least risky of all assets." Indeed, in the Australian market these securities are regarded as highly risky in comparison to nominal bonds — though this is partly because of their relative illiquidity.

In all countries where inflation-linked bonds are actively traded, real yields have, historically, been quite volatile. For example:

- In the U.K., real yields on long index-linked gilts fluctuated between 2% and 4.5% in the period 1981–1993 (Eichholtz et al.) In the period 1984–1994, real yields on short index-linked gilts fluctuated between 1.5% and 5.75%, partly reflecting instability in monetary policy (Brown and Schaefer).
- In Israel from 1984–1993, long dated real yields fluctuated between − 1.5% and 3.3%; however, they more typically trade in the range ±1% (Eichholtz et al.)
- In Australia, real yields have varied from a high of 5.75% in 1986 and 1994, to a low of 3.25% in 1993 (Carmody and Mason).

Thus, like nominal yields, market real yields trade in ranges of hundreds of basis points. This translates into very significant price volatility, which is sometimes experienced over a very short period — e.g., Australia, moving from 1993 to 1994. (Of course, the existence of real yield volatility should be no surprise, since real bond returns have always been volatile: see Chapter 4.)

Since there was no U.S. market in inflation-indexed bonds before 1997, it is not possible to observe a long history of market real yields. Real yields are often estimated by subtracting current inflation from current nominal bond yields; but this procedure is obviously illogical, as it assumes that expected inflation is equal to current inflation. One can get a better idea of what market real yields would have been by taking nominal yields and subtracting a consensus inflation forecast.

Exhibit 3–2 shows the 10-year nominal Treasury yield minus the 10-year consensus CPI forecast, as reported in the Philadelphia Fed's Survey of Professional Forecasters. This measures investors' expectations of real returns on 10-year Treasury bonds, and is therefore a reasonable estimate of the 10-year real yield.

Even though using consensus data has a number of drawbacks — as explained at the end of this chapter — this rough analysis yields some useful results. The graph shows clearly how long-dated real yields soared in the early 1980s, due to the extreme instability in monetary policy. They stabilized after 1985, once monetarism was discarded and a more stable approach to monetary policy was instituted. Since then they have fluctuated between 5% (in the overheated economy of the late 1980s) and 2% (in the depths of the recession). Note the apparent link during this latest period between long-term real yields and current GDP growth.

Although the U.S. inflation-indexed bond market is extremely young, the extant history of TIPS real yields already displays some interesting phenomena. Exhibit 3–3 shows TIPS real yields since issuance. During this 6-month period, market real yields traded in a 50 bp range. TIPS yield volatility was 10.3%, compared to 11.6% for 10-year nominal bonds.

Exhibit 3–3 also shows the yield spread between the 10-year TIPS and the 10-year CMT nominal yield. This may be regarded as a rough measure of the market's inflation expectations over the next ten years. We will describe more accurate ways to measure this implied market inflation forecast later in the chapter.

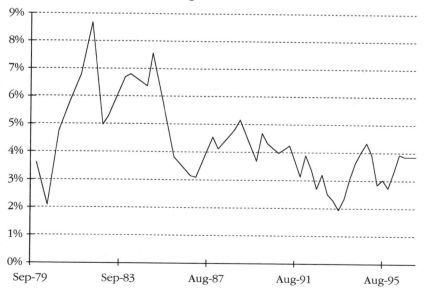

Exhibit 3–2: U.S. 10-Year Real Yield, Estimated from Consensus Long-Term CPI Forecasts

Exhibit 3–3: TIPS Real Yield History and Spread to Nominal Yield Curve

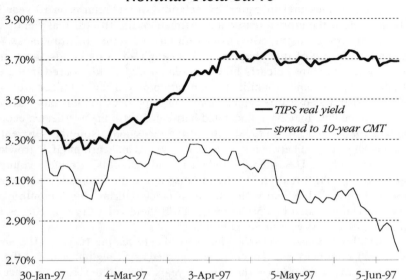

This brief history already illustrates some important points. For example, in the early part of February both real yields and inflation expectations fell. From the beginning of March, however, concerns about inflation caused nominal yields to rise. Note that long-term inflation expectations remained capped at around 3.2%, while real yields continued to rise; this reflects the market's view that if inflation were to rise much above 3%, the Fed would act to lower it by raising real interest rates.

In early April, both real yields and inflation expectations were stable. At the end of April, the employment cost index was released and was significantly lower than market forecasts. This caused market participants to revise their inflation forecasts downwards and inflation expectations to fall to around 3%. However, real yields remained stable since the market did not anticipate that this new economic data would result in any change to Fed policy.

Existence of an Inflation Risk Premium

It is often asserted that real yields on inflation-linked bonds should reflect an inflation risk premium, since investors are not exposed to inflation risk as they are with nominal bonds. Note that if future inflation were known — not necessarily zero — there would be no inflation risk premium; it is uncertainty about inflation that creates a risk premium. The more volatile inflation is expected to be, the higher the inflation risk premium on nominal bonds should be, and the lower real yields should be in relation to nominal yields.

It is important to note that it is uncertainty about future inflation which should determine the risk premium, not the historical volatility of inflation. For example, the inflationary episode of the 1970s is not relevant unless investors think it may be repeated. Investors' expectations about the future volatility of inflation are not directly observable (although, see below), but it may be helpful to look at economists' estimates. It is also useful to compare expected inflation volatility with expected volatility in real interest rates, since both factors are relevant to the risk/return opportunities offered by inflation-indexed bonds.

Note that if the inflation risk premium exists, one would not expect it to be unvarying. Since it is related to market expectations about potential uncertainty in inflation, it is comparable to option implied volatility. One would thus expect the inflation risk premium to depend on bond maturity, and also to vary over time; for example, if the market lost confidence in the Fed's ability to control inflation, the inflation risk premium would rise, causing nominal yields to rise relative to real yields. However, since the inflation risk premium is determined by inflation uncertainty over a long period (ten years for the 10-year TIPS), sudden changes would be unusual. The inflation risk premium should experience moderate fluctuations, like long-dated swaption implied volatilities, and not sharp ones, like short-dated exchange-traded option implied volatilities.

In the absence of an inflation-linked derivatives market, the inflation risk premium is not directly observable. Naive attempts to measure it can lead to grossly overstated estimates. A number of proposed methods for measuring it turn out to be spurious. For example, it has been asserted that the differential between money market and bond yields arises because of an inflation risk premium, which can thus be estimated by looking at the long-term average spread between the Fed Funds rate and the 2-year bond yield (about 70 bp in the period since deregulation). This argument has a grain of truth, but the conclusion is incorrect as it stands. As we observed in Chapter 1, there are other reasons why money market yields are usually lower than bond yields: liquidity preference and the impact of capital charges both have important effects. Furthermore, if the spread between money market and bond yields reflects a risk premium, this not just an inflation risk premium but a real rate risk premium as well.

Also, the argument that the difference between the Fed Funds rate and the 2-year bond yield equals the inflation risk premium implies that the yields of money market securities reflect no inflation risk premium, while this risk premium is fully priced into 2-year bond yields. This would only be plausible if money market securities were not (perceived to be) subject to inflation risk, and this is far from obvious, particularly since real money market returns were frequently negative during the 1970s.

Thus we must look for more valid ways of estimating what the inflation risk premium should be. One approach, which we describe later in this chapter, is based on an analysis of historical real and nominal yields. It suggests that the market inflation risk premium on a 10-year nominal bond is somewhere between −15 bp and 25 bp.

A second approach is sometimes possible. If there were an efficient market in both conventional and index-linked bonds with a range of maturities stretching from 10 years to 30 years, one could in principle use the methods described in the first section of Chapter 4 to determine the market's long-term expectations about nominal and real yield volatility as reflected in the observed convexity bias, and hence to deduce the market's long-term expectations about inflation volatility. For reasons mentioned in Chapter 4, a reasonably long yield history would be required to obtain reliable results. At the moment this procedure would only be practicable in the U.K., and the applicability of this procedure to yields on index-linked gilts is questionable because of their favorable tax treatment. Once a 30-year TIPS has been issued in the United States, and has been actively traded for some time, it will be possible to carry out this analysis.

A third approach is to try to observe inflation uncertainty directly. Exhibit 3–4 shows the probabilities attached by economists to various GDP growth and inflation scenarios; it is taken from the Survey of Professional Forecasters (first quarter, 1997). Although subjective uncertainty is not identical to expected volatility, the survey results are consistent with a short-term volatility of around 1% p.a. in both inflation and GDP growth; that is, they are about equally volatile.

Economists' forecasts recognize that both inflation and real yields are volatile, and that they have comparable volatilities. It is tempting to conclude that nominal bond yields should indeed reflect an inflation risk premium, since returns on nominal bonds are affected by both inflation volatility and real yield volatility, while returns on inflation-linked bonds are only affected by real yield volatility. But this conclusion is not necessarily correct.

Based on an analysis of 30 years' worth of cross-country panel data, Judson and Orphanides have shown that — as one might expect — there is a strong negative correlation between inflation and growth. Thus, as inflation rises, real yields should fall, and vice versa; in other words, the risks arising from fluctuations in inflation and fluctuations in real yields at least partly offset each other, at least over the medium to long term. It is therefore conceivable that, over the medium to long term, a portfolio of nominal bonds may be less risky, not more risky, than a portfolio of inflation-linked bonds. Certainly the situation is more complex than it seems at first.

We can actually use the earlier "economists' estimates" of volatility in real GDP growth and inflation, together with the implied volatility of short-term rates, to compute a rough estimate of the correlation between inflation and growth. Assuming that nominal rates are solely determined by growth and inflation, we have:

$$\sigma^2_{nominal} = \sigma^2_{growth} + \sigma^2_{inflation} + 2\rho\sigma_{growth}\sigma_{inflation}$$

If all three volatilities are around 1% per annum, then solving this formula for ρ gives the estimate $\rho \approx -0.5$. However, it would not be meaningful to try to compute a more precise estimate this way.

Exhibit 3-4: Economists' Uncertainty about Future Inflation and GDP Growth

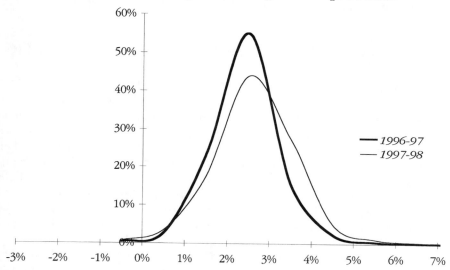

Probability attached to possible changes in GDP price index

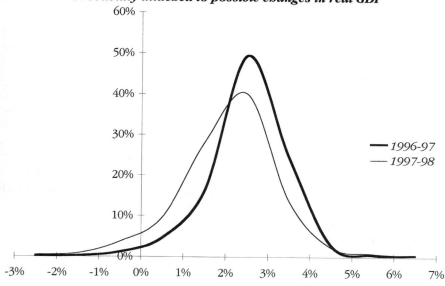

Probability attached to possible changes in real GDP

Incidentally, Judson and Orphanides also found a strong negative correlation between inflation volatility and growth. In other words, if inflation is expected to become more volatile, real yields should fall, i.e., inflation-indexed bond prices should rally. However, in this senario inflation-linked bonds should outperform nominal bonds, since the inflation risk premium should rise.

INFLATION-INDEXED BONDS IN A NOMINAL PORTFOLIO

What is the Duration of an Inflation-Indexed Bond?

Inflation-indexed bonds are often used for specialized purposes (e.g., asset/liability management for insurance companies offering inflation-linked life annuities), and may thus be segregated from other fixed-income holdings. However, if they are held in the same portfolio as nominal bonds, an interesting problem arises when attempting to define their "duration." We first examine the simplest possible definition of duration, and its consequences; then we look at some alternative definitions.

It is easy to compute the duration of an inflation-indexed bond using exactly the same method as one would use for a nominal bond. Because of its low real coupon and low real yield, an inflation-indexed bond tends to have a much longer duration than a nominal bond of comparable maturity.

But what does this duration mean? The duration of a nominal Treasury bond measures its sensitivity to changes in nominal yields, i.e., to changes in inflation and real interest rate expectations. By contrast, the duration of an inflation-linked bond measures its sensitivity to changes in real yields, i.e., to changes in real interest rate expectations alone. In other words, the two durations are not comparable: they are measuring different things. So, for example, it does not make sense to look for a "reference" nominal yield for the TIPS real yield: while the TIPS yield may appear to trade off the 10-year Treasury during some periods, or off the 5-year Treasury during other periods, there is no fundamental reason why any such relationship should persist.

This creates a problem on the portfolio level. If we try to compute a portfolio duration by adding up the durations of nominal and inflation-indexed bond holdings, what does the resulting figure mean? Two portfolios could have the same duration but, depending on the relative weighting of index-linked bonds, might have a very different response to a change in investor's economic expectations. A simple duration target is no longer an effective way of controlling portfolio interest rate risk.

Thus, when a portfolio contains both nominal and inflation-linked bonds, it is critical to monitor and report the relative weights and durations of the "nominal" and "real" components of the portfolio separately. One approach is to report two durations for the portfolio, which distinguish two sources of risk:

1. A "portfolio real yield duration" equal to the sum of the durations of both nominal and inflation-indexed bond holdings. This shows how the port-

folio value will respond to a change in market real yields (which also affect nominal yields).

2. A "portfolio inflation duration" equal to the duration of the nominal bond holdings alone. This shows how the portfolio value will respond to a change in market inflation expectations (which affect nominal yields but not real yields).

Similarly, care must be taken when carrying out portfolio simulations. For example, when carrying out parallel interest rate simulations, it is standard practice to apply an identical yield shift to all securities in the portfolio. For a portfolio containing both nominal and inflation-indexed bonds, this actually corresponds to a "real yield simulation." One should also carry out "expected inflation simulations," where the yield shift is applied to nominal but not inflation-indexed bond yields.

There is one practical situation in which it makes sense to compare the durations of a nominal and inflation-indexed bond directly: when designing trading strategies based on expected inflation. Suppose the central banking authority is targeting a long-term inflation rate of no more than 3%; and suppose that the 10-year nominal yield is 7.50% while the 10-year real yield is 4.00%. This means that the market is predicting an average inflation rate, over the next ten years, of 3.5%. If one had faith in the central bank's ability to meet its inflation target, nominal bonds would look undervalued relative to inflation-indexed bonds.

How should one exploit this perceived opportunity without changing exposure to other sources of risk? The correct way is to execute a duration-matched swap, selling 10-year inflation-indexed bonds and buying 10-year nominal bonds. If inflation expectations fall, the strategy would realize a profit. If real interest rate expectations change (i.e., if real yields change), there would be no effect — which is the intention. Later in this chapter, we develop more accurate ways to derive market inflation forecasts from the real and nominal yield curves, and discuss some further implications for portfolio strategy.

The above duration calculation is based on the (known) real cashflows, and discounts at the real yield. There are other potential ways to compute the "duration" of an inflation-linked bond, which involve forecasting the (unknown) nominal cashflows and discounting using nominal yields, on a zero coupon curve basis. The three most obvious alternatives are:

1. Using a fixed inflation forecast, generate projected bond cashflows (one should use a forecast which ensures that the net present value of the forecast cashflows, discounted using the current nominal zero coupon curve, is equal to the current bond price). Compute the duration of this fixed cashflow stream using ±100 bp shifts in the nominal zero coupon curve.

2. The same, except that when shifting the zero coupon curve by ±100 bp, one recalculates the bond cashflows based on a new inflation forecast, adjusted by ±1%. That is, the cashflow stream is assumed to depend on the level of nominal yields.

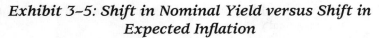

Exhibit 3–5: Shift in Nominal Yield versus Shift in Expected Inflation

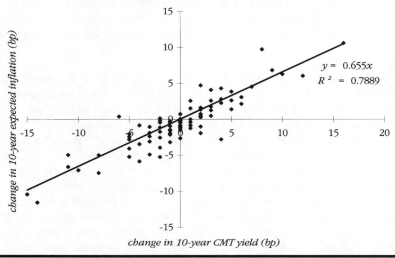

change in 10-year expected inflation (bp)

$y = 0.655x$
$R^2 = 0.7889$

change in 10-year CMT yield (bp)

3. The same, except that one adjusts the inflation forecast by an amount different from ±1%. For example, Exhibit 3–5 shows that in early 1997, a 10 bp rise in U.S. nominal yields corresponded, on average, to an 0.06%–0.07% rise in market long-term inflation expectations (we explain later in this chapter how the "expected inflation" figures were derived). Thus one might adjust the inflation forecast by (say) ±0.65%. The precise number depends on the reference Treasury yield, and historical period used to estimate the relationship.

In each case, some minor variations are possible; for example, either constant or time-varying inflation forecasts could be used. These calculations can be related to the above concepts of "real yield duration" and "inflation duration" in the following way:

1. Assuming a fixed cashflow stream (i.e., a fixed inflation scenario) amounts to assuming that the ±100 bp shift in nominal yields is due to a change in real yields, not a change in inflation expectations. Thus, this calculation determines the sensitivity to a change in real yields, i.e., it is essentially computing a *real yield duration*, and produces an answer very close to the duration calculation described above.

2. Assuming an inflation scenario that varies by ±1% amounts to assuming that the ±100 bp shift in nominal yields is due to a change in inflation expectations. Thus, this calculation measures an *inflation duration*, i.e., a sensitivity to a shift in market inflation expectations, which is conceptually different from the real yield duration. The inflation duration of a

TIPS will be approximately zero, but may depend on the precise way the calculation is carried out.

3. Assuming an inflation scenario that varies by some amount based on the empirical relationship between nominal yields and market inflation expectations amounts to calculating a *nominal yield duration*, which attempts to measure the sensitivity of an inflation-linked bond to a shift in nominal yields.

Real yield duration is the most important of these risk measures — and, as we have seen, it can be calculated without using an inflation forecast. The inflation duration of a TIPS is not a useful risk measure; however, in the U.K. and Australian markets, where inflation-indexed Treasuries have some residual inflation sensitivity due to the lag in inflation indexation, inflation duration is perhaps worth monitoring. The definition of nominal yield duration makes essential use of an estimate about an empirical relationship which is probably unstable, severely limiting the usefulness of this risk measure.

Note that if inflation-indexed Treasury bonds did have stable nominal durations — i.e., if they did respond in an absolutely predictable way to a change in nominal yields — then there would be no point in issuing them, since they could be perfectly replicated by nominal bonds. In fact, experience shows that inflation-indexed bonds cannot be hedged perfectly with nominal bonds.

One can also attempt to compute a "tax-adjusted duration" for an inflation-linked bond, which takes its tax treatment into account; this may be of importance in the U.K., where inflation accruals are not taxed. In the U.S. market inflation-linked and nominal bonds are taxed on a broadly consistent basis; in particular, by analogy with Treasury STRIPS, the inflation adjustment to the bond principal is taxable as it occurs, and not simply at bond maturity. Thus, just as one continues to use pre-tax durations for Treasury STRIPS despite their tax treatment, it seems reasonable to use pre-tax durations for TIPS as well. Additionally, the Australian experience suggests that pre-tax duration measures suffice for most day-to-day interest rate risk management. However, it is worth discussing tax briefly.

The Impact of Taxation: An Outline

Inflation-indexed bonds attempt to eliminate inflation risk, but it reappears on an after-tax basis. We begin with the fact that tax affects returns on both nominal bonds and inflation-indexed bonds in an unfortunate way: high inflation results in lower after-tax real returns. For inflation-indexed bonds, an investor would reason as follows (see Roll for more details):

forecast after-tax real yield

= forecast after-tax nominal yield − forecast inflation

= tax rate · forecast pre-tax nominal yield − forecast inflation

= tax rate · (pre-tax real yield + forecast inflation) − forecast inflation

= tax rate · pre-tax real yield − (1 − tax rate) · forecast inflation

For nominal bonds, the reasoning is similar:

> forecast after-tax real yield
> = forecast after-tax nominal yield − forecast inflation
> = tax rate · forecast pre-tax nominal yield − forecast inflation
> = tax rate · (pre-tax real yield + market inflation) − forecast inflation
> = tax rate · pre-tax real yield − (forecast inflation − tax rate · market inflation)

where "forecast inflation" refers to the investor's inflation forecast and "market inflation" refers to the market's inflation forecast as reflected in the spread between market nominal yields and market real yields. Thus an investor who agrees with the market's inflation forecast and who is thus indifferent between inflation-linked bonds and nominal bonds on a pre-tax basis will also be indifferent an after-tax basis.

The arguments show that projected after-tax real returns on both inflation-indexed and nominal bonds depend on forecast inflation. For example, assuming a tax rate of 40%, after-tax real yields will be negative unless expected inflation is less than 1.5 times the pre-tax real yield. In the second quarter of 1997, market real yields were around 3.60%. Thus an investor forecasting inflation of 5.4% or greater would expect negative real after-tax returns. Of course, the market inflation forecast, as reflected in the spread between nominal and real yields, is much lower than this.

An important consequence is that since U.S. inflation-indexed bonds and nominal bonds are affected equally, *inflation-linked bonds do not protect investors against the negative after-tax impact of high inflation*. Thus, TIPS real yields reflect only a premium for "pre-tax inflation risk." By contrast, since U.K. index-linked gilts receive preferential tax treatment, their yields also reflect a premium for "after-tax inflation risk." The price paid by U.K. investors, as observed by Roll and by Brown and Schaefer, is illiquidity: the market for index-linked gilts is confined to investors with high marginal tax rates. (By the way, this provides a neat example of the tax clientele effects analyzed by Dybvig and Ross.)

Roll points out a further consequence: if the demand for inflation-indexed or nominal bonds is a function of expected after-tax returns, pre-tax real yields should rise as expected inflation rises, to maintain a constant after-tax real yield. It is not clear whether real yields on inflation-indexed bonds actually behave in this way, although the Australian experience in 1994 suggests that they do. In any case, this introduces a further source of uncertainty about the future behavior of real yields.

Inflation-Indexed Bonds and Portfolio Efficiency

Inflation-indexed bonds have a risk profile quite different to that of nominal bonds. In fact, it could be argued that for asset allocation purposes, they should not be grouped with nominal bonds but should be treated as an entirely separate asset class. We will use portfolio theory to explore the consequences of adopting this point of view. More specifically, we will try to determine what weight TIPS should have in efficient portfolios with varying degrees of risk, and what impact their inclusion has on expected returns.

Exhibit 3-6: Assumptions Used in Efficient Portfolio Analysis

	Bills	Bonds	TIPS	Equities
Expected return	5.5%	6.5%	6.5%	10%
Return volatility	1%	8.5%	7.5%/4.5%	16%
Correlations				
Bills	1.0	0.1	0.0	−0.1
Bonds		1.0	0.5	0.1
TIPS			1.0	0.3
Equities				1.0

For simplicity, we focus on maximizing nominal returns in the U.S. market, and we work in a total return framework. Other kinds of analysis are possible: for example, Eichholtz, Naber and Petri discuss the problem of matching inflation-indexed liabilities in the U.K. and Israeli markets. We summarize their results below.

The results of any Markowitz-style analysis are always highly dependent on the expected returns, volatilities and correlations used. The assumptions we use are set out in Exhibit 3–6, and are broadly based on market data and presumed market expectations. They were derived as follows:

- Expected nominal returns for bills and nominal bonds are based on current market yields — this is more meaningful than using historical returns. We assume that nominal bonds and TIPS have the same expected return (since they are generally viewed as less risky, TIPS are unlikely to have a higher *expected* return than bonds). The expected return for equities is obtained by adding a risk premium of 3.5% to that for bonds; this roughly corresponds to the average historical excess return in the period 1970–1995.
- Return volatilities for bills, nominal bonds and equities are historical, calculated over the period 1970–1995. Since there is no meaningful return history for TIPS in the US, two different volatility assumptions are made: a "realistic" 7.5% volatility (which is somewhat lower than the historical return volatility of inflation-indexed bonds in Australia) and a "low" 4.5% volatility (the most optimistic scenario, which assumes that real rates will be quite stable).
- Correlations between returns on bills, nominal bonds and equities are historical. Correlations with TIPS returns are based on those observed in the Australian and U.K. markets (see Eichholtz et al. for the latter). In particular, we assume a small positive correlation of 0.3 with equities, which is consistent both with the historical data and with the observation, made earlier in this chapter, that inflation-indexed bonds and equities are somewhat related.

Exhibit 3-7: Composition of Efficient Portfolios, 7.5% Volatility Assumption

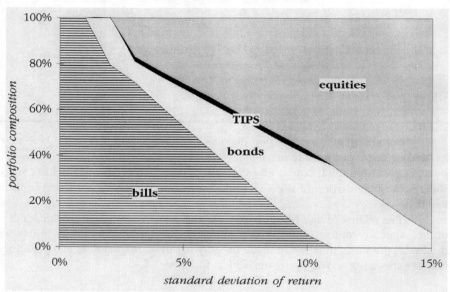

For simplicity, we focus on maximizing nominal returns, and we work in a total return framework. Other kinds of analysis are possible: for example, Eichholtz, Naber and Petri discuss the problem of matching inflation-indexed liabilities.

At first glance, the results seem highly dependent on the volatility assumption used for TIPS. Exhibit 3–7 shows the composition of theoretically efficient portfolios with varying degrees of risk, using the realistic volatility assumption; Exhibit 3–8 shows the same, using the low volatility assumption. Using a 7.5% volatility, TIPS play almost no role in any efficient portfolio; for example, at moderate risk levels, nominal bonds are preferred because of their lower correlation with equities. However, using a 4.5% volatility, TIPS have a much more important role to play. They partly displace bills at low risk levels, and largely displace nominal bonds at moderate to high risk levels. Only the equity weightings remain more or less unchanged.

But how much value do TIPS actually add? Exhibit 3–9 shows the efficient frontier, i.e., expected returns from efficient portfolios, calculated using both the realistic and low TIPS volatility assumptions. Above the 2% risk level, they are very close: expected returns differ by no more than 14 bp. That is, even assuming that TIPS will have a very low return volatility does not significantly increase their expected value added to portfolio returns.

Exhibit 3-8: Composition of Efficient Portfolios, 4.5% Volatility Assumption

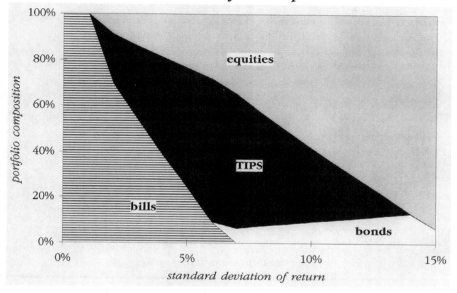

Exhibit 3-9: Efficient Frontier for the Two Different Volatility Assumptions

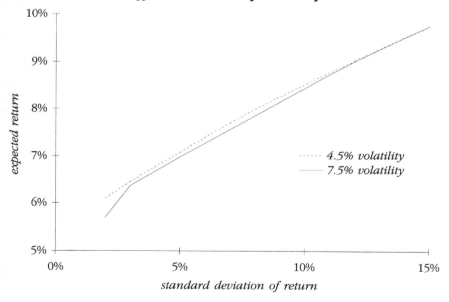

Exhibit 3–10: Efficient Portfolios Including and Excluding TIPS

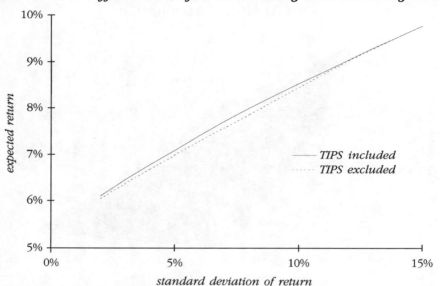

Exhibit 3–10 is even more telling. It shows expected returns from efficient portfolios under the low TIPS volatility assumption, for both unconstrained portfolios and portfolios from which TIPS have been excluded. Even at moderate risk levels, where TIPS are most important, the difference in expected returns is only 14 bp. Moreover, an investor who currently held a TIPS-free portfolio, and who wanted to capture this additional 14 bp by purchasing TIPS, would have to turn over 60% of the portfolio to achieve the optimal asset class weightings.

The overall conclusions are that (a) a realistic TIPS return volatility assumption, consistent with historical experience, implies that TIPS do not add value to asset allocation; and (b) even under a very optimistic TIPS return volatility assumption, the value added by TIPS is very modest. The main reasons are that TIPS do not have a higher expected return than nominal bonds, but have a slightly higher assumed correlation with equities.

These results should be compared with the findings of Eichholtz et al., who used data from 1983–91, and discovered a significant difference between relatively low inflation countries such as the U.K., and countries such as Israel where inflation has been extremely high and volatile.

- Results for the U.K.: If the goal is to maximize total return, inflation-linked bonds do not appear in any efficient portfolio. If inflation-linked liabilities are included in the problem, they appear in very low risk efficient portfolios, but with negligible weight (less than 1%).

- Results for Israel: If the goal is to maximize total return, inflation-linked bonds play a minor role in low risk portfolios but a major role in risky portfolios, sometimes having a weight of over 50%. If inflation-linked liabilities are included in the problem, inflation-linked bonds play a major role at all levels of risk, with weights between 44% and 88%.

U.S. investors will have to decide which set of results provides more useful guidance. Readers are encouraged to run the analysis themselves, based on their own portfolio objectives, and using volatility and correlation assumptions derived, not just from historical data, but from their own views on the nature of the U.S. economy. The computing resources required are very modest, and the exercise is likely to yield valuable insights.

ADVANCED ANALYTICAL APPROACHES TO INFLATION-INDEXED BONDS

Deriving a Term Structure of Inflation Forecasts and Real Yields

Exhibit 3–3 showed the spread between the TIPS real yield and the 10-year CMT nominal yield, which provided an estimate of the market's implied inflation forecast. While this simple measure has been reasonably accurate, it has the following shortcomings:

- it ignores the maturity mismatch between the TIPS and the 10-year CMT, and it also ignores the cashflow mismatch between the TIPS and nominal coupon streams; and
- it assumes a constant nominal yield and a constant real yield over the whole 10-year period, and produces a single, constant inflation forecast for that whole period.

Better results can be obtained by adopting a zero coupon approach, which analyzes securities on a cashflow-by-cashflow basis and which recognizes that real and nominal interest rates and inflation can vary as we move forward in time. This gives a more accurate estimate than taking a simple yield spread and, more importantly, gives additional information about the term structure of inflation forecasts and real yields, and (to some extent) the inflation risk premium.

In the Australian market, where inflation-linked Treasuries have been issued across a range of maturities, one can build a real zero coupon or forward rate curve using methods similar to those used to construct a nominal zero coupon or forward rate curve. (There are some complications, mostly arising from the indexation lag.) The spread between the real and nominal forward rate curve may be interpreted as the market's implied inflation forecast — possibly incorporating an inflation risk premium. This forecast need not be constant, but can vary through time.

The difficulty in the U.S. market is that, at the time of writing, there is only one TIPS outstanding: only the 10-year real yield is observable. How can we reconstruct an entire real forward rate curve or an entire implied inflation curve? This can be done in two steps:

1. Estimate short-term real interest rates by comparing short-dated nominal Treasury yields to short-term consensus inflation forecasts. This assumes that market short-term real rates should be consistent with these consensus forecasts, which seems reasonable since these forecasts are based on a great deal of data and analysis. Later on, we will discuss how sensitive the analysis is to a variation in the consensus forecasts used.

2. Interpolate between these short-term real interest rates and the observed long-term market real yield using a macroeconomic model, such as the one described in Chapter 1. More precisely, we assume that the forward real interest rate curve has the functional form implied by such a model, and fit this functional form to the given short- and long-term real yields. Note that this procedure only relies on the structure of the model; there is no need to estimate the model parameters separately since they are (implicitly) determined by market data.

One refinement is required. Recall from Chapter 1 that the short end of the yield curve can be idiosyncratic, and often has an unusual shape. This occurs partly because monetary policy is often perceived to be in disequilibrium compared to where the market thinks it currently "should be," and partly because short-dated yields can be based on detailed short-term economic forecasts: that is, short-term economic expectations can be more complex than long-term expectations. Thus, it is useful to allow for additional structure at the short end of the curve.

Step 1 does this by using consensus inflation forecasts for both the next quarter and for the next year. Step 2 does this by assuming that the real yield curve can have a more complex form than described in Chapter 1. More precisely, if:

r^e is the market forecast long-term equilibrium real interest rate;

r_0 is what the market thinks the short-term real interest rate should be; and,

$r_0{}'$ is what the short-term real interest rate actually is.

then we assume that the real forward rate curve has the form:

$$r^e + (r_0 - r^e)\exp(-\delta t) + (r_0{}' - r_0)\exp(-\delta 't)$$

The first two terms of this expression are derived from the economic model presented in Chapter 1; the last term is chosen for its simplicity, and seems to give quite good results in empirical testing. To simplify the analysis, we also assume that the nominal forward rate curve (and hence the forward inflation curve) has the same functional form.

Here δ is estimated as described in Chapter 4 and δ' is estimated in an *ad hoc* fashion; in fact, the analysis is not too sensitive to the choice of δ and δ'. We choose to fit 3-month, 2-year and 10-year nominal Treasury yields precisely, and observe that this generally gives a good fit to intermediate nominal yields. As we observed in Chapter 1, mid-range nominal bond yields can be distorted by maturity-specific supply/demand factors. Mid-range real yields are unlikely to be affected by these factors, and so we adopt a method which does not transmit these distortions to the estimated real yield curve.

Recall that nominal yields may reflect an inflation risk premium. This must either be modeled separately, or absorbed into the market implied inflation curve, which then represents a "risk-adjusted inflation forecast." It is preferable to adopt the latter approach, in the absence of additional information enabling us to estimate the risk premium separately. This ensures that the estimation procedure is stable and does not rely on any assumptions about an unobservable (and possibly maturity-dependent) variable. However, one must remember that the resulting inflation forecast is risk-adjusted.

Exhibit 3–11 shows the results of this analysis, as of 1/31/97, 5/12/97 and 6/13/97. This exhibit has the following interpretation. On 1/31/97, the implied market forecast said that inflation would rise from a current level of around 3% to a long-term equilibrium rate of around 3.4%, while short-term real interest rates would rise from a current 2.5% to around 3.4% (note that this level is consistent with historical long-term real yields as shown in Exhibit 3–2). These estimated market forecasts are consistent with a long-term scenario of moderately strong growth leading to some upward pressure on inflation. The market forecast for 10-year average inflation was around 3.25%, significantly higher than the consensus forecast produced by the Society of Professional Forecasters.

By 5/12/97, after a monetary tightening and the release of economic data which eased inflation concerns, the situation had changed. The implied market inflation forecast said that inflation would remain relatively stable: it would rise moderately over the remainder of the cycle and then drift down to an equilibrium level somewhat lower than 3%. Short-term real interest rates would rise from a current 2.8% to around 3.7% (reflecting expectations of slightly more aggressive monetary policy). These estimated forecasts are consistent with a long-term scenario of strong growth but muted inflation. Note that the market forecast for 10-year average inflation was now very close to the consensus forecast.

By 6/13/97, inflation expectations had eased even further; in fact, the implied 10-year average inflation forecast was by then somewhat lower than the SPF consensus forecast, which had itself been revised downwards since the previous quarter. In detail, inflation was expected to rise from 2.5% to 3%, and then ease back to around 2.6%. Since real interest rates had not changed appreciably, the fall in long-term inflationary expectations was not due to a belief that the Fed would act more aggressively to contain inflation, but was probably due to a positive reassessment of the economy and its ability to sustain non-inflationary growth.

Exhibit 3–11: Estimated Forward Real Rates and Inflation on 1/31/97

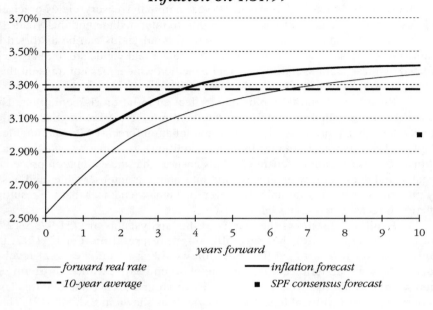

5/12/97

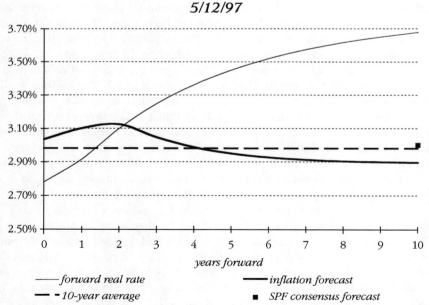

Exhibit 3-11 (Continued): 6/13/97

Legend:
— forward real rate
- - 10-year average
— inflation forecast
■ SPF consensus forecast

This interpretation ignores the fact that the market inflation forecast is risk-adjusted, and incorporates an inflation risk premium. However, one can see that this risk premium cannot be large: for example, if it were 70 bp then this would imply that market participants were expecting a long-term inflation rate of around 2% on 6/13/97, which seems improbable. In fact, a possible interpretation is that on both 1/31/97 and 5/12/97, market participants expected long-term inflation to average 3%, but that nominal yields on 1/31/97 reflected a 25 bp inflation risk premium while nominal yields on 5/12/97 reflected no inflation risk premium. This would seem reasonable, since when inflation expectations are muted, inflation risk is dominated by real interest rate risk. Thus, nominal yields on 6/13/97 appeared to reflect a "negative inflation risk premium," arguably due to the fact that in investors' minds, real rate risk by then assumed significantly more importance than inflation risk.

We thus conclude that, if market long-term inflation expectations are assumed to agree with the economists' consensus forecast, *the inflation risk premium in nominal bond yields has fluctuated between 25 bp and −15 bp.* However, we will see in a moment that the discrepancy between the observed market long-term inflation forecast and the economists' consensus forecast can be explained in other ways. Therefore, this evidence about the inflation risk premium is inconclusive. (In a forthcoming paper, Evans uses different methods to measure time-varying inflation risk premia in the U.K. market.)

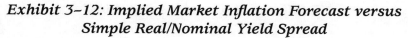

Exhibit 3–12: Implied Market Inflation Forecast versus Simple Real/Nominal Yield Spread

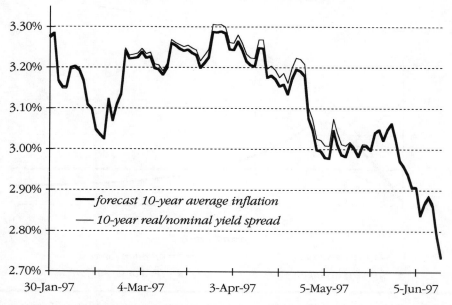

Note that, while the long-term equilibrium real rate and inflation forecasts are somewhat sensitive to the short-term consensus inflation forecasts fed into the analysis, the 10-year average market inflation forecast is not; varying the short-term inflation forecasts has little effect on the 10-year forecast. Therefore, it is probably more valid to focus on this figure than on the long-term equilibrium forecast. Exhibit 3–12 compares the 10-year market inflation forecast, computed as above, with the simple yield spread between the 10-year TIPS and the 10-year CMT nominal yield. The yield spread actually provides quite a good measure of expected inflation. However, note that the discrepancy would be much wider if the yield curve were very steep, if the short end of the yield curve had an unusual shape, or if there were a larger maturity mismatch. The zero coupon approach gives more accurate results under all yield curve environments, and also provides additional information.

One useful application of the analysis is the estimation of real yields: this can be done by integrating the estimated forward real rate curve. Exhibit 3–13 shows estimated semi-annual par real yields for various maturities, again on 1/31/97 and 5/12/97. While the nominal curve flattened between January and May 1997, the real yield curve actually steepened. This illustrates how the dynamics of the real yield curve may differ from that of the nominal curve.

Exhibit 3–13: Estimated Real Yield Curves on 1/31/97 and 5/12/97

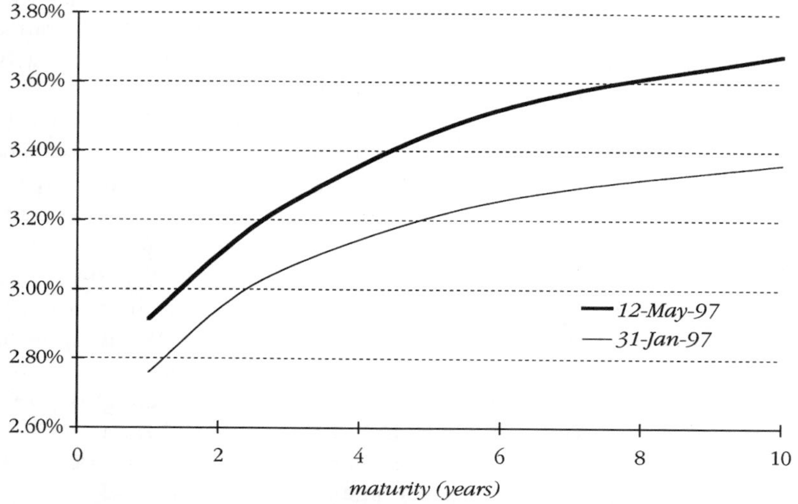

Real yield curves are useful to investors in a number of ways. Here are some applications which arise in insurance investment management and corporate finance:

1. They can be used to value inflation-linked liabilities, such as inflation-indexed annuities.
2. They can be used to value inflation-linked revenue streams, such as toll-road revenues; this is helpful when assessing potential returns from infrastructure projects.
3. They can be used to estimate the present value of a company's future wage costs, which are broadly linked to inflation.

In each case, tradition valuation methods use nominal discount rates and an inflation forecast, which is usually taken to be constant. Using estimated market real yields is equivalent to using nominal discount rates together with the implied market inflation forecast, which need not be constant. This valuation method is consistent with the way nominal and inflation-linked bond holdings are valued.

For example, suppose a project will be completed in 1 year's time, and will generate quarterly real revenues of $25m in today's dollars, for 5 years following. An investor wishes to value the project as at 5/12/97. Using a constant real rate of 3.66% (the TIPS market real yield) values the project at $439m, whereas using the estimated real yield curve values the project at $444m — that is, using more accurate real yields makes a $5m difference. The discrepancy remains if we add a risk premium to the discount rates. The discrepancy would be larger if the yield curve were very steep, or oddly shaped.

Risk-adjusted market inflation forecasts are also useful in a number of ways, not all of them obvious. For example, if a prepayment model had to make certain assumptions about future house price levels (which affect LTV ratios and thus prepayment rates), these assumptions should not be specified arbitrarily, but should be derived from market inflation forecasts.

The analysis will be considerably sharpened once the Treasury has issued TIPS with a range of maturities, preferably including at least 2-, 5-, 10-, and 30-year maturities. This will make it possible to construct more accurate real yield curves and inflation curves. The availability of a 2-year TIPS real yield will also reduce the reliance of the analysis to the short-term consensus forecasts used, and thus improve the construction of a real yield curve. Note that if a 30-year TIPS is included, the estimation procedure must be modified to take the convexity bias into account: Chapter 4 explores this issue in more detail, and the analysis there is applicable to inflation-linked bonds as well as nominal bonds.

Quality spreads in the inflation-indexed bond market are also worth analyzing. At the time of writing, inflation-indexed bonds have been issued by Federal agencies, financial institutions and corporates. Since quality spreads depend on maturity, one would like to construct quality-specific real yield curves which permit accurate comparisons between different curves. This will suggest how new issues should be priced, and may also be used to identify arbitrages in quality spreads between the real and nominal markets.

Note that even once a range of TIPS maturities is outstanding, it is likely that bond yield data for lower qualities will remain sparse. Thus, the interpolation method described above will still be useful for constructing real yield curves for lower qualities, even if it is no longer required to construct a Treasury real yield curve.

Economists' Forecasts versus Market Implied Forecasts

Why is there often a discrepancy between economists' inflation forecasts and market implied inflation forecasts? One obvious explanation is that traders and investors do not necessarily agree with economists. One must be careful here: this is only an explanation if one believes that the consensus between investors can differ from the consensus between economists, which is a much less obvious assertion. In fact, if this is true, it says something remarkable: that in making economic forecasts, market participants do not always rely on the skills and resources of the "experts" which (in effect) they themselves have selected. On the face of it, this would seem to contradict market efficiency, i.e., the hypothesis that investors make use of all available information in what they believe to be an optimal way. One might argue that in an efficient market, either bond yields would reflect economists' predictions, or economists would be considered unreliable and would therefore not have jobs.

A second explanation is as follows. Investors do not make a single inflation forecast, but attach probabilities to future inflation scenarios; and this probability determines future bond yields (including the inflation risk premium, if it exists). Roughly speaking, if i is the unknown long-term inflation rate, which we regard as a random variable to which economists and market participants assign some probability distribution, then:

$$\textit{market implied inflation forecast} \approx \textbf{mean}(i) + \lambda \cdot \textbf{variance}(i)^{1/2}$$

where the second term represents the inflation risk premium, i.e., λ is the market price of inflation risk. On the other hand, one could argue that:

$$\textit{economists' consensus forecast} \approx \textbf{median}(i)$$

where the median is perhaps taken over a "trimmed" distribution, i.e., eliminating outliers. (The actual story is probably more complex than this, since different market participants and economists are using their individual probability distributions.)

Even if economists and market participants are using the same probability distribution, these two expressions need not be equal if this distribution is skewed. For example, if there is an upside skew, then the market implied forecast can be appreciably higher than the economists' consensus forecast, for three reasons:

- the mean will be higher than the median, if there are wide outliers on the upside;
- the inflation risk premium may be relatively more significant; and,
- the "trimming" in the median will have eliminated more outliers on the upside.

When inflation is low (below around 3%), there tends to be an upside skew and thus the market implied forecast is very often higher than the economists' consensus forecast. There are two main reasons for this skew. First, it is harder to cut real wages when inflation is very low, since workers tend to resist nominal wage cuts; this makes lower inflation scenarios seem less likely. Second, if low inflation is perceived to be the result of domestic policy rather than, e.g., an external currency standard, political risk poses a threat to continued low inflation.

This seems to be the explanation advanced by Carmody and Mason. It is important to note that wage stickiness and the absence of an external currency standard need not be unchangeable features of the economy; cf. the historical observations in Chapter 4. That is, the tendency for probability distributions to be skewed when inflation is low is not universal, but arises from particular institutional features of Western economies. These may be changing even now; for example, it is much more plausible that real wages should fall in the USA over the next few years than it was in the early 1960s, when inflation was similarly low.

Note that the discrepancy between the market forecast and the consensus forecast may vary over time. For example, we saw earlier that it was around 0.25% on 1/31/97, but close to zero on 5/12/97; and on 6/13/97 it was –0.15%. An investor who believed that this discrepancy should theoretically be constant or nearly constant (e.g., because it reflects an inflation risk premium), might monitor the discrepancy from day to day, to detect potential trading opportunities.

For most practical applications, one should use market implied forecasts rather than economists' consensus forecasts. This ensures that one will obtain valuations of inflation-linked revenue streams or liability streams which are consistent with observed market prices of traded securities. In other words, using market implied forecasts ensures arbitrage-freeness, while using economists' forecasts admits the possibility of arbitrage.

Selected References

Brown, R. and Schaefer, S., "Ten Years of the Real Term Structure: 1984–1994," *J. Fixed Income*, March 1996.

Brynjolfsson, J. and Faillace, A., *Inflation Protected Bonds*, Frank J. Fabozzi Associates, New Hope, 1997.

Carmody, S. and Mason, R., *Analysis of Australian Index-Linked Securities*, Deutsche Morgan Grenfell (Sydney) research report, June 1996.

Dybvig, P. and Ross, S., "Tax Clienteles and Asset Pricing," *J. Finance*, July 1986.

Eichholtz, P., Naber, P. and Petri, V., "Index-Linked Bonds in a Liability Framework," *J. Fixed Income*, December 1993.

Elmendorf, D., "The Effect of Deficit-Reduction Laws on Real Interest Rates," *Federal Reserve Board*, October 1996.

Evans, D., "Real Rates, Expected Inflation and Inflation Risk Premia," to appear in *J. Finance*.

Federal Register, Vol. 62, No. 3, Monday, January 6, 1997; see Appendix B to Part 356.

Judson, R. and Orphanides, A., "Inflation, Volatility and Growth," *Federal Reserve Board*, May 1996.

Keynes, J. M., *The General Theory of Employment, Interest and Money*, Macmillan, London, 1936.

Roll, R., "US Treasury Inflation-Indexed Bonds: The Design of a New Security," *J. Fixed Income*, December 1996.

Chapter 4

Long Bond Pricing Paradoxes and Long-Term Yields

ANALYSIS OF THE CONVEXITY BIAS

The Convexity Bias in Long Bond Yields

This chapter explores the impact of convexity on long bond yields. Although the results are relevant to all bonds, option-embedded or not, we will focus mainly on non-callable Treasuries. Excluding bonds with option features helps bring out the issues more clearly.

If two portfolios have the same duration and yield, the one with the higher convexity will outperform if there is a parallel shift in yields. Does this mean that portfolios with higher convexity always outperform? Empirical research — for example, the study carried out by Lacey and Nawalkha — suggest that they do not, because these portfolios tend to have lower yields. Intuitively, investors are prepared to pay for convexity by giving up yield. This is exactly what one would expect in an efficient market.

This yield give-up can be observed in the shape of the Treasury curve. For example, one might naively expect the 30-year yield to be higher than the 20-year yield, particularly when the yield curve up to 20 years has a positive slope. In fact, the yield on a 30-year Treasury bond is almost always lower than the yield on a 20-year bond: see Exhibit 4–1. The usual explanation is that the 30-year bond has about 1.8 times the convexity of the 20-year bond, and that the "cost" of this convexity is about 10–15 bp.

The convexity bias in observed yields has been the subject of much attention in the swap market. For example, Burghardt and Hoskins observed that the 10-year swap rate is significantly lower than the yield on an equivalent 10-year strip of Eurodollar futures. This is because the swap has convexity while the futures position does not; a dealer who is receiving swap and short Eurodollar futures benefits from being long convexity.

Since convexity only delivers benefits if yields are volatile, the size of the convexity adjustment depends on how volatile yields are expected to be. Exhibit 4–2 graphs the convexity adjustment versus bond maturity, based on a rule of thumb commonly used by traders, and assuming an absolute yield volatility of 80 bp per annum. (We will derive this rule of thumb in a moment.) For example, the convexity adjustment is around 30 bp for a 20-year bond, and around 50 bp for a 30-year bond; thus, the theoretical yield give-up when moving from a 20-year bond to a 30-year bond is around 20 bp, although this is partly offset by the general upward slope of the yield curve along its length.

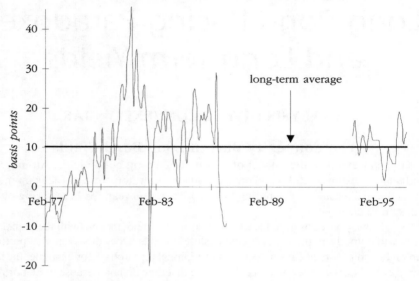

Exhibit 4–1: Slope of the Long End of the Curve
(20-Year Yield minus 30-Year Yield)

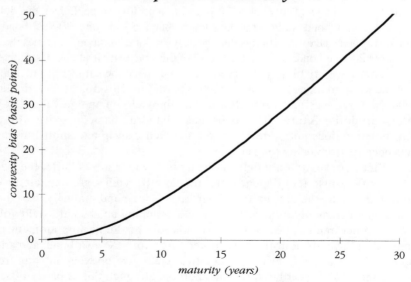

Exhibit 4–2: Theoretical Convexity Bias versus Maturity,
80 bp Annual Volatility

As an example of the convexity bias, recall from Chapter 1 that a long FRA/ short Eurodollar futures position resembles a hedged long option position, where volatility results in profits from rehedging. Thus one would expect the FRA yield to be lower than the futures rate, reflecting the "option cost;" and over time, the FRA yield should converge to the futures rate, reflecting the "option time decay." The difference between the FRA yield and the futures rate is, by definition, the convexity bias.

The traders' rule of thumb for computing the convexity bias can be derived as follows. Consider an arbitrary bond without embedded options. If the yield of the bond at some future date t is y, write $B(y)$ for the corresponding bond price. For example, the current t-forward price of the bond is:

$$B_{\text{fwd}} = B(y_{\text{fwd}})$$

where y_{fwd} is the current t-forward yield. Now, the expected bond price at time t is just $E[B]=B_{\text{fwd}}$; but if the bond yield is volatile, it is not the case that $E[y]=y_{\text{fwd}}$; in fact, the difference between the forward yield and the expected future yield is precisely the convexity adjustment to the bond yield.

If the actual yield of the bond at time t is y rather than y_{fwd}, then we can write:

$$B(y) \approx B(y_{\text{fwd}}) + D \cdot (y_{\text{fwd}} - y) + C \cdot (y_{\text{fwd}} - y)^2$$

where D is the duration of the forward bond position and C is its convexity divided by two. Taking expected values, this gives us:

$$B_{\text{fwd}} \approx B_{\text{fwd}} + D \cdot (y_{\text{fwd}} - E[y]) + C \cdot E[(y_{\text{fwd}} - y)^2]$$

Now $E[(y_{\text{fwd}} - y)^2]=\sigma^2 t$ where σ is the basis point volatility of bond yields. Thus we obtain the following expression for the convexity bias.

$$E[y] - y_{\text{fwd}} \approx (C/D)\sigma^2 t$$

For example, the convexity adjustment for a FRA is approximately $\frac{1}{2}\sigma^2 t^2$. Assuming an absolute volatility of 100 bp per annum, this works out to only 2 bp for a 2-year FRA, but 12.5 bp for a 5-year FRA and 50 bp for a 10-year FRA. This explains the significant discrepancy between the Eurodollar strip and the swap curve at long maturities.

Implicit Volatility and How to Estimate It

What volatility σ should be used to compute the convexity bias? There are two approaches one can take. First, one can estimate volatility separately, and then use this to calculate what the appropriate convexity adjustment should be. Alternatively, one can attempt to observe the convexity bias directly and derive a volatility from it: that is, one observes actual swap or bond yields, and attempts to deduce what level of volatility is implied by those yields, i.e., market participants' expectations about future (medium to long-term) volatility, as reflected in observed yields. In this chapter, we refer to such a volatility estimate as the *implicit volatility.*

Implicit volatility is clearly different from historical volatility. The market's expectations about future volatility are only partly determined by historical experience. However, since changes in long-term volatility — as opposed to short-term volatility spikes — tend to be triggered by structural shifts in the economy, any large discrepancy between historical volatility and implicit volatility should be regarded as surprising, and worthy of further investigation.

Implicit volatility may also be different from the implied volatilities observed in the interest rate derivatives markets. The value of the convexity in a long bond is only fully realized over a long period of time — 10 years or more. (Note that it is irrelevant that the bond may change hands over this period, provided the potential future value of convexity is priced into each transaction.) Short dated implied volatilities of bond futures options are clearly irrelevant; cap/floor volatilities are not directly relevant, because they are the implied volatilities of money market rates and not bond yields. A comparable implied volatility would be that on (say) a 10-year swaption on a 10-year swap, but prices on such long-dated contracts are not routinely quoted.

Furthermore, because the importance of the convexity bias has only been appreciated relatively recently, there may well be a discrepancy between implicit volatility and OTC option implied volatilities even where they are directly comparable, such as in the swap market. In theory, this gives rise to an arbitrage opportunity; in practice, it may be difficult to exploit a convexity arbitrage efficiently. This chapter focuses on bond market data and attempts to estimate implicit volatility from long bond yields.

Trying to estimate implicit volatility simply by looking at the 20-year/30-year yield spread turns out to be a bad idea. First, it would restrict us to studying periods where both 20-year and 30-year historical yields are available. Second, we need to take the overall slope of the yield curve into account. If the yield curve as a whole is nearly flat, the convexity bias will lead to an appreciable downward slope from the 20-year to the 30-year point; if it is steeply positive, and the same convexity bias is present, the curve may be flat or even upward sloping from 20 years to 30 years. Thus short bond yields are relevant to the analysis.

Third, any analysis which relies too heavily on the yields of specific bonds is vulnerable to yield anomalies which affect those particular bonds. These may arise from temporary supply/demand or liquidity conditions, or may be more persistent (as in the case of the on-the-run 10-year note, as noted by Carayannopoulos). Thus it is desirable to somehow take all bond yields into account in the analysis. However, yields on short maturity bonds should be used with caution, as the short end of the curve can behave idiosyncratically — see Chapter 1.

In order to incorporate the effect of overall yield curve slope, to discount the effect of yield anomalies on specific bonds, and to take into account the sometimes aberrant behavior of the short end of the yield curve, we will again use a theoretical model of the yield curve based on the macroeconomic model of interest rate expectations sketched in Chapter 1. This states that the expected path of future interest rates (which can be identified with current Eurodollar futures rates) must, in theory, have a certain functional form; to obtain a theoretical functional form for the forward curve, we simply add an extra term corresponding to the convexity bias. Here is a brief review of the model we will use.

The short rate s is defined to be the expected short-term nominal return on bonds; this assumes that since the bond market is liquid and homogeneous, any difference in expected short-term returns between bonds will be arbitraged away (i.e., it assumes LEH, see Chapter 1). The short rate need not be equal to any specific bond yield, since the expected short-term return on a bond incorporates not just an income effect but an expected price effect as reflected in observed forward bond prices. The short rate is determined by the market's expectations of imminent monetary policy, as influenced by near term inflation and growth prospects; clearly, it is related to the short term money market yield.

The long rate l is defined to be the expected long-term rate of return on bonds. That is, it is the "expected rate of return on a bond with infinite duration," i.e., the limit of the expected return on a zero coupon Treasury bond as the maturity approaches infinity. The long rate is not equal to the limiting zero coupon yield, since yields incorporate a convexity adjustment. The long rate is determined by the market's expectations of long run inflation and growth in the economy.

We saw in Chapter 1 that the rationally expected path of short-term nominal rates must have the form:

$$g(t) = l + (s - l)e^{-\kappa t}$$

The coefficient κ is a rate of adjustment parameter which is derived from the elasticity parameters appearing in the macroeconomic model. Note that this framework can easily accommodate an expected bond market risk premium: one can add a risk premium to s and l. Note that the expected risk premium need not be constant by maturity, but it is constrained to vary smoothly with maturity, with the same rate of adjustment parameter κ.

To obtain a theoretical expression for the forward rate, we add a term representing the convexity bias $\frac{1}{2}\sigma^2 t^2$ for a FRA:

$$f(t) = l + (s - l)e^{-\kappa t} - \frac{1}{2}\sigma^2 t^2$$

This description of the yield curve may seem rather abstract: none of the four parameters l, s, κ, and σ can be observed directly. However, they can be estimated from observed Treasury yields: it is possible to find the "best fit" parameters corresponding to a given yield curve.

In particular, this estimation procedure gives us, for each Treasury yield curve, an estimate of the implicit volatility σ. We will follow the paper of Phoa in adopting this approach. It has the advantage, emphasized in Chapter 2 in a different context, of using cross-sectional data: that is, rather than obtaining a single estimate of (say) σ from an entire time series of yields, we obtain estimates for σ for each daily or monthly yield curve, and we can thus observe how it behaves over time. This turns out to be important.

This theoretical description of the forward curve has the undesirable feature that very long forward rates become negative, causing very long forward bond prices to explode. However, this is not a significant problem in practice. Taking $l = 6\%$ (i.e., a historical low for the post-1970 period) and $\sigma = 0.75\%$ (corresponding to 12.5% proportional volatility, a high estimate for long-term volatility), forward rates only become negative at a forward date of 46 years, and the 30-year forward rate is approximately 3.5%. Thus, it may be hoped that the model gives reasonable answers when applied to Treasury bonds, although more sophisticated methods would have to be devised to analyze 100-year bonds.

We will return to this issue later in the chapter. For the moment, we note that more reasonable asymptotic behavior could be obtained by assuming that long bond yields were mean reverting. Unfortunately, this introduces another parameter which is extremely difficult to estimate — much more so than κ, which is itself hard to estimate, as pointed out in the next section. Moreover, the mean reversion time scale would necessarily be long (for example, long bond yields broadly trended upwards from 1953 to 1982). Thus, the practical impact on the analysis of Treasury bond yields would be minimal.

The point is that even though the above formulation has implausible asymptotic properties, it may still do a good job of modeling the investor expectations which determine Treasury bond yields. In fact, as a model of the structure of investor expectations, it is probably more plausible than one based on a mathematically sophisticated term structure theory with a larger number of unobservable parameters, even if the latter is mathematically more consistent. The test, of course, is to fit the model to historical Treasury yields and see whether the results are meaningful.

In this chapter, we use 1-, 2-, 3-, 5-, 7-, 10-, 20-, and 30-year CMT yields provided by the Federal Reserve Board (available monthly from 1953, and daily from 1977). As we shall see, the results of the study suggest some techniques for relative value analysis and security selection; in order to apply these seriously, one would have to use traded yields on actual coupon bonds.

Historical Analysis of the Convexity Bias

The forward rate curve in the previous section can be integrated to obtain the following formulas for the discount function and par yield curve:

$$PV(t) = \exp\left(-lt - (s-l)\kappa^{-1}(1 - e^{-\kappa t}) + \frac{1}{6}\sigma^2 t^3\right)$$

$$\text{theoretical } n\text{-year CMT yield} = \frac{2(1 - PV(n))}{\displaystyle\sum_{i=1}^{2n} PV(i/2)}$$

In principle, then, the estimation problem is simple: given a set of CMT yields, find l, s, σ, and κ which give the best fit to those yields. The first question is: what is the meaning of "best fit?" We will adopt the normal procedure of initially using χ^2 estimation, and then reviewing the distribution of errors to determine whether this was in fact a reasonable thing to do.

It is helpful to make some observations before proceeding. Firstly, provided the model of investor expectations is realistic, one would not expect serious outliers. Deviations from the model may be thought of as indicating anomalous liquidity or supply/demand conditions, and under this interpretation a discrepancy no larger than 5–15 bp (and generally less than this for longer bonds) would be expected. Thus it should not be necessary to use more robust statistical estimators.

However, as noted above, the model need not be realistic for short-dated bonds. Thus, if 1-year CMT yields are included in the data set, much larger discrepancies would be expected under certain circumstances — for example, at times where there was a sharp divergence between Fed policy and the market's views. It should also be noted that, in economic terms, the same basis point error is less significant for a shorter than for a longer bond. It might thus be possible that somewhat larger discrepancies could arise for shorter bonds.

The solution adopted was to weight basis point errors by bond duration, i.e., to minimize price errors rather than yield errors. This turns out to give empirically good results for 2–30 year bond yields. It gives the 1-year CMT minimal weight without discarding it from the dataset altogether.

Details about the estimation process appear in the paper of Phoa. Since they are not really relevant to an interpretation of the results, we simply observe that the estimation problem is a constrained nonlinear optimization problem, and can be solved reasonably efficiently using recently developed algorithms. However, care is required, since some apparently natural methods — for example, attempting to estimate all four parameters simultaneously using a Levenberg-Marquardt algorithm — are unstable and yield unreliable results.

The first question is how well the yield curve model fits observed CMT yields. Exhibit 4–3 shows the distribution of basis point errors for the 5-, 10-, and 30-year CMT yields. Errors are small and unbiased except for the 10-year CMT yield, which was generally overestimated by the model; this however is consistent with the findings of Carayannopoulos regarding the systematic overpricing of the 10-year Treasury note. A graph of the model error over time, for various maturities, shows that it appears to be a stationary process which is uncorrelated with the level or slope of the yield curve, or with any other obvious economic variable. It may be concluded that the yield curve model we have adopted is a realistic one.

Exhibits 4–4, 4–5, and 4–6 show the results of the estimation process for monthly data. The long and short rates appear plausible, and — as expected — move up and down with observed changes in the level and slope of the yield curve. Interestingly, the fitted mean reversion coefficient tends to hover around either 0.5 or zero; we will discuss this phenomenon later. Implicit volatility has been estimated in two different ways: with a fitted mean reversion coefficient (the preferred method), and assuming that the mean reversion equals 0.5 (which is quicker, but less reliable).

Exhibit 4-3: Yield Curve Model Estimation, Distribution of Errors

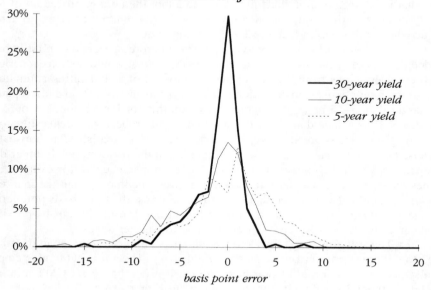

Exhibit 4-4: Yield Curve Model Estimation, Long and Short Rates

Exhibit 4–5: Yield Curve Model Estimation, Mean Reversion Coefficient

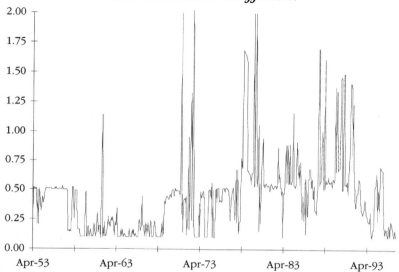

Exhibit 4–6: Yield Curve Model Estimation, Implicit Volatility

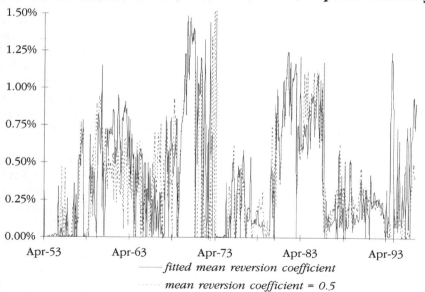

—— fitted mean reversion coefficient

······ mean reversion coefficient = 0.5

Exhibit 4–7: Historical 24-Month Correlation between Level Shifts and Slope Shifts

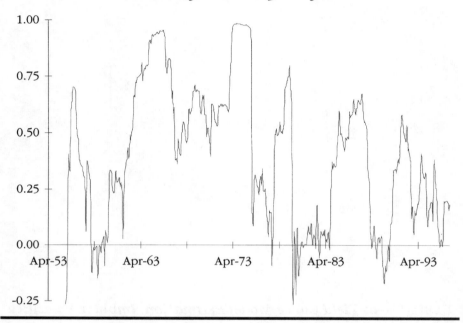

As an aside, we can now tie up a loose end from the very beginning of Chapter 1. There, we observed that on economic grounds, there was no reason why parallel and slope shifts (i.e., changes in the long rate, and in the spread between the long and short rates) should be uncorrelated. Exhibit 4–7 shows the historical correlation between parallel and slope shifts; more precisely, between a rise (respectively, fall) in the long rate and a steepening (respectively, flattening) in the yield curve. The correlation is usually positive, and was significantly positive in the 1960s and early 1970s. A positive correlation implies that short bond yields are "stickier" than long bond yields.

Exhibits 4–8 and 4–9 show the results of the estimation process for daily data. This gives a more detailed picture for the period since 1977. Note that it is difficult to estimate κ when the yield curve is nearly flat, and the estimates on these dates are quite unstable; however, when the curve is flat, the value of κ is irrelevant, so this does not taint our estimates of σ.

Interpretation of the Results: Volatility Regimes

The major observation is that implicit volatility is not constant, nor does it seem to be a continuously varying random quantity. Instead, it seems to be either switched "on" or "off:" there appear to be two distinct regimes. See Exhibit 4–10.

Exhibit 4–8: Mean Reversion Coefficient, Daily Estimates

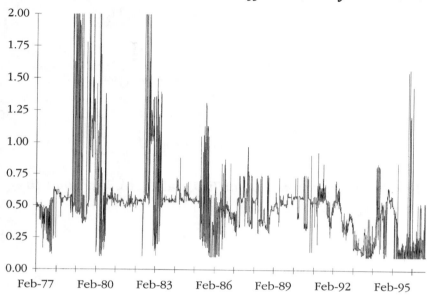

Exhibit 4–9: Implicit Volatility, Daily Estimates

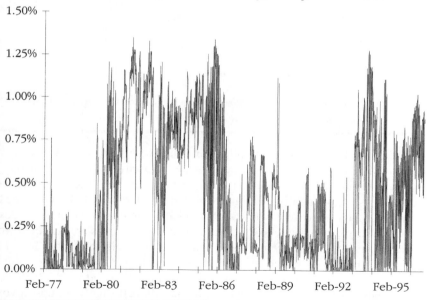

Exhibit 4-10: Implicit Volatility Regimes

Period	Regime	Implicit volatility
1954–57	off	—
1958–65	on	≈ 70 bp p.a.
1966–67	off	—
1968–72	on	≈ 100 bp p.a.
1973–79	(mostly) off	—
1980–83	on	≈ 80 bp p.a.
1984–93	off	—
1994–96	(mostly) on	≈ 80 bp p.a.

Exhibit 4-11: Implicit Volatility and Historical Volatility

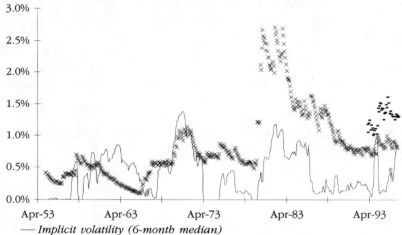

— Implicit volatility (6-month median)
× Historical volatility of 10-year Treasury yield (exponentially weighted)
- Option implied volatility (5-year caps)

Exhibit 4–11 compares implicit volatility with historical 10-year bond yield volatility, both expressed in percent per annum. (Implicit volatility is smoothed by taking an annual median, to make the graph easier to read.) Historical volatility is exponentially weighted with a decay factor of 0.9, and is thus a reasonably long-term measure, while still responding quickly to volatility shocks. Implicit volatility can be switched "off" even while bond yields are still quite volatile. However, a volatility *shock* tends to switch implicit volatility "on." The most recent examples of this occurred in 1979–80 and 1993–94.

The other interesting observation is that in basis point terms, historical volatility tends to be higher when yields are higher, while the level of implicit volatility (when it is "on") seems to be independent of absolute yield levels. Remembering that implicit volatility is meant to encapsulate the market's volatility expectations over long time frames, during which outright yields will vary greatly, it seems *a priori* reasonable that the fact that yields are currently high or low should not unduly bias implicit volatility, and this does in fact appear to be the case.

If one believes that the volatility of yields is proportional to the outright level of yields, then an implicit volatility of 70–80 bp is consistent with the hypothesis that the market expects long-term proportional volatility to be around 11%, and that long bond yields will fluctuate around 7.5%, i.e., are mean reverting. But the evidence for this interpretation is not very strong.

Although not much data was not available for this study, it appears that implicit volatility is not closely related to long-dated OTC implied volatilities. This is not surprising, for the reasons mentioned in the introduction. However, a shock to implied volatilities tends to coincide with a shock to historical volatilities (as in early 1994), and thus also coincides with implicit volatility being switched on: see Exhibit 4–11.

Finally, recall from Exhibits 4–5 and 4–8 that the mean reversion coefficient itself seems to exhibit a kind of regime-switching behavior. During the periods 1953–57, 1972–92 and 1994 it appears to fluctuate around 0.5, while during 1958–71 and 1993–96 (excepting 1994) it appears to fluctuate around 0.1–0.2. A very tentative interpretation would be that a low value of κ appears to coincide with long-term expectations of strong growth coupled with low inflation and a belief that the business cycle no longer applies — these are clearly secular, rather than cyclical, shifts in attitudes.

However, it would be unwise to attempt to draw any definitive conclusions since, as mentioned in the previous section, the estimation procedure was not optimized to generate the most accurate possible estimates of κ. A more refined procedure would probably employ different weights. As mentioned earlier, it should also make use of the yields of traded bonds, rather than interpolated constant maturity Treasury yields.

Some Consequences of the Analysis

We saw in Chapter 1 that the most important kinds of yield curve shift are a parallel shift in the yield curve and a shift in yield curve slope, with a curvature shift generally emerging as the third factor. These may be interpreted, in terms of our model, as changes in l, $(l–s)$, and κ. The above analysis suggests the existence of an additional source of yield curve risk — fluctuations in implicit volatility σ — which should be taken into account in the risk monitoring process.

This source of risk may not be apparent from a principal component analysis since, as we have seen, σ does not exhibit small random fluctuations like a "typical" random quantity, but instead seems to be switched "on" or "off." Furthermore, studies tend to use data sets whose observations are much more closely clustered at short maturities, thus reducing the statistical weight given to observed fluctuations in long bond yields. Thus a short-end "hump" factor is much more likely to be detected, and will appear relatively more important than a "convexity bias" factor driven by changes in implicit volatility.

Volatility risk is, of course, very familiar from the interest rate derivatives markets. In fact, in those markets, where volatility shows a distinct term structure, it is necessary to subdivide volatility risk by, for example, separating exposure to short-dated and long-dated volatility. In the present study, by contrast, it does not make practical sense to introduce more than one volatility parameter. Although theoretically attractive, this would make the estimation process unstable, and would probably lead to meaningless results. (Note that mean reversion implies that physical bond yield volatilities have some term structure anyway; i.e., the model is already realistic in that it does not predict flat volatilities.)

The present line of investigation has potential applications to fixed income portfolio management. For example, it could be argued that when implicit volatility is low, as it was in 1987–1993 except for brief periods, 30-year bonds are undervalued relative to shorter bonds. This has implications for an active portfolio strategy with a relatively long time horizon: in effect, in periods such as these, long-dated long bond volatility can be bought very cheaply.

There are a number of reasons why this strategy is not entirely obvious, which may explain why such "anomalies" can persist for long periods of time. In particular, note that one cannot exploit the opportunity simply by executing a duration-matched switch from, say, 20-year bonds into 30-year bonds, as this would change the exposure of the portfolio to a shift in yield curve slope. Instead, one must adopt a neutral strategy which leaves slope risk as well as duration unaffected: a 20-year position must be rebalanced into 10-year and 30-year holdings, with a correspondingly smaller convexity pickup. Thus the trade is only worth executing in volume. Incidentally, this strategy ignores curvature risk; κ-immunization is possible via "condor" rather than "butterfly" trades, but is unwieldy and subject to additional execution risk.

Note that the fact that these "anomalies" may persist for a long time, combined with the costs of funding short bond positions, means that it probably does not make sense to execute this kind of convexity arbitrage on a leveraged basis. Thus one would not necessarily expect hedge fund activity or proprietary trading to drive such anomalies away.

Alternatively, rather than regarding low implicit volatility as an anomaly, one might choose to interpret it as suggesting a risk premium for 30-year bonds over and above the overall bond market risk premium (versus money market returns). Thus during 1987–1993 this implied risk premium would have averaged 40–50 bp. But it is difficult to see why this risk premium should vanish at points when long bond yields become very volatile, which is what it seems to do. One would also be forced to conclude that long bonds had a negative risk premium in the early 1960s. Although this is possible — in recent experience they had certainly been much less volatile than short rates — it is somewhat counterintuitive.

A final practical observation is that the shape of the long end of the curve — which is mainly determined by σ — is, to a large degree, independent of the shape of the mid part of the curve — which is mainly determined by κ. That is, investment managers may be justified in assuming that long bond "value" and mid-range bond "value" are not too closely coupled, and adopting different methods to analyze different parts of the curve.

The present study potentially sheds some light on alternative theories of the term structure, in particular the preferred habitat theory. It may be possible to relate regime switching to structural changes in the fixed-income market triggered by volatility. However, this would require a detailed institutional analysis, and is beyond the scope of this paper.

We conclude by noting the usefulness of examining a long historical time period when carrying out any analysis of bond market behavior. In the present case, the data exhibited noticeable patterns over time frames longer than an economic cycle, presumably related to secular changes in the structure of the economy or the U.S. bond market. Furthermore, an analysis of (say) 1990–1996 data alone would have been potentially misleading. This observation should be borne in mind when extending the analysis to bond markets other than the U.S.

THEOREMS ABOUT VERY LONG-TERM INTEREST RATES

"Very Long-Term Yields Must Reflect the Most Bullish Scenario"

We have seen that for bonds with maturities up to 30 years, convexity effects have an important impact on market yields. Bonds with much longer maturities are also actively traded: for example, century bonds in the US, and perpetual annuities — "consols" — in the UK market. (Indeed, there are Dutch perpetuals which have been making regular interest payments for the past 350 years.) Here convexity effects are even more important, and can affect long bond yields in quite unintuitive ways. In particular, there are two remarkable theorems about very long-term interest rates, which hold for any sensible model of interest rates. The precise statements are technical, but the meaning of the theorems is as follows:

1. Very long-term yields are not an unbiased average of expected future interest rates, but must be calculated using a disproportionate weighting of the most bullish interest rate scenarios; in fact, higher interest rate scenarios become totally irrelevant at sufficiently long maturities (Dybvig and Marshall/Dybvig, Ingersoll and Ross).

2. Extremely long-term forward rates and zero coupon yields can never fall, even when expected long-term future interest rates fall; and this limits how much very long dated bonds can participate in an interest rate rally (Dybvig, Ingersoll and Ross).

(The "extremely long zero coupon yield" here means the *infinite maturity zero coupon yield*, i.e., the limiting yield of a default-free zero coupon bond as the maturity approaches infinity. This should intuitively exist, although some term structure models imply that it does not exist. Note that it is not the same as the yield on a consol, which has intermediate cashflows and is thus "shorter;" nor is it the same as the "long rate" defined earlier in this chapter, as it incorporates a convexity bias whereas the long rate l — which is an expected future rate of return rather than a present bond yield — does not.)

Both of these theorems are extremely general. In particular, they apply to inflation-indexed bonds as well as nominal bonds, and do not assume that interest rates must be positive. The proofs use arbitrage arguments, and can be interpreted in terms of trading strategies — albeit very long-term strategies.

Although these theorems have been folklore since around 1986, their implications are not yet widely appreciated. Since the proofs are a little technical and unenlightening, we will concentrate on giving the intuition behind the results. We will also try to assess their practical importance to valuing long-dated bonds and liability streams, although it is difficult to be precise because most of the relevant parameters are unknown. For further technical details, see the original papers.

We have seen that when interest rates are uncertain, forward rates must be lower than expected future short rates. To derive a formula for forward rates, we begin with the following formula, derived in Chapter 2, which expresses the price at time t of a zero coupon bond maturing at a later time T as a mathematical expectation involving the (unknown) future short rates:

$$P(t, T) = E_t \exp\left(-\int_t^T r_s ds\right)$$

If we think of as being the discount factor from time t to time T under a particular interest rate scenario, then this formula says that the price of a zero coupon bond is equal to the expected discount factor to its maturity date — that is, the average of the discount factors under all scenarios, weighted by their probabilities.

Now, the T-forward rate quoted at time t is:

$$f(t, T) = -\frac{d\log(P(t, T))}{dT} = -\frac{1}{P(t, T)} \frac{dP(t, T)}{dT} = \frac{E_t\left[r_T \exp\left(-\int_t^T r_s ds\right)\right]}{E_t\left[\exp\left(-\int_t^T r_s ds\right)\right]}$$

Intuitively, this expresses the T-forward rate in terms of the possible future values of the time T short rate r_T under all possible interest rate scenarios (i.e., along all possible random inerest rate paths). These values are weighed by:

1. the scenario probabilities; and,
2. the scenario-specific discount factors from time t to time T.

For example, suppose there are only three possible interest rate scenarios, with probabilities $p_{(1)}, p_{(2)}, p_{(3)}$. Then the T-forward rate is the weighted average:

Exhibit 4-12: Impact of Weighting by Discount Factor in Forward Rate Calculation

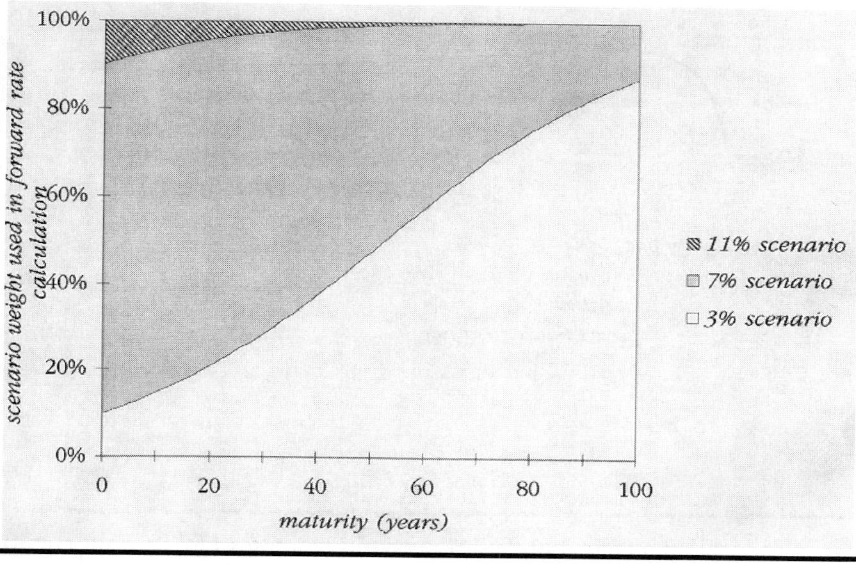

$$f(t, T) = \frac{P_{(1)}D_{(1)}(t, T) \cdot r_{T, (1)} + P_{(2)}D_{(2)}(t, T) \cdot r_{T, (2)}}{P_{(1)}D_{(1)}(t, T) + P_{(2)}D_{(2)}(t, T) + P_{(3)}D_{(3)}(t, T)}$$

$$+ \frac{P_{(3)}D_{(3)}(t, T) \cdot r_{T, (3)}}{P_{(1)}D_{(1)}(t, T) + P_{(2)}D_{(2)}(t, T) + P_{(3)}D_{(3)}(t, T)}$$

Now, weighting by discount factors makes lower interest rate scenarios relatively more important, since discount factors are higher under those scenarios. That is, low rate scenarios are more relevant than high rate scenarios when calculating the forward rate. This effect becomes more pronounced as the forward rate grows more distant, since the difference between the discount factors becomes larger.

To illustrate this point, suppose there are only three possible interest rate scenarios:

- with probability 0.1, the short rate remains constant at 11%, forever;
- with probability 0.8, the short rate remains constant at 7%, forever; and
- with probability 0.1, the short rate remains constant at 3%, forever.

The expected future short rate on any future date is obviously 7%, but the forward rate is lower than 7%, because in calculating it, we must weight each scenario by the relevant discount factors. Exhibit 4-12 shows the relative weight given to each scenario, for different maturity dates.

Exhibit 4–13: Behavior of Bond Yields at Very Long Maturities

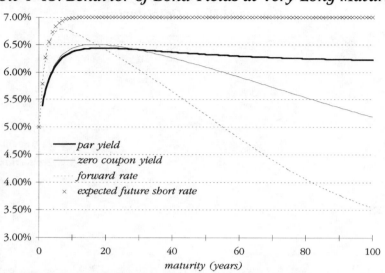

The weight attached to the 3% scenario increases rapidly with maturity, while the weight attached to the 11% scenario becomes negligible beyond 40 years. As a result, the 30-year forward rate is around 6%, and the 100-year forward rate is around 3.5%. By 200 years, the forward rate is virtually equal to 3%; i.e., the 7% and 11% scenarios are irrelevant, and only the most bullish (3%) scenario is relevant.

This tendency of forward rates to fall with maturity is basically the same effect as the convexity bias studied above. It feeds through into zero coupon yields and par yields, which are also dragged down towards the most bullish interest rate scenario. To take a slightly more realistic example, suppose that the short rate is currently 5%, and suppose there are only three possible interest rate scenarios:

- with probability 0.1, the short rate rises from 5% to a long-term level of 11%;
- with probability 0.8, the short rate rises from 5% to a long-term level of 7%; and,
- with probability 0.1, the short rate falls from 5% to a long-term level of 3%.

In each case we assume that the short rate approaches the given long-term level exponentially, as described in Chapter 1. It is clear that in expectation, the short rate will rise from 5% to an expected long-term level of 7%. However, Exhibit 4–13 shows that forward rates look quite different from expected future short rates: they peak at less than 10 years and then start to fall as maturity rises. The zero coupon and par yield curves, which can be derived from the forward curve, slope down beyond about 20 years.

Exhibit 4–14: Par Yields versus Yields under Unbiased Expectations Hypothesis

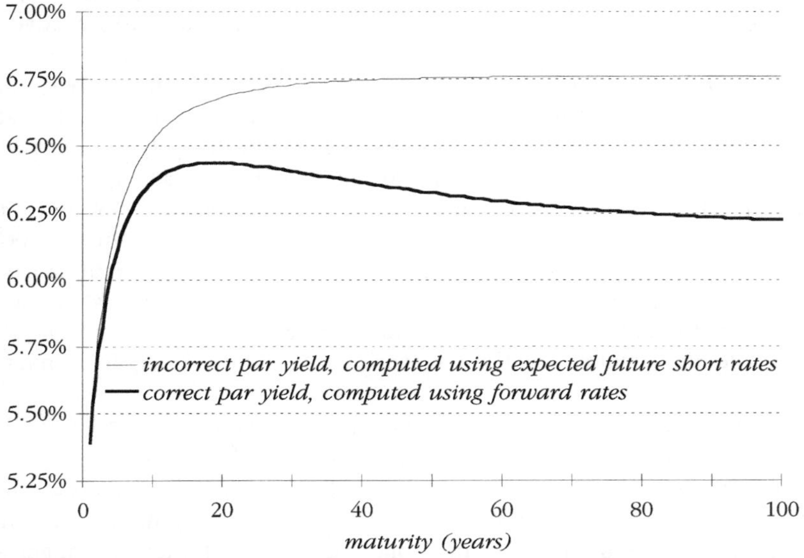

Therefore, the unbiased expectations hypothesis — which states that forward rates are equal to expected future short rates — is false, and it is not correct to compute par yields using expected future short rates rather than forward rates. The error is substantial: Exhibit 4–14 shows that this procedure will overstate par yields by up to 50 bp.

Exhibit 4–14 also shows that pricing 100-year bonds off the 30-year Treasury yield can lead to errors. The (incorrect) unbiased expectations hypothesis implies that 100-year yields are virtually the same as 30-year yields, whereas they should in fact be around 20 bp lower. This difference may be interpreted as the additional convexity bias reflected in 100-year bond yields.

These examples were based on an oversimplified term structure model, which allowed only three random interest rate scenarios rather than an infinite number. However, Dybvig and Marshall obtained similar results using a plausible model with realistic parameters, implemented via Monte Carlo simulation. Thus the theorem is not only true but has practical relevance, irrespective of the specific term structure model one happens to believe in.

The analysis seems to suggest that an investment grade century bond priced at 75 bp over the 30-year Treasury yield may be significantly undervalued. The instinctive response is that, while this theoretical result may be relevant for default-free bonds, the yields of very long corporate bonds are driven up because investors demand substantial compensation for assuming 100-year credit risk. However, the "fair" yield spread for assuming credit risk is not necessarily higher for a 100-year bond than for a 30-year bond. For example, if a bond has a 1% chance of defaulting each year, with a 50% recovery rate, then a yield spread of approximately 50 bp is sufficient compensation for diversified investors, irrespective of the bond's maturity.

Even if we assume that default probabilities rise dramatically beyond 30 years, the required yield spread on a 100-year bond does not rise much. Suppose we compare a 30-year bond with a 1% p.a. default probability, with a 100-year bond, with a 1% p.a. default probability for the first 30 years and a 5% p.a. default probability thereafter. The 100-year bond appears substantially more risky, but in fact an investor requires only an additional 20 bp yield spread for the 100-year bond as theoretical compensation (assuming a 0% recovery rate in either case; the appendix to Chapter 6 describes the calculation). The reason is that when assessing the impact of future loss scenarios, they must be weighted by the discount factor to the loss date; thus, more distant loss scenarios are proportionally less important.

"Extremely Long-term Forward Rates Can Never Fall"

The first theorem had unexpected implications about the fair yield of a 100-year bond; the second theorem has unexpected implications about its interest rate risk. To explain the intuition behind it, we make a simplifying assumption. (The formal proof does not depend on the assumption, but uses an arbitrage argument which applies whenever the infinite maturity zero coupon yield exists.)

The assumption is that along every random interest rate path ω, the short rate tends to some long-term equilibrium level r_ω^∞, which may depend on the path ω. Consider the lowest possible value $\mathbf{r}^\infty$ of the long-term equilibrium level r_ω^∞, i.e.,

$$\mathbf{r}^\infty = \operatorname*{essinf}_\omega \; r_\omega^\infty$$

(In more intuitive terms, a particular long-term level r is "possible" if the set of paths ω for which

$$r_\omega^\infty \leq r$$

has positive probability, and $\mathbf{r}^\infty = \inf r$.) In this context, the first theorem tells us that very long yields are basically determined by $\mathbf{r}^\infty$. Formally, it states that as the maturity approaches infinity, both the forward rate and the zero coupon yield tend to $\mathbf{r}^\infty$; that is, "extremely long" forward rates and zero coupon yields are essentially equal to this lowest possible long-term interest rate level $\mathbf{r}^\infty$.

Now, as time goes by and events unfold, a particular long-term level r_ω^∞ which was formerly possible may become impossible; thus, $\mathbf{r}^\infty$ can rise over time. However, a particular long-term level r_ω^∞ which was formerly impossible must remain impossible; if it is possible now, it must have been possible before. Thus, $\mathbf{r}^\infty$ cannot fall over time. This means that *extremely long forward rates and zero coupon yields can never fall*.

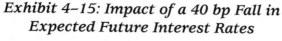

Exhibit 4-15: Impact of a 40 bp Fall in Expected Future Interest Rates

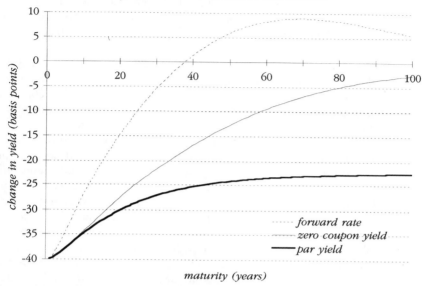

Thus extremely long yields are anchored to the level implied by the most bullish scenario; and this also limits the degree to which very long yields (30 to 100 years) will respond to a change in expected future interest rates. Intuitively, since a 100-year bond yield is predominantly determined by the most bullish interest rate scenario anyway, a fall in expected interest rates due to a change in the probabilities of higher interest rate scenarios will not have much effect. This is the real practical impact of the theorem.

To illustrate this, recall the second example above, where the short rate starts at 5% and approaches a long-term level of either 11%, 7% or 3%. Suppose now that the short rate falls by 40 bp, and that the probabilities of the three long-term interest rate scenarios changes as follows:

- the 11% scenario is now assigned a probability of zero;
- with probability 0.9, the short rate rises from 4.6% to a long-term level of 7%; and,
- with probability 0.1, the short rate falls from 4.6% to a long-term 3%.

It is easy to see that this corresponds to a 40 bp fall in all expected future interest rates, at all future dates. However, this does not cause all bond yields to rally by 40 bp. The impact on bond yields is more complex than this, and is shown in Exhibit 4–15.

At the short end of the curve, forward, zero coupon and par yields all fall by 40 bp as expected. However, the 100-year par yield falls by only 22 bp, and the 100-year zero coupon yield falls by only 3 bp. Even more surprisingly, long-dated forward rates actually *rise*, since (under these probabilities) the 7% scenario gets a higher weight at these forward dates: e.g., a weight of 47% at 60 years, compared to 44% under the former probabilities.

The conclusion is that if the Treasury market rallies, yields on 100-year bonds should in theory respond in a muted fashion. The effect should certainly be taken into account when assessing the interest rate risk of a portfolio containing 100-year bonds, but unfortunately one cannot be more precise about this without using a more realistic term structure model and realistic parameters.

The theorem has important implications for term structure modeling itself, for the simple reason that any term structure model which allows extremely long-dated forward rates to fall is inconsistent with the theorem, and is thus incorrect because it permits arbitrage. Thus, even if the model works well for bonds with maturities up to 30 or even 40 years, it may be unreliable when used to value 100-year bonds. For example, Dybvig, Ingersoll and Ross showed that under the continuous-time Ho-Lee model, the infinite maturity zero coupon yield can be set to a reasonable value at time zero, but it immediately rises to infinity thereafter — intuitively, the convexity bias explodes as maturity rises, as it did for the yield curve model used earlier in this chapter. Note that, by contrast, the CMS model is consistent with the theorem: mean reversion implies that the infinite maturity zero coupon yield is constant in this model.

It must be emphasized that these long-term interest rate results have no necessary connection with mean reversion. Of course, a model which assumes that long bond yields mean revert to a single constant long-term level will be consistent with the theorem, but it is hard to say what this level should be. Deriving it from the current Treasury yield curve is of dubious validity, since this curve does not extend past 30 years; in fact, the theorem of Dybvig and Marshall suggest that the long-term level must be the "lowest possible level of average interest rates" (which we try to estimate later in this chapter).

More seriously, a model which assumes a single fixed long-term level will ignore the risk arising from the fact that this level is unknown, and this may introduce biases in pricing. Ingersoll, Skelton and Weil have constructed a model which allows random upward jumps in the infinite maturity zero coupon yield, and their model might form a suitable basis for assessing this risk. However, although their work dates back to 1978, empirical tests of the model are still missing — probably because there is not enough relevant market data.

Therefore there are serious difficulties in modeling the behavior of 100-year bonds satisfactorily, and thus in estimating their "fair" yields and their sensitivity to shifts in Treasury yields. Investors in these bonds are exposed to substantial model risk, and also to the risk that the bonds will behave differently once the market becomes more efficient. Perhaps this is the reason why their yields are so high relative to the levels which seem theoretically justified.

Exhibit 4–16: Long Government Bond Yield in Britain and the United States

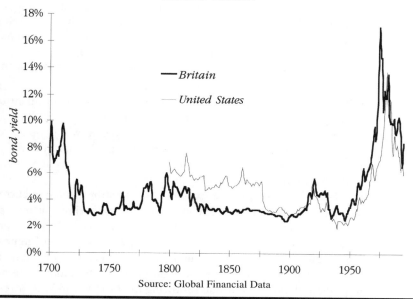

Source: Global Financial Data

A VERY LONG-TERM ANALYSIS OF THE BOND MARKET

Long Bond Yields, Inflation and Real Bond Returns since 1700

The long-term interest rate theorems discussed above reveal the practical importance of understanding how interest rates are distributed over the very long run. If there is a positive probability that they will be very low, the implications for century bond valuation are significant. To attack this question, we adopt an empirical approach: we will (a) look at what the very long-term historical behavior of bond yields has been, and (b) determine whether this historical experience may be relevant in the long-term future. Note that we are primarily interested, not in determining what long-term interest rates are *expected* to be, but in identifying the *most bullish scenario*, even if this scenario may be quite improbable. For recall that in the previous examples, although the 3% scenario was only assigned a probability of 0.1, it turned out to be a primary determinant of long-dated yields.

The need to focus on the most bullish (but still reasonable) scenario actually makes our task easier. To identify the expected scenario, or the most probable scenario, would require an impossible amount of foresight. To identify the most bullish scenario merely involves determining what is possible.

Active secondary markets in Government debt have existed for a very long time. Exhibit 4–16 shows historical Government bond yields in Britain since

1700, and in the United States since 1800. In Britain, bond yields stabilized at around 3%–4% from around 1724, when political and financial stability was achieved under Walpole's Whig administrations, and remained in that range (except in wartime) until 1950 — a period of over 200 years. In the United States, bond yields traded at 5%–6% until Reconstruction was well underway, when the more promising economic outlook allowed them to fall to British levels. An important point is that, apart from one-off effects such as this, global shifts in bond yields tend to dominate country-specific shifts.

Exhibit 4–17 shows the distribution of historical long Government bond yields. In Britain, yields have been lower than 4% around 60% of the time, and lower than 5% around 80% of the time. The results for the U.S. would be the same if the period up to the Reconstruction era were excluded. Historically, the high levels of bond yields observed since the 1960s have had no precedent, even in wartime, since the beginning of the eighteenth century.

Exhibit 4–18 shows part of the explanation. Inflation, which is currently regarded as normal, is a relatively new phenomenon; except during wartime, price stability has been the norm in both Britain and the United States. (Whether prices remain stable during and immediately after a war depends on the willingness of the Government to enforce rationing.) Thus inflation expectations have historically been very low, depressing the level of bond yields. It should also be noted that, at least until the inflationary episode following the First World War, investors appeared to demand no premium for inflation volatility.

Exhibit 4–17: Distribution of Historical Bond Yields in Britain and the United States

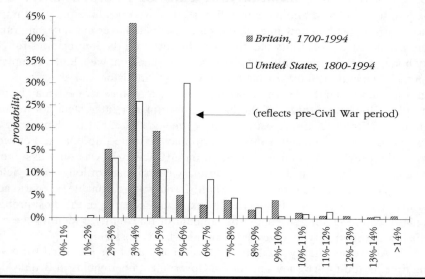

Exhibit 4–18: Historical Price Level in Britain and the United States

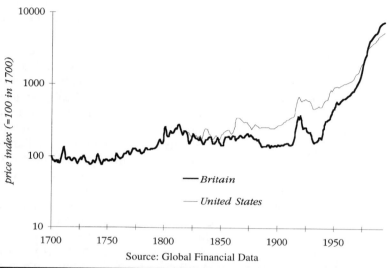

Source: Global Financial Data

On the basis of the historical evidence, one could argue that a long-term average nominal interest rate of 3% represents the most bullish scenario. Although recent experience makes 3% appear to be an absurdly low level, it seems more reasonable if we take a longer view — and remember, this scenario does not have to be likely, but only possible.

The difficulty with using long-term historical data is that there may have been some fundamental change in the structure of the economy, or the financial markets, which makes this data irrelevant. Therefore, in order to argue that 3% represents a reasonable scenario, we need to argue that there is enough continuity between the past and the future (or a potential future) to justify using the historical data as a guide to the future.

Very Long Cycles in the Global Economy: A Theoretical Account

Our argument is based on Arrighi's analysis of long-term cycles in capitalist accumulation. This work is part of a project to explain the development of capitalism since the early Renaissance, initiated by the structuralist historian Fernand Braudel. The theoretical analysis is supported by extensive empirical evidence, particularly on international trade; full details have been presented by Arrighi. Our own contribution is to use bond yield and price data as supporting evidence, and to draw out some of the practical implications for the bond market.

The global financial markets have existed since about 1500. By then, expatriate Genoese had set up an international clearing system to facilitate cross-border payments and settlements, based on an early version of the gold standard; there was an active and liquid market in negotiable bills of exchange; there were highly developed foreign currency markets, with arbitrageurs ready to exploit any anomalies; and a capital base for international finance was provided by *compere*, or government revenue bonds.

Since then, capitalism has undergone several long cycles of development under a succession of financial powers: first Genoa, then Holland, then England, and finally the USA. A new cycle starts when a new power gains control of the global financial system. Genoa took control of the system from Venice around 1450, modernized it, and ran it for nearly 200 years. Holland took it over in the early 1600s, and ran it for over 150 years. Britain took charge around 1800, and stayed in control for over 100 years. Finally, the U.S. took control around 1920. Exhibit 4-19 shows the history of Government bond yields throughout this series of long cycles.

Each cycle has followed a consistent pattern, overlapping with the previous cycle. In an initial period of financial turmoil, a particular country — which was already a major center of productive capacity — moves into a position of economic dominance by developing a key competitive advantage (see below) which attracts external capital; it thus gradually becomes the focus of high finance. In this first phase, its economic growth and financial activity is driven by excess global liquidity. Consolidation of power is achieved by taking control of the international payments system and currency standards. There follows a period of strong growth in productive capacity and global trade. Eventually efficiency, globalization and competition drive down real returns: production and trade are expanding too rapidly for profits to be maintained.

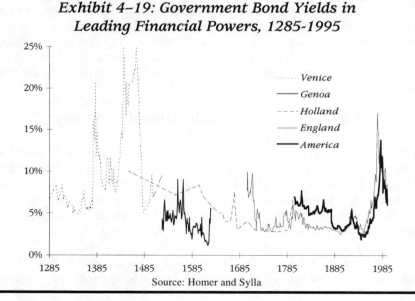

Exhibit 4-19: Government Bond Yields in Leading Financial Powers, 1285-1995

Source: Homer and Sylla

Exhibit 4–20: Historical Real Returns from Government Bonds

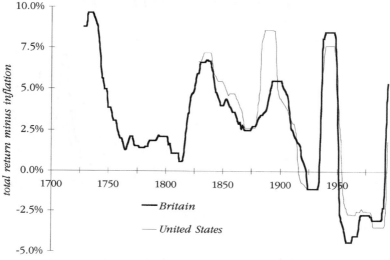

This triggers a "signal crisis" in which the focus shifts from production and trade to finance, and global liquidity explodes. Then there is a brief golden age when extraordinary profits in the financial sector feed the rest of the economy. However, as this financially driven growth cannot be sustained once other sites have received enough capital to make their autonomous growth possible, there is eventually a "terminal crisis" in which, in a period of extreme market volatility, control shifts to the next dominant power.

There is a lot of evidence to support this story. For example, the monopoly of liquidity: in 1947, the U.S. controlled 70% of the world's gold reserves. Or increasing globalization of trade: as a proportion of all trade, international trade was higher in 1900 (the British golden age) than it was at any time between 1920 and 1980. And the key process, the explosion in global liquidity, can be documented in every cycle.

Exhibit 4–20 shows real returns from long Government bonds in Britain and the United States, while Exhibit 4–21 shows the historical volatility of real returns. The real return series appear to show cycles of around 50 years, while the volatility series show cycles of around a century, with turning points around the late eighteenth century, around the early twentieth century, and around the present.

These cycles have a natural explanation in terms of the cycles of capitalist accumulation discussed by Arrighi. Real returns are initially high, then decline as production and trade become less profitable; there is some recovery after the signal crisis as activity shifts to high finance, but decline follows. Return volatility declines as power becomes entrenched, and continues to decline after the signal crisis because the existence of global liquidity smoothes returns; however, the terminal crisis triggers market turmoil.

Exhibit 4–21: Historical Volatility of Real Government Bond Returns

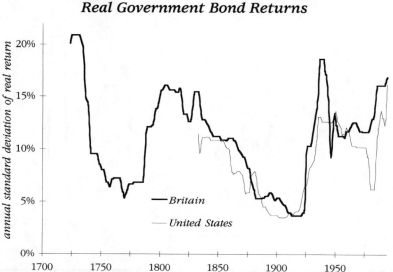

However, not every cycle is identical. Firstly, as we mentioned, each new power gained an initial advantage by working out how to make certain costs lower and more stable: Genoa internalized the payments system; Holland internalized protection costs (the armed forces); Britain internalized production costs via its colonies; the USA internalized transaction costs via vertical integration. Secondly, cycles tend to alternate between expansionary, finance-centered powers which focus on opening new markets — Genoa and Britain — and state-centered powers which focus on consolidating known markets — Holland and the USA.

The charts, and history, suggest that we are coming to the end of the American cycle. What comes next? One candidate is the East Asian capitalist archipelago. This is already a focus of economic activity: trans-Pacific trade is, by value, over 150% the size of trans-Atlantic trade. The region is, as we would expect, finance-centered and expansionary: China and now Eastern Europe are beginning to play the same role for East Asia as India did for Britain, or Spain and its American colonies did for Genoa.

But East Asia may simply not be big enough to become the new world financial power. Perhaps something more complex will emerge: an alliance between East Asia and the trans-national sites of political and financial power — e.g., the international banking system, the IMF, and a Security Council no longer dominated by the United States — resembling the alliance between Genoese capital and the trans-national Habsburg dynasty. This would offer a new key competitive advantage: the internalization of financial risk, via broad and liquid derivatives markets and international coordination between political and monetary authorities.

Recall that cycles tend to alternate between state-centered and finance-centered powers. The U.S. regime, like the Dutch and Venetian regimes before it, was state-centered: it was based on a strong internal market, vertical integration, and consolidation of existing markets. All these factors favor huge, multi-faceted, inward-looking companies. The next regime, like the British and Genoese regimes, is likely to be finance-centered: based on free trade, outsourcing and subcontracting, and expansion into new markets such as Eastern Europe, Central Asia and Africa.

In any case, it seems at least possible that history — or at least the history of bond yields and inflation — will continue to repeat itself. That is, one can argue that the phenomena which explain the price stability and low bond yields which persisted for many centuries, up to 1950, may well continue to be relevant in the coming centuries.

Selected References

Arrighi, G., *The Long Twentieth Century: Money, Power and the Origins of Our Times*, Verso, London, 1994.

Burghardt, G. and Hoskins, B., "A Question of Bias," *Risk*, March 1995.

Carayannopoulos, P., "A Seasoning Process in the U.S. Treasury Bond Market: The Curious Case of Newly Issued Ten-Year Notes," *Financial Analysts Journal*, January/February 1996.

Dybvig, P., Ingersoll, J. and Ross, S., "Long Forward and Zero Coupon Rates Can Never Fall," *J. Business*, vol. 69, no. 1, 1996.

Dybvig, P. and Marshall, W., "Pricing Long Bonds: Pitfalls and Opportunities," *Financial Analysts Journal*, January/February 1996.

Homer, S. and Sylla, R., *A History of Interest Rates* (3rd edition, revised), Rutgers University Press, New Brunswick, 1996.

Keynes, J. M., *The General Theory of Employment, Interest and Money*, Macmillan, London, 1936.

Kirikos, G. and Novak, D., "Convexity Conundrums," *Risk*, March 1997.

Lacey, N. and Nawalkha, S., "Convexity, Risk and Returns," *J. Fixed Income*, December 1993.

Phoa, W., "Can You Derive Market Volatility Forecasts from the Observed Yield Curve Convexity Bias," *J. Fixed Income*, June 1997.

Chapter 5

Prepayment Analysis and Prepayment Model Risk

PREPAYMENT MODELS: GOALS, CONSTRUCTION, FITTING, EVALUATION

Goals and Non-Goals of Prepayment Analysis

"Research on prepayment modeling may be compared to research on the treatment of cancer or AIDS, or indeed, any other obstinately incurable disease, on two counts. First, experts in the field are probably only marginally more effective than lay people (since they really do not have a remedy). Second, the activity is seemingly hopeless (and all the while unavoidable)." [Ani Sanyal]

Keeping up with prepayment research is a frustrating activity for most investors. On the one hand, the volume of data is overwhelming, as is the volume of high quality analysis and interpretation; on the other hand, after nearly two decades of effort and more or less extravagant claims, no-one has ever come up with the "right" model. It is hard to steer a course between blind faith in some specific prepayment model, and complete disillusionment with all such models.

No prepayment model can ever be as precise as investors would like. Borrower behavior is complex, affected by a multitude of economic and non-economic factors, and changes continually. Prepayment forecasting is comparable to forecasting inflation, economic activity or the market share of a product line, and about as accurate. In fact, given that prepayment models are required to forecast prepayments for the next thirty years, it is not obvious that any plausible models should exist at all. It is now widely accepted that the quest for the perfect model is a delusion.

There are at least three implications for investors. First, since one cannot simply choose to use the "right" model, one must find criteria for choosing between different models which are all imperfect — criteria which are based on the practical goals of prepayment modeling. Second, since prepayment model risk is unavoidable, one must find ways to understand it, quantify it and determine its potential impact on the risk/return profile of different securities. Third, one must determine how detailed prepayment research can add value to an investment strategy by helping to control prepayment model risk.

141

We begin by focusing on the goals of prepayment modeling. There are many different criteria which one might use to evaluate a prepayment model. For example, we might require any or all of the following:

1. It is a good fit to the historical data.
2. It is consistent with dealer PSA estimates.
3. It is consistent with dealer OAS figures.
4. It matches dealer effective durations.
5. It predicts bond cashflows accurately.
6. It predicts bond price changes accurately.

There are other possible criteria — e.g., can the model be used to identify relative value opportunities? does its structure allow different aspects of model risk to be measured? does it match the published mortgage index durations? — but the criteria listed above are the most obvious and, at first sight, the most fundamental.

These six criteria are inconsistent; it is impossible for a single prepayment model to satisfy them all simultaneously. Before showing why this is the case, we discuss each of these criteria in a little more detail. This will help us determine their relative importance.

1. This is the simplest test that can be applied to a model. If a model is incapable of matching observed historical prepayment trends, this raises questions about the validity of its assumptions; however, a good fit to historical data does not imply good predictive power — the past may be a poor guide to the future.
2. Published dealer PSA estimates provide some indication of the "market consensus" on prepayments. However, it must be remembered that they vary widely between dealers, and that even where two dealers release the same PSA estimates, they may be using very different models which yield different results under scenario analysis. Dealer PSA estimates have essentially no economic significance.
3. The calculation of OAS requires the use of a prepayment model (and a term structure model), and discrepancies must indicate differences in the models being used. But this relationship is complex, and it is rarely possible to explain discrepancies without detailed knowledge of the relevant models. Thus, while OAS does have an economic meaning, dealer OAS figures do not contain sufficient information in themselves to form a basis for evaluating a prepayment model.
4. Similar remarks to 3 apply. Dealer effective durations are of greater significance than dealer OAS figures, since they shed light on how observed MBS price quotes may respond to shifts in Treasury yields. However, dealer effective durations, like PSA estimates, vary widely and are also subject to bias. The link between a dealer's effective durations and observed price shifts needs to be tested empirically.

5. Prepayment behavior is extremely noisy, and while one can hope that a model will provide accurate cashflow forecasts on average, it is unrealistic to expect it to yield accurate month-by-month forecasts. Note that forecasting cashflows is only important in itself to clients who require these cashflow forecasts for asset/liability matching or solvency testing.

6. The ability to use a model to predict performance under different interest rate scenarios is critical; it forms the basis for portfolio risk management, and is also an important tool in analyzing trades. However, note that no model can capture all possible sources of MBS price risk.

Note that the immediate response of an MBS price to a change in interest rates depends, not on the *actual* effect this will have on prepayments, but on the *market's expectations* about the effect on prepayments. That is, criterion 6 says that the model should be consistent with the dynamic prepayment forecasts held by market participants "as a group."

To sum up, the different criteria essentially demand that the model match:

1. historical experience;
2. one aspect of dealer forecasts;
3. another aspect of dealer forecasts;
4. a third aspect of dealer forecasts;
5. actual future experience; and
6. the implied market consensus forecast.

Regarding 2–4, it should be pointed out that published dealer forecasts are subject to a number of potential sources of bias:

- Dealers can be tempted to skew forecasts to shed a favorable light on existing long or short positions held in inventory, or imminent deals in the primary market.
- Dealers often wish to show high OAS figures. For example, when the curve is positively sloped, there is a temptation to use higher prepayment speed forecasts so that bonds are being evaluated against shorter-dated Treasury yields. Note that this can bias the dealer median forecast as well as an individual dealer's forecast.

Regarding 6, note that, on a literal level, the term "implied market consensus forecast" has no meaning. Different market participants are observed to have widely differing prepayment expectations. More importantly, these expectations are formed within different frameworks which may be incomparable — they are not all just plugging different parameters into the same model.

This is why focusing on median PSA forecasts is misleading. For example, consider two investors, only one of whom believes that the yield curve slope affects fixed rate mortgage prepayments (independently of the overall level of the yield curve). Both may come up with identical PSA forecasts, and possibly even identical PSA forecasts under ±300 bp rate shocks, but they are still using different and probably incomparable models, which may give radically different results under more complex yield curve scenarios.

In any case, it is clear that 1–6 can be mutually inconsistent. For example, 1 and 5 will be inconsistent if future prepayment patterns do not match those observed in the past — e.g., if borrowers have become more sophisticated in evaluating refinancing opportunities. 5 and 6 will be inconsistent if the market is wrong about future prepayment behavior — for example, if borrowers turn out to be more (or less) sensitive to refinancing opportunities than generally predicted. Similarly, 5 and 2–4 will be inconsistent if dealers as a group are wrong about future prepayments.

1 and 6 (or 1 and 2–4) will only be consistent if market participants (or dealers) are basing their prepayment forecasts entirely on historical analysis. If they have made adjustments based on an informed judgment that the future will differ from the past, there will be a discrepancy. 2–4 and 6 will be inconsistent if there is a bias in dealer forecasts, as noted above. In particular, it is entirely possible that 4 and 6 can be inconsistent — if dealer effective durations are not cross-checked against actual market moves, this can persist for some time. Finally, 2, 3 and 4 can be mutually inconsistent: dealer *median* PSA, OAS and effective duration may be unrelated, since there is almost certainly no single model which gives rise to all the median numbers observed across different coupons.

Given that these criteria are inconsistent, it is necessary to decide which are important. From an economic point of view, it is reasonably clear that:

- 6 is important to all investors concerned about mark-to-market risk.
- 5 is important to asset/liability managers such as banks and insurance companies, who may need to carry out solvency testing under different interest rate scenarios, or synthetic GIC managers who may wish to forecast future crediting rates.
- 4 is not generally important; however, for investors whose performance is measured against a benchmark, and who are often under- or overweight mortgages, a large discrepancy from an index manufacturer's overall index duration is inconvenient from the point of view of performance measurement and performance attribution.
- 3 is useful, but not necessary, for investors attempting to evaluate trade proposals put forward by dealers.
- 1 and 2 have no practical importance to most investors.

We conclude that for most investors, the major goal of prepayment modeling is to forecast how MBS prices will respond to changes in interest rates: that is, to compute interest rate risk measures such as effective duration, and to enable investors to carry out yield curve stress testing. Of course, if a model turns out to have other uses — such as generating OAS figures which help investors to assess relative value — then so much the better. Chapter 6 discusses this in considerable detail.

It follows that one should test a prepayment model by seeing how well it would have predicted observed price changes — that is, by seeing whether it produces realistic effective durations. Unfortunately, although this helps us determine how accurate the model is on a week-to-week basis, it does not tell us how the model may perform under an extreme scenario like those used to stress test MBS portfolios. In this case, investors must make a partly subjective judgment about how realistic the model is.

In order to make such a judgment, statistical tests against historical data are insufficient; an investor needs a detailed understanding of the structure of the model and where the parameters came from, and enough insight to determine whether this structure and these parameters seem reasonable. Therefore, before explaining how to test a prepayment model against the market, we discuss how a prepayment model should be constructed, and how parameters can be fitted to available data. This is also highly relevant to assessing prepayment model risk.

Building a Prepayment Model

Just as an economic model makes use of a set of basic economic variables, and a model of a business begins with a list of factors relevant to the business, so a reliable prepayment model must be based on an understanding of what causes prepayments, and how to forecast future prepayments due to each cause. That is, a model is not simply a "black box" statistical relationship, but must focus on specific causes of prepayments. Although this approach has been around for some time (cf. the work of Mason since 1992–93), it is only recently that its importance has been widely understood; it will be illustrated at various places in this chapter.

The most important distinction is between interest rate sensitive and non interest rate sensitive prepayments. Exhibit 5–1 shows a detailed list of the various causes of prepayments, classified according to whether their occurrence is linked to changes in interest rates.

How can a prepayment model take all these causes of prepayments into account without becoming unwieldy? To answer this, note that a model typically has both *parameters*, which are estimated from historical data and change relatively infrequently, and *inputs*, which vary from day to day. We can set out the general principles that (a) a model should only include parameters and inputs which have an appreciable impact on bond value, and (b) its inputs should include only market rates, which can be hedged using traded securities. That is, a model should be parsimonious, and an investor should only require market data to use the model.

However, prepayment research must examine a multitude of factors, not all of them ultimately important, in order to decide on the structure of the model — e.g., which causes of prepayments should be grouped together for modeling purposes — to determine what the parameters and inputs should be, and to find optimal parameter values. This is why prepayment research looks at many sources of data which are not explicitly represented in the resulting model, and why it differentiates between causes of prepayments which may be lumped together in the model.

Exhibit 5-1: Causes of Mortgage Prepayments

I. *Non interest rate sensitive prepayments*
   A. relocation
      1. trading up to more expensive property
      2. moving to different city
   B. refinancing
      1. to increase loan size (i.e., to release equity in product)
      2. lower rate available due to improvement in credit rating
      3. switch to product with different terms and conditions
      4. dissatisfied with service
   C. voluntary principal paydown
      1. partial prepayments (curtailments)
      2. lump sum paydown of entire loan
   D. debt servicing problems
      1. default followed by formal foreclosure
      2. loan written off by servicer
      3. borrower liquidates voluntarily due to financial stress
   E. involuntary prepayments
      1. death
      2. divorce
      3. destruction of property
   F. negative prepayments (which influence prepayments at the pool level)
      1. additional draw-downs from home equity lines of credit
      2. withdrawal of prepaid principal from a redrawable mortgage
II. *Interest rate sensitive prepayments*
   A. refinancings
      1. lower rate on the same lending product
      2. lower rate obtained by switching to another lending product
   B. relocations
      1. trading up, made possible by increased home loan affordability
   C. debt servicing problems
      1. higher adjustable rate no longer affordable

It is well known that macroeconomic factors such as house prices or unemployment affect prepayments. But it does not follow that these should explicitly appear in a prepayment model as parameters or inputs. In fact, recalling that the model is trying to predict the *future* behavior of prepayments rather than understanding their historical behavior, one could say that:

- current house prices or unemployment may affect future prepayments, but to the extent that they are relevant, their impact is already observable in current prepayment rates and current bond market rates; and,
- future house prices or unemployment may affect future prepayments, but they are unknown, and the only fully objective information about them is that implicitly contained in bond market data, i.e., the extent to which the current yield curve reflects market expectations about house prices/unemployment.

Therefore, *if the model is correctly specified*, the current and historical prepayment rates and other relevant prepayment data (which are used to estimate the model parameters) and bond market rates (which appear as model inputs) implicitly contain all relevant information about house prices, unemployment and other macroeconomic variables.

As an illustration of what a prepayment model actually looks like, and how it takes the different causes of prepayments into account, we will now give a brief description of a model (which is similar but simpler in structure to the CMS fixed rate prepayment model). The full mathematical specification is omitted. In any case, the precise mathematical description of the functions used in the prepayment model is less important than the procedure used to fit parameters to the model. The example model takes account of the following kinds of prepayments:

Non interest rate sensitive, including:
    "relocations, non interest rate sensitive refinancings" [1(a), 1(b), 1(c)(ii)]
    "defaults and abandonments" [1(d)]
    "curtailments and miscellaneous" [1(c)(i), 1(e),1(f)]
Interest rate sensitive [including 2(a)(i), 2(b), 2(c)]

The model ignores some prepayments of type 2 (a) (ii); that is, it recognizes that a borrower with a 30-year mortgage may refinance when fixed mortgage rates fall, but ignores the fact that if fixed rates remain stable but adjustable rates fall, the borrower may refinance into an ARM. At the end of the chapter, we will discuss how reasonable this assumption may be. For the moment, observe that it allows us to make an important simplification: the model forecasts interest rate sensitive prepayments based on only a single reference rate, and can thus be hooked up to a one factor term structure model.

The reader may wonder why non interest rate sensitive prepayments are broken down into three categories, when it is only their overall level which matters to the investors. The reason is that, oddly enough, this makes it possible to fit parameters to the model when only limited data is available; we will discuss this point in more detail later in the chapter.

The structure of the model is as follows:

- The rate of *non interest rate sensitive prepayments* is assumed to depend only on pool seasoning. It is modeled by specifying a function of time alone.
- The rate of *interest rate sensitive prepayments* is assumed to depend on the difference between the initial pool WAC and the 10-year CMT yield (which is assumed to determine the 30-year mortgage rate); in particular, if the interest rate differential is below a certain threshold level, a zero rate for these prepayments is assumed. Interest rate sensitive prepayments are modeled by specifying a function of the interest rate differential; this function is zero below the threshold rate.

Exhibit 5–2: Prepayment Model, Non Interest Rate Sensitive Prepayments versus Seasoning

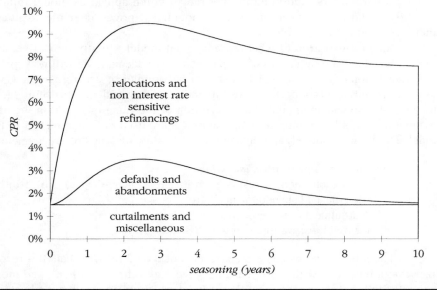

- *Burnout* — the tendency of pools which have already experienced heavy refinancings to be less interest rate sensitive — is modeled by multiplying the predicted level of interest rate sensitive prepayments by a *burnout multiplier*. This is equal to one for newly originated pools; for seasoned pools it is a function of the pool's *factor ratio*, defined to be the actual pool balance divided by what the pool balance would have been had it only experienced non interest rate sensitive prepayments as forecast by the model (i.e., had it experienced no interest rate sensitive prepayments).

Exhibits 5–2, 5–3, and 5–4 show the prepayment model functions for a typical set of parameters.

As an aside, this is not the most plausible way to model burnout. The usual explanation for burnout is that "faster" (more interest rate sensitive) borrowers tend to leave the pool at the first favorable opportunity, leaving behind the "slower" (less interest rate sensitive) borrowers. "Faster" borrowers might include those who are more financially sophisticated, who have lower LTV ratios or better credit histories, who have paid fewer points, or — if the pool has significant WAC dispersion — who have lower mortgage rates. Thus, some prepayment models attempt to model burnout by explicitly assuming that there are two or more populations of borrowers, which prepay in different ways; e.g., McConnell and Singh divide borrowers into different "refinancing cost categories."

Exhibit 5-3: Prepayment Model, Interest Rate Sensitive Prepayments versus Rate Differential

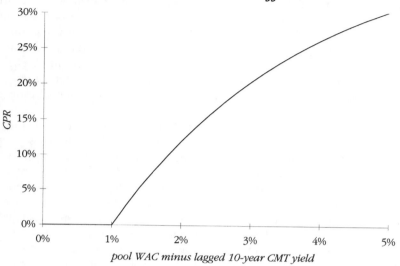

pool WAC minus lagged 10-year CMT yield

Exhibit 5-4: Prepayment Model, Degree of Burnout versus Refinancings Already Experienced

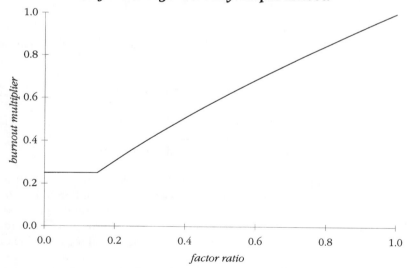

factor ratio

If detailed information is available on the composition of the pool, this can be a very powerful way to model burnout. If not, the approach is much less useful. The reason is that one then has to infer how many different categories of borrower are, how many borrowers fall in each category, and how each category behaves, all on the basis of very incomplete data. Statistical estimation is very unstable, while using subjective judgment is arbitrary; in either case there is no assurance that the categories one has come up with have any meaning. Therefore, where pool composition data is not available and one only has access to aggregate prepayment data, the "burnout function" approach used in the model turns out to be much more robust.

One might expect a burned-out pool to prepay, not just more slowly, but more unpredictably. The reason is that borrowers who were formerly "slow" may now have become "fast" — they may have become more financially sophisticated, rising house prices may have improved their LTV ratios, or they may have better credit scores than before. That is, burned-out pools may or may not become "refreshed" over time, and this phenomenon is not purely a function of seasoning, interest rates or the initial pool characteristics. Of course, if detailed pool composition data is available, and is properly analyzed, this source of uncertainty can be mitigated.

Note that "negative burnout" is also possible. In the model described above, if the factor ratio is greater than 1 — i.e., forecast non interest rate sensitive prepayments have exceeded actual prepayments — then the burnout multiplier is greater than 1. The reasoning is that if housing turnover has been unusually low, there is pent-up demand which will result in a surge of prepayments when a fall in interest rates makes new home loans more affordable.

Fitting Parameters to a Model

There are at least five ways to fit parameters to a prepayment model, which can be used either separately or in combination:

1. Making up parameters (the "educated guess" method).
2. Fitting to a time series of aggregate prepayment data.
3. Fitting to cross-sectional aggregate prepayment data.
4. Fitting to detailed prepayment data.
5. Fitting to market price data ("implied prepayments").

All these approaches have their problems, and we will discuss each of them briefly. The intention here is not to give a detailed description of how to fit a prepayment model, but to offer some guidance on how to interpret and assess prepayment research whose aim is to fit a model. No single procedure is correct — the best procedure depends on the nature of the collateral and the available data.

Making up Parameters Based on an Educated Guess: If prepayment data on a particular collateral type is entirely missing, it is generally still better to make some plausible assumptions than to assume that prepayment risk does not exist.

For example, plausible parameters might be devised by looking at data on related collateral types, together with more general statistical data such as housing turn-over figures. However, this procedure is obviously very unsatisfactory, and should only be used as a last resort: i.e., when there is no data, or when one is sure that the historical data is irrelevant.

Fitting to a Time Series of Aggregate Data: This is the traditional way to fit a prepayment model; Schwartz and Torous give a useful account of the statistical methods which should be used. It is assumed that most readers are familiar with this approach, at least in general terms. There are three important points which ought to be made.

First, prepayment data is notoriously noisy — partly because of anomalies in reporting, but mostly because borrower behavior is often erratic. If least squares estimation is used, the presence of many outliers seriously distorts the estimation process. One solution is to smooth the data, e.g., by using quarterly rather than monthly prepayment figures; unfortunately, this makes it difficult to measure interest rate sensitivity accurately. A better solution is to use a more robust statistical estimation procedure, which gives less weight to outliers.

Second, one must use some judgment when determining which historical data is relevant. Prepayment behavior changes over time, and data from the 1970s or even the 1980s may not be relevant (e.g., because tax laws, borrower demo-graphics, the range of lending products and borrower attitudes to debt were very different); including this data might simply make the results less reliable. On the other hand, using too short a period might also yield unreliable results, because too narrow a range of interest rate environments has been sampled.

Third, blindly fitting to the data can sometimes yield parameters which are clearly implausible, or which generate results (e.g., effective durations) which appear unrealistic. There may be alternative parameter sets which provide a poorer statistical fit but which are nonetheless "better." That is, one has to confine the parameter search process to "realistic" regions of the parameter space, and this means making a judgment based on market knowledge.

> "The existence of several phenomenologically indistinguishable but conceptually different situations with different consequences calls for a diagnostic approach... followed by alternative 'what if' analyses... Not only must the estimator and a procedure for computing it be specified, but also the situations for which it is supposed to be appropriate or inappropriate and criteria for judging estimators and procedures must be given... The *M*-estimate approach is not a panacea..." [Peter Huber]

Fitting to Cross-Sectional Aggregate Data: The prepayment model described above predicts that prepayments are a function of the pool seasoning, the pool WAC and the current reference Treasury yield. For a given collateral type, there are generally many pools outstanding at any given time, with varying WACs and varying degrees of seasoning, and varying current prepayment speeds. Thus, one can attempt to fit parameters to a single month's prepayment data, across the range of different pools; this is really a special case of a time series fit, where the time series is only one month long. This method corresponds to taking a snapshot of the current prepayment behavior of that collateral type.

The main advantage of the method is that, because it does not mingle data from different historical periods, it is (by definition) very responsive to the most recent prepayment trends. In particular, it is a useful way of detecting a shift in borrower behavior: the impact on the fitted model parameters is immediate, whereas if one is fitting to a long historical time series, the fitted parameters will respond only gradually to a change in prepayment patterns.

A disadvantage of the method is that, if one is trying to fit a large parameter set to a relatively small dataset, the results can be unstable. It is often advisable to fit only a few key parameters to cross-sectional data, keeping the rest fixed (e.g., at values derived from a time series fit, as above). Also, prepayments often display month-to-month volatility and also strong seasonal variations, and some allowance must be made for this.

Exhibit 5–5 shows the result of fitting the above prepayment model to a single month's FNMA data (May 1997), consisting of prepayment speeds on 105 different WAC/seasoning combinations. Both actual and model prepayments are plotted versus seasoning and versus WAC. The in-sample fit is quite good, although it deteriorates for highly seasoned, very high coupon issues. Note that these all have very low balances and are quite burned out; as argued above, one would expect such pools to exhibit less predictable prepayment behavior there is no noticeable bias in the errors.

This method can be particularly useful for fitting prepayment model parameters to ABS data, such as home equity loan data. Here, historical data may be largely missing, or of dubious relevance, whereas current prepayment speeds may be available for a range of deals with varying pool WAC and pool seasoning. A cross-sectional fit can sometimes yield surprisingly good results, provided sensible constraints are imposed on the parameter search to ensure that only "realistic" parameter sets are permitted.

For agency mortgages, for which a much greater volume of data is available, a cross-sectional parameter fit should be used mainly for monitoring current trends in prepayments, rather than to generate model parameters which are used to calculate portfolio risk measures. It is difficult to manage portfolio risk on the basis of parameters which are oversensitive to short term prepayment trends, and which may thus fluctuate widely from month to month — the resulting effective durations are too unstable.

Fitting to Detailed Prepayment Data: Recall that the prepayment model described earlier had separate parameters describing relocations, defaults, curtailments and refinancings. If we have, for a given pool, a detailed loan-by-loan breakdown of prepayments — for example, if we know which borrowers moved house in each month, which borrowers defaulted, or which borrowers refinanced, why they refinanced, and what products they refinanced into — then we can use this information to generate parameter estimates directly.

This approach is extremely powerful, and is the preferred method when it is feasible. Unfortunately, it requires access to detailed, loan-level prepayment data, which is not always collected by servicers. The sheer volume of survey data at the loan level, combined with the need to interpret it in an informed manner, also means that this approach involves a great deal of work.

Exhibit 5–5: Results of Cross-Sectional Prepayment Model Fit (May 1997 FNMA Data)

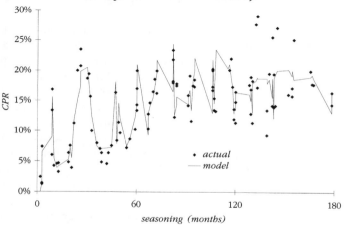

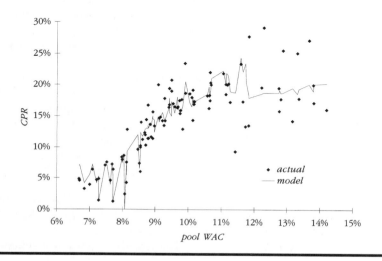

Fitting to Market Price Data: This approach has been described by Chen and Cheyette, and is often referred to as the "implied prepayments hypothesis." The idea is that market prices themselves contain information about investors' prepayment expectations; thus, instead of fitting parameters to historical data, one can try to extract an "implied prepayment model" by fitting parameters to observed market prices. (The name is meant to suggest an analogy with the distinction between historical volatility and implied volatility in options markets.) It would not be appropriate to go into the technical details here, but we can make the following observations.

- The approach does not involve constructing a model from market data, but using market data to fit parameters to a pre-specified model. Choosing this model requires judgment. If it is poorly specified, the results will be poor; also, if a model with a different structure is substituted, the results will differ.
- Market prices reflect both prepayment expectations and risk premia, and these must be disaggregated; to do this, more or less arbitrary assumptions must be made about the OAS of the securities, i.e., about the patterns which market risk premia display across different securities. As we will see in Chapter 6, the structure of market risk premia is arguably quite complex.
- The resulting prepayment forecasts can be unintuitive, because they may also reflect investor risk aversion: for example, Cheyette's implied forecasts are 2–3 times as rapid as the prepayment speeds predicted by an econometric model. This makes it hard to tell whether an implied model is reasonable. It also means that implied models cannot be used for cashflow forecasting and solvency testing, or forecasting crediting rates on a synthetic GIC.
- If there is temporary market segmentation — for example, if discount and premium passthroughs are being held by different classes of investors — observed market prices may not be consistent with a single set of prepayment expectations, and thus the results may be meaningless.
- Market prices give us little information about prepayment expectations under extreme interest rate scenarios (e.g., a ±200 bp shift) because these scenarios are very improbable, and thus have a very low weight in determining prices. Thus, the forecasts generated by an implied model under extreme interest rate scenarios are of questionable validity.
- Volatility in MBS prices can make the estimation of an implied prepayment model very unstable, and the fitted parameters may fluctuate significantly from day to day. This is a particular problem when one is attempting to estimate several different parameters.

The overall conclusion is that, while a market implied prepayment model might be useful for analyzing relative value — between different MBS, or between the mortgage-backed sector and other sectors of the fixed-income market — it is unsuitable for portfolio risk management. The effective durations it computes will not be stable from day to day, making duration management difficult or impossible. Also, an implied prepayment model cannot reliably be used for stress testing.

Empirical Duration as a Tool for Monitoring Model Performance

As stated earlier, a key goal of prepayment modeling is to generate realistic effective durations. That is, the model should accurately predict how MBS prices respond to changes in Treasury yields. Thus a model should be tested against observed price shifts.

Since MBS option-adjusted spreads are themselves volatile, it is clearly impossible for effective durations to predict price changes perfectly on a day-to-day basis. Furthermore, since there can be short-term correlations between OAS shifts and Treasury yield shifts (either coincidental, or due to temporary psychological factors), model effective durations can appear to be biased in the short term even if they are in fact realistic. The best we can hope for is that:

- prediction errors are smaller over longer periods, i.e., a week or a month;
- there is no systematic bias in predictions over longer periods; and
- prediction errors correspond to intuitively plausible shifts in OAS.

For example, the prediction error over a given week should be consistent with market intelligence, e.g., that excess supply pushed out spreads on premium coupons, or that a specific TBA rallied relative to other coupons because a dealer was covering a large short position. Of course, since market intelligence is always incomplete, one will not always be able to find an explanation for an observed prediction error, even if an explanation exists.

Here are some more details on the testing procedure. Define the empirical duration of an MBS, over a given period and relative to a given reference Treasury yield, to be the change in price over that period divided by the change in the reference yield. Note that the empirical duration will vary from period to period. The effective duration computed by the model is "realistic" if, on average, it is consistent with the observed empirical duration.

What period should we use to compute empirical durations? Using too long a period (say, a month) yields blurred results, because yields may have traded in too wide a range, making it unreasonable to assume that the security has had a single "duration" during the period. On the other hand, using too short a period (say, a day) yields highly unstable results, since the impact of OAS shifts tends to dominate that of yield shifts; also, when the change in the reference yield is only a few basis points, the result will be unstable anyway.

A reasonable compromise is (i) to measure empirical durations over a rolling 1-week period, which still gives rather unstable results, (ii) to look at a moving average or median of these 1-week empirical durations, and (iii) to monitor this moving average over time. For example, Exhibit 5–6 shows the empirical duration of the 7.5% FNMA 30-year TBA measured in this way (using the 10-year CMT yield as the reference yield).

Exhibit 5–6: Empirical Duration of 7.5% FNMA 30-Year TBA

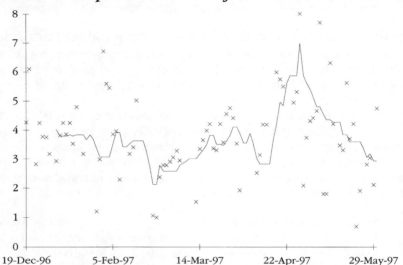

What reference yield should we use to compute empirical durations? In theory, if one is using a prepayment model which uses (say) the 10-year CMT yield as a reference rate, one should be consistent and use the same reference rate to compute empirical durations. In practice, one might want to pick the reference yield which gives the most stable-looking empirical durations over time, and as yields shift. For example, Exhibits 5–7 and 5–8 show empirical durations for 6.5% and 8.5% coupon GNMA passthroughs, using both the 5-year and 10-year CMT yield as the reference rate. For the longer, discount security, the 10-year CMT yield gives more stable, consistent results; for the shorter, premium security, the 10-year CMT also gives more stable results, but the difference is marginal.

Intuitively, since most passthroughs have negative convexity, their empirical durations should be higher when yields are at a higher level. Exhibits 5–9 and 5–10 plot observed empirical durations versus yield levels for the 6.5% coupon and 8.5% coupon passthroughs. In both cases the relationship has been somewhat unstable. The discount security seems to have an empirical duration of around 5.0, with only mild negative convexity. The premium security shows more evidence of negative convexity, with an empirical duration of around 2.0 at a yield level of 6.40%, rising to around 3.0 at a yield level of 6.90%.

Empirical durations may be compared to effective durations calculated by a prepayment model in the following way. First, select a historical period, and measure empirical durations over that period. Second, carry out a linear regression (see Exhibit 5–11 for an example); this can be used to derive a "best estimate" of the empirical duration at a fixed yield level, say 6.50%. Third, compare this "best estimate" to the model effective duration, computed at the same yield level.

Exhibit 5–7: Empirical Duration of 6.5% GNMA 30-Year TBA

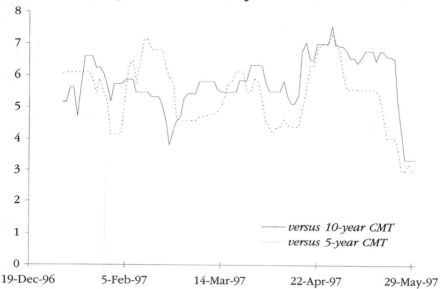

Exhibit 5–8: Empirical Duration of 8.5% GNMA 30-Year TBA

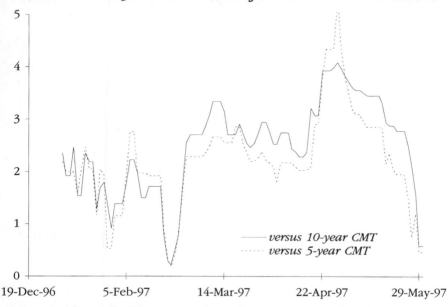

Exhibit 5–9: Empirical Duration versus Yield, 6.5% GNMA

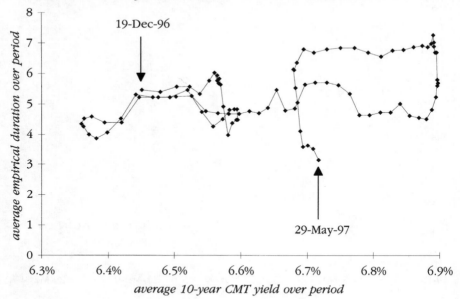

Exhibit 5–10: Empirical Duration versus Yield, 8.5% GNMA

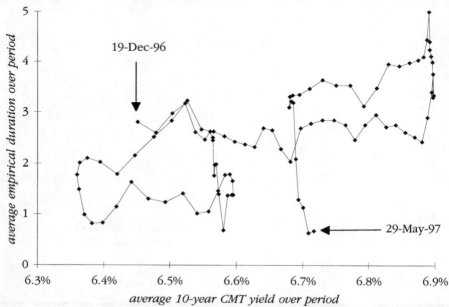

Exhibit 5–11: Empirical Durations of 6.5% GNMA, and Linear Regression (12/96–3/97)

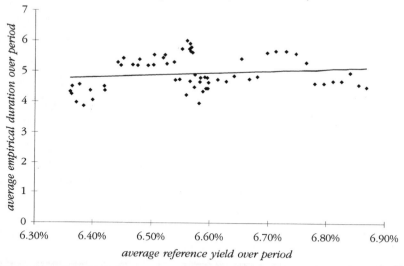

For the CMS prepayment model, the results of this comparison are shown in Exhibit 5–12; the agreement is quite close across all coupons. Note that the discrepancy would probably be much larger if data from April and May 1997 were included, since empirical durations were very unstable during that period. Thus it is advisable to keep updating the comparison, and not to place too much reliance on the most recent results — whether they show good agreement or poor agreement.

It has sometimes been suggested that when managing the duration of a portfolio, empirical durations should be used instead of model effective durations — this would make it unnecessary to rely on a prepayment model. This is not feasible, for the following reasons:

- Empirical durations are very unstable.
- It is impossible to calculate stable and reliable empirical convexities.
- Empirical durations cannot be used for stress testing (±200 bp scenarios).
- Empirical durations cannot be calculated reliably for illiquid securities.

However, the instability of empirical durations tells us one very important thing: any attempt to calculate a perfectly accurate duration for a mortgage-backed security is misguided. The price of an MBS does not respond in a mechanical way to changes in yields, and its duration is inherently "fuzzy." This fact is related to the existence model risk (as discussed below); and we will explore the implications of this fact in Chapter 6.

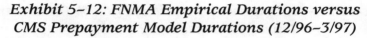

*Exhibit 5–12: FNMA Empirical Durations versus
CMS Prepayment Model Durations (12/96–3/97)*

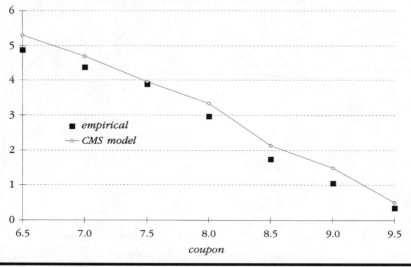

Finally, it should be noted that although the concept of empirical duration appears related to the concept of "implied prepayments," they are actually quite distinct. If a prepayment model has been fitted to market price data for a single day, there is no guarantee that it will generate effective durations which agree with observed empirical durations. If it has been fitted to market price data over some historical period, the effective durations it generates may agree with the historical empirical durations measured over that period — depending on how the model was constructed — but they need not agree with future empirical durations.

PREPAYMENT MODEL RISK

Prepayment Model Risk versus
Other Sources of Prepayment Risk

Prepayment risk comes from a variety of sources, which — in the context of a given prepayment model — may be grouped under two main headings: (a) sources of uncertainty which appear as stochastic factors within the model, and (b) sources of uncertainty about whether the model or its parameters are valid. Prepayment model risk is a specific kind of type (b) risk.

Here is a more detailed classification of prepayment risk factors.

General Factors, Treasury-Linked: The most notorious cause of prepayments is refinancing: when mortgage rates fall, borrowers tend to refinance. Since mortgage rates are closely linked to Treasury yields, market yield volatility contributes to prepayment risk; this component of the risk can, by definition, be hedged using bond market instruments — *but only to the extent that one assumes a fixed relationship between bond yields and refinancing.*

General Factors, Other Market-Linked: Mortgage rates can also be affected, though to a much lesser extent, by changes in MBS spreads, i.e., in the cost of securitization: thus a large shift in spreads might (but might not) affect mortgage rates and hence refinancings, a risk which is much more difficult to hedge.

General Factors, Other Macroeconomic: Relocations are influenced by non-market economic variables such as house prices and wages growth, which cannot be hedged directly using market instruments. Traditionally, prepayment modeling has been treated as a form of macroeconomic modeling: the inputs are market and non-market economic variables, and the outputs are forecasts of refinancings and relocations under different scenarios (random interest rate paths).

Product-, Issuer-, or Pool-Specific Factors: Prepayments may also be triggered for more specific reasons. In this case, only a single product, issuer or group of borrowers may be affected. For example, product-specific refinancings occurred in Australia in late 1995 and early 1996: when Citibank first introduced home equity loans in Australia, the product was unique; however, the availability of lower rate products from competitors, and especially the proliferation of redrawable P&I mortgages, caused rapid refinancings, so that by 1996–97 CPRs sometimes exceeded 80% — far higher than for any other product.

Fitting Error: Even if a prepayment model is, in principle, a good one, poor data or poorly interpreted data can lead to a mis-estimation of the model's parameters. Taking care with statistical estimation procedures can minimize error, but not eliminate it entirely. Furthermore, if a model has more parameters, the estimates for these parameters will be less robust.

Sampling Error: Observed prepayments will tend to fluctuate for purely random reasons. For larger pools this random effect will not be great, but especially for smaller pools it may appreciably contribute to the risk of a small CMO tranche.

Incomplete Data: Pool-specific characteristics such as gross WAC and average points paid can affect prepayments. If this data is missing, arbitrary assumptions must be made (for example, using net WAC plus an assumed servicing margin, or using MBA aggregate statistics on average points paid); if these are inaccurate, the model forecasts will be less reliable. This problem can be particularly severe when attempting to model home equity loan prepayments.

Numerical Error: Accurate prepayment models are typically difficult to implement efficiently, and generally require Monte Carlo simulation of interest rate paths and prepayment vectors. Naive Monte Carlo methods are notoriously inaccurate, so one must take care to verify that the numerical implementation is in fact reliable. Furthermore, the reliability of a method may differ for different classes of securities. For example, the CMS Representative Path methodology has been designed to achieve fast, accurate valuation of securities backed by fixed-rate mortgage collateral; it converges more slowly for ARM-backed securities.

Model Risk: Finally, a good prepayment model, implemented reliably, can turn into a bad model simply because borrowers start behaving differently. *This can happen no matter how sophisticated the model is.*

Note that only the first risk factor is of type (a); the rest are of type (b). (However, for current coupon and premium fixed rate mortgages, the first risk factor is the most important.) Of the remaining risk factors, model risk is the most difficult to control: it is difficult or impossible to hedge, and although better data or research can mitigate it, it cannot be eliminated, for reasons explained below. Thus it will occupy us for the rest of this chapter, and a large part of Chapter 6.

Sources of Prepayment Model Risk and its Potential Impact

Borrower behavior may change for at least the following reasons:

1. *Short-term non-economic factors affecting refinancing:* Some models recognize this by incorporating, e.g., a "media effect" in projecting refinancings, but the timing and impact of future media effects (more accurately described as marketing effects) is impossible to predict.

2. *Increasing borrower sophistication in general:* Most models predict that a certain proportion of borrowers will not refinance even when it is rational to do so, or attempt to explain this behavior in terms of the cost of refinancing. Empirically, some borrower behavior appears to be genuinely irrational, and cannot be plausibly explained in terms of refinancing cost; but it is impossible to predict how irrational borrowers will be in the future.

3. *Product innovation in the home lending market:* A broadening in product range can affect prepayments on existing mortgage products; for example, the introduction of 15-year mortgages and balloon mortgages and the popularization of adjustable-rate mortgages contributed to accelerated prepayments. To take a more recent example, the availability of second lien home equity loans has made it less attractive to undertake a "cash-out refi," i.e., a refinancing whose purpose is to release equity in the house (although the higher interest rates on home equity loans mean that cash-out refis are still attractive under certain circumstances). Macroeconomic factors play only a secondary role in financial product innovation, whose pace is more often driven by factors such as competition in the retail lending market, consumer trends or improved technology.

4. *Broader changes in the consumer finance sector:* For example, tax deductibility of mortgage interest has meant that curtailments have historically been a minor source of prepayments. However, very low bank deposit rates tend to stimulate curtailments once they offer comparable after-tax returns. More broadly, an increased desire for liquidity, combined with a widening variety of investment and lending products (and hybrids of the two), can stimulate both higher curtailments and more frequent refinancing. Conversely, increased regulation, or the general withdrawal of unprofitable finance products, may have the opposite effect.

5. *Tax changes:* Since the Tax Reform Act of 1986, interest on personal loans has not been tax-deductible. This change in the tax code was an important incentive for homeowners to consolidate their debt into their mortgage. In the short to medium term, it increased the level of cash-out refis executed for the purpose of debt consolidation (rather than interest rate savings). In the medium to long term, it resulted in the creation of the home equity loan market, whose existence has potentially important consequences for future prepayment patterns — as discussed below.

6. *Demographic trends such as changes in mobility:* These are frequently due, not solely to economic factors, but to cultural factors which cannot be predicted.

These, or other considerations, can invalidate any prepayment model no matter how many inputs it uses, and no matter how accurately it reflects current and historical borrower behavior patterns.

It is clear from this discussion that investors relying on any specific prepayment model are exposing themselves to significant model risk. In practice, this can lead to losses in the following way. As new information reveals a change in homeowner behavior, such as an increased propensity to prepay (other factors being equal), market participants begin to revisit their prepayment models and eventually to revise them. This causes a revision in their assessment of security values, and thus in market bids and offers.

The effect is exacerbated because the process tends not to be smooth. Analytical and technical resources are required to develop a new prepayment model. On the other hand, relatively high liquidity (at least of agency passthroughs) acts as a disincentive to revise models, since market participants reason that positions can be unloaded quickly if something goes wrong. Furthermore, a market participant who has adopted a new model giving markedly different security valuations will either be reluctant to trade, or, if the market is sufficiently liquid, may even be arbitraged against in the short term; this is particularly true for market makers.

However, once sufficient consensus has begun to emerge, there is increasing pressure to revise one's model *if* one believes that others will. And in fact, once the process begins, lagging participants will tend to mirror newly observed quotes even when their model development is incomplete. That is, everyone implicitly revises their models at the same time, leading to a discontinuous jump in market prices generally accompanied by extreme illiquidity. This situation could be described as a "model shock;" these shocks are infrequent, but quite painful when they do occur. Less dramatically, minor revision and fine-tuning of prepayment models occurs constantly, causing market prices to drift away from those which may have been predicted by earlier versions of the models.

Some historical examples of model revision, very commonly cited (cf. Bartlett, for example), are:

1. In 1988–89, most prepayment models overestimated prepayments by failing to take into account a general decline in housing turnover. This decline had both cyclical and secular components, and was also related to an increased consumer focus on debt reduction.
2. GNMA prepayments in early 1992 were much slower than predicted because of the newly imposed FHA insurance premium, and also because of the impact of the recession; however, the streamlined refinancing program in October 1992 pushed prepayments towards rates on conventional programs.
3. The refinancing surge of 1991–93 was more dramatic and more prolonged than most analysts predicted. A major reason seems to have been the wider availability of 15-year balloon mortgages and the growing popularity of ARMS, as alternatives to standard 30-year fixed rate mortgages. This was a function, not simply of the steepness of the yield curve, but of product innovation, marketing and changing consumer preferences.

A vivid example of model shock occurred in the Australian market in 1991–1994. Many holders of fixed-rate passthroughs issued from the FANMAC program used prepayment models derived from U.S. experience, incorporating a burnout effect on prepayments. In fact, no burnout was ever observed in Australia. This experience, of course, has no direct relevance to the U.S. market. However, it should be remembered that since burnout depends on borrower irrationality to a large extent, it is one of the most problematic aspects of any model.

Quantifying Prepayment Model Risk

Just as prepayment analysis is often treated as an exercise in statistical estimation from historical time series, it has also been suggested that model risk can be quantified by analyzing historical data, e.g., to derive "standard errors" which measure potential forecasting errors. This is a fallacy. *One should not attempt to estimate model risk by comparing model forecasts with historical prepayments.* This is because:

• Over short periods, prepayments are always noisy and a model will tend to show a poor fit. However, only a medium-term model bias — over, say, five years or more — will significantly affect valuations (except for very high premium passthroughs and short CMO tranches). Thus, model errors measured over short time scales will overstate risk. On the other hand, there is usually insufficient historical data to make statistically significant statements about any bias occurring over longer time scales.

- If the model was fitted to the historical data, the comparison is post hoc and thus invalid. On the other hand, if previous model forecasts are compared to subsequent prepayment experience, this arguably gives us little information about the model currently being used.
- Most prepayment models performed very badly in 1993, and it could be argued that this experience was atypical. Including this period in an analysis of model risk would possibly be overstating this risk quite drastically.
- At a time when the consumer lending market is evolving rapidly, and when the economy and housing market are experiencing major structural changes, the historical experience of 1976–1996 provides at best an incomplete guide to the future.

How else can model risk be quantified? One can start by determining how much disagreement there is between different dealers. Assuming that major dealers all have access to comprehensive data and have all invested resources in analyzing it thoroughly, any dealer's forecast may be regarded as expressing a competent opinion about future prepayment patterns, and any discrepancy between dealer forecasts will represent a reasonable difference of opinion between experts. Exhibits 5–13 and 5–14 show the typical variation in reported dealer PSA forecasts.

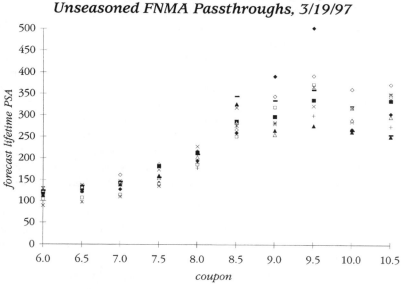

Exhibit 5–13: Dealer PSA Forecasts for Unseasoned FNMA Passthroughs, 3/19/97

Exhibit 5–14: "Standard Error" in Reported Dealer Forecasts versus Consensus Forecast

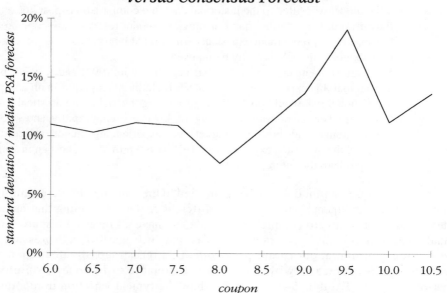

These graphs show that it is normal for dealer forecasts to disagree by 10%, or 15% for premium mortgages — refinancing speeds are harder to predict, so the scope for disagreement is greater. Thus, when estimating potential return volatility due to model risk, it might seem reasonable to vary prepayment forecasts by 10% to 15%, depending on the collateral.

Unfortunately, this approach will usually understate model risk. The reasons are that (a) the range of dealer forecasts does not cover all reasonable prepayment scenarios, and in fact that (b) for reasons described above, there is considerable pressure on dealers not to report forecasts which stray too far from the consensus. That is, even though in theory different dealers are using independent models, in practice the reported results tend to be variations on a single theme. Thus the range of forecasts may give us some — incomplete — idea about the extent of possible model drift, but we must find other ways, perhaps more subjective, of estimating the potential effect of model drift or model shock which has not been reflected in any dealer's reported forecasts.

There is an alternative approach which was originally developed by Mason for use in the Australian market where dealer forecasts are not so readily available (for simplicity, we omit all technical details and refinements in this account). The idea is to translate prepayment speeds into a more intuitive scale. Rather than using PSA or CPR, we measure prepayments in terms of *the average life of a mortgage*.

Exhibit 5-15: Effect on Average Mortgage Life of 20% Revision to Forecast Speeds

Collateral Type	Forecast Avg. Mortgage Life	Revised Avg. Mortgage Life
FHA	12 years	10.7 years/13.6 years
whole loan	7 years	6.1 years/8.3 years
premium	4 years	3.5 years/4.7 years

For example, if a pool prepays at 260% PSA throughout its life, then the average life of a mortgage in the pool is 7 years; while if another pool prepays at 125% PSA then the average life of a mortgage is approximately 12 years. (Note that this is not the same as the usual definition of average life, which refers to the average life of $1 principal in the pool, and thus depends on scheduled amortization as well as prepayments. For these two pools, the average life of $1 principal would be 6.5 years and 10.5 years respectively.)

The advantage of measuring prepayments in terms of average mortgage life is that it is an intuitive scale which can be easily related to information from a wide variety of sources, such as long-term housing turnover data or even anecdotal information from mortgage bankers or loan servicers. For example, if a bank reports that whole loans in its portfolio appear to have about a 7 year turnover rate, this is consistent with a 260% PSA; while if housing data suggest that FHA borrowers relocate about once every 12 years, this is consistent with a 125% PSA.

Average mortgage life is a useful way of understanding the "real-world" meaning of a revision to prepayment forecasts. Exhibit 5-15 shows the impact on average mortgage life, for three examples, of a 20% upward or downward revision in forecast prepayment speeds.

It is hard to say, on the face of it, whether ±20% is a reasonable band of uncertainty in prepayment speeds. However, it is easier to assess more concrete statements such as:

- "We expect that the average time to relocation for FHA borrowers will remain around 10.5–13.5 years."
- "We expect that the average time to turnover for mortgages in our whole loan portfolio will stay around 6–8.5 years."
- "We expect that over the next 3.5–4.5 years, half of these premium mortgages will have prepaid."

Each of these statements represents an intuitively reasonable degree of uncertainty. Thus, when viewed this way, the use of a ±20% band of uncertainty, as in Exhibit 5-15, seems to be reasonable. For example, the slower the loans are expected to prepay, the greater the corresponding uncertainty in average mortgage life — which is what we would expect.

The other advantage of this point of view is that it emphasizes that there is a degree of imprecision inherent in judgments about model risk. The use of

PSA and CPR, and statistical measures such as standard error, can give a misleading impression of accuracy. Average mortgage life is a more intuitive scale which emphasizes the unavoidable fuzziness of the judgments involved.

Thus, to derive an initial estimate of prepayment model risk, it is usually realistic to use the same ±20% band for different securities. However, more detailed prepayment research may suggest a more refined approach. For example, an investor may believe that housing turnover may remain stable, but that changes in technology and marketing may have a very uncertain impact on future refinancings. Thus prepayments on premium mortgages may be regarded as intrinsically more difficult to forecast. On this view, it might be reasonable to use (say) a ±15% band for discount mortgages and a ±30% band for premium mortgages. Similarly, for reasons discussed above, one might use a wider band for burned-out pools. The reasonableness of an assumed band of uncertainty can be assessed by interpreting it in terms of average mortgage life.

For whole-loan and especially asset-backed deals, a further aspect of prepayment model risk becomes important. The perceived degree of prepayment model risk may depend, not just on the nature of the collateral, but on the extent of information disclosed. For example, suppose an investor holds two securities backed by home equity loans and believes that the underlying loan pools have essentially identical characteristics; however, suppose that monthly prepayment and credit performance data is available on the first pool but not the second. From an investor's viewpoint, both pools are subject to prepayment model risk. However, if the first pool starts to behave in an unpredicted way, investors will be able to revise prepayment forecasts and recalculate average lives, effective durations and convexities; thus, the security should remain liquid. If the second pool starts to behave in an unpredicted way, the security is likely to become illiquid, as investors have no way of revising their prepayment forecasts and durations. Thus prepayment model risk has a much greater potential impact on the second security, since it introduces potential liquidity risk.

Case Study: A CMO Auction

Now that we have some idea of how to quantify prepayment model risk at the level of the underlying collateral, we still need to determine what economic impact it might have on bondholders. This topic will be addressed in detail in Chapter 6, but it may be useful to describe a case study of the dollar impact of model risk on mortgage-backed securities — more specifically, CMOs.

Risky CMO tranches often have leveraged exposure to prepayment risk, and model risk is particularly significant for these tranches. Also, the fact that the market for these securities is highly illiquid means that observed bids tend to reflect market participants' theoretical valuations. If bidders are assumed to have the same access to market data and option pricing technology, any discrepancy between bids must be due to differences in valuation methodology and prepayment modeling. Thus, CMO auctions provide a way of observing model risk in action.

Exhibit 5-16: Results of CMO Auction, Summary

Lot	Bids	Type	Index	Multiplier	Cap	Lowest	Highest	Std. Dev.
#20	4	SEQ				$32.00	$37.00	$2.18
#22	5	FLT	10yT-50bp	1		$90.00	$94.16	$1.65
#1	16	INV	6m LIBOR	−2	22.10%	$87.13	$96.13	$2.75
#2	16	INV	1m LIBOR	−2.749	25.00%	$80.75	$97.94	$5.20
#3	13	INV	1m LIBOR	−3.415	29.88%	$79.50	$99.50	$7.19
#8	12	INV	COFI	−1.857	16.53%	$55.00	$79.00	$8.57
#11	12	INV	1m LIBOR	−2.148	17.19%	$70.00	$86.50	$5.01
#18	12	INV	1m LIBOR	−2.6	19.27%	$27.75	$47.00	$6.14

Exhibit 5-17: Results of CMO Auction, Individual Bids

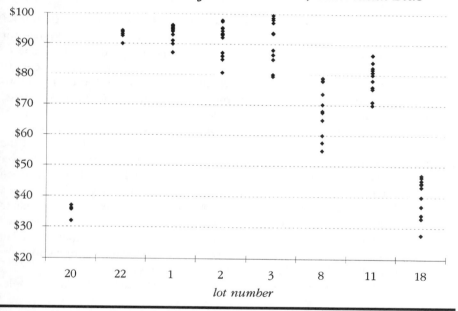

Bernardo and Cornell have analyzed the results of a first price, sealed bid CMO auction held in 1995. The securities were all backed by FHLMC or FNMA collateral, and were mostly inverse floaters. The bidders were all major dealers or large institutional investors. The results of the auction, for selected lots, are summarized in Exhibits 5-16 and 5-17.

The degree of dispersion between bids is remarkable, and not just for the lots displayed here: omitted lots showed similar dispersion. In general, the riskier the security, the higher the dispersion of bids. For example:

- Most lots were potentially long-dated inverse floaters, subject to a high degree of prepayment risk; these all showed high dispersions.

- Lot 1, though an inverse floater, was less risky because of its very short maturity (March 1997); the dispersion of bids was correspondingly lower.
- Lot 20 (a sequential tranche) and Lot 22 (a CMO floater) were both less risky tranche types than inverse floaters; the dispersion of bids was again correspondingly lower.

Using auction theory, Bernardo and Cornell show that under reasonable assumptions, the variance of valuations is at least as high as the variance of bids. Thus different bidders were coming up with drastically different valuations for the securities, despite having equal access to market data and prepayment data. The study also confirms that there is a direct relationship between valuation uncertainty and liquidity — itself a relevant factor in assessing value.

Yield Curve Slope: A Model Factor or a Source of Model Risk?

One specific source of model risk is worth singling out. It has been known for some time that there is a relationship between refinancing speeds and the slope — not just the level — of the yield curve. This is because borrowers have access to lending products priced off different parts of the yield curve. For example, 30-year mortgages often experience refinancings when the yield curve steepens, making ARM rates look more attractive, while ARMs often experience refinancings when the curve flattens, making 30-year mortgages look more attractive.

Note that in a perfectly efficient home lending market, the slope of the curve would be irrelevant. For suppose that the curve is currently steep. A borrower who intends to repay a mortgage over the full 30 years should be indifferent between paying a fixed rate for 30 years and an adjustable rate which, though initially lower, is expected to rise (as indicated by the forward curve). A borrower who intends to move house in three years might prefer the ARM; but this implies, not that borrowers should be switching back and forth between ARMs and fixed rate mortgages, but that the lending market should segment between less mobile and more mobile borrowers, who would prefer fixed rate mortgages and ARMs respectively.

In fact, for various reasons, borrowers do not behave like this; for example:

1. The availability of ARMs with low teaser rates complicates the decision to refinance into ARMs. In particular, refinancing into ARMs can be more attractive if the borrower adopts a strategy of regularly refinancing from one teaser rate to the next (and if lenders continue to permit this).
2. Borrowers may evaluate their options irrationally, e.g., they may believe that ARM rates cannot rise, or they may assign an unrealistically low probability to a rise in rates.
3. Borrowers may have a view on interest rates different from that reflected in the market forward curve. This may have been the case in 1993.
4. Borrowers under financial stress may opt for an ARM simply because it offers the lowest current interest rate and thus makes immediate debt ser-

vicing easier (this was probably an important factor in 1992–93). Borrowers who do not face this financial pressure may make decisions based on a longer time horizon.

5. Borrower risk aversion influences the decision to refinance. For instance, ARM borrowers will refinance into a higher fixed rate because known repayments offer extra security, but the extra interest which they are prepared to pay depends on their degree of risk aversion — which in turn depends on their other financial obligations relative to income, and their subjective assessment of their own financial prospects and risks.

Thus borrowers do refinance between ARMs and fixed rate mortgages, and the slope of the curve is indeed relevant. However, it is vital to note that *the slope of the curve does not fully determine the relative attractiveness of ARMs and fixed rate mortgages*. For example, neither the current level of ARM teaser rates, the willingness of lenders to permit refinancing without penalty, or the degree of borrower rationality, financial stress or risk aversion are solely determined by the slope of the yield curve; in fact, most of them are largely independent of the yield curve slope.

If borrower preferences for ARMs were determined purely by yield curve slope, i.e., by a mechanical comparison of interest rates, one would expect a stable relationship between ARM originations and the spread between the 30-year fixed and ARM mortgage rates. The Mortgage Bankers' Association publishes a survey of mortgage applications which, among other things, monitors the market share of ARMs. Exhibit 5–18 plots ARM market share versus the 30-year/ARM mortgage rate spread. It shows that although a strong relationship does exist, it has not remained stable over time. The ARM market appears to have gone through several different phases since 1990.

These phases may be summarized as follows:

- From 1990 up to the first Fed tightening in 1994, ARMs were moderately popular. ARM originations were triggered at an interest rate saving of around 180 bp versus the 30-year fixed mortgage rate, and market share rose by about 10% for each additional 50 bp saving.
- During the series of tightenings in 1994, ARM market share hovered around 30% regardless of the mortgage rate differential. This high market share was due to the fact that ARM applications remained relatively stable while fixed rate mortgage applications had fallen significantly.
- From late 1994 to late 1995, ARMs continued to be a popular product, with borrowers showing a higher degree of interest rate sensitivity: savings of less than 150 bp versus the 30-year fixed rate triggered originations, and market share rose by about 15% for each extra 50 bp saving.
- Since 1996, ARMs have been somewhat less popular, with borrowers appearing to be less interest rate sensitive. ARM originations were still triggered at a 30-year/ARM spread level significantly below 150 bp, but market share rose by only 10% per 50 bp saving.

Exhibit 5-18: ARM Market Share, Showing Changing Popularity of Adjustable Rate Mortgages

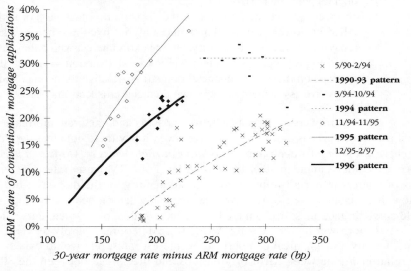

It is clear that there is no direct, stable relationship between the slope of the yield curve and ARM originations, and that constructing a model which takes yield curve slope into account will be difficult. If a prepayment model assumes some stable relationship, it implicitly makes assumptions about future borrower attitudes towards the ARM lending product, and these assumptions require justification. Note that a prepayment model fitted to 1990–1993 data may not have performed well in 1994–1996.

The existence of balloon mortgages and 15-year mortgages complicates the picture, by introducing potential sensitivity to different parts of the yield curve. And again, potential interest rate savings are not the sole criterion. For example, borrowers take out 15-year mortgages, not simply to capture a lower interest rate, but because they wish to build up equity more rapidly.

Selected References

Bartlett, W., *The Valuation of Mortgage-Backed Securities*, Irwin, New York, 1994.

Bernardo, A. and Cornell, B., *Bidding for Derivative Securities*, UCLA Anderson School of Management Working Paper #17–95 (sponsored by CMS), October 1995.

Chen, S., "Understanding Option-Adjusted Spreads: The Implied Prepayments Hypothesis," *J. Portfolio Management*, Summer 1996.

Cheyette, O., "Implied Prepayments," *J. Portfolio Management*, Fall 1996.

Fabozzi, F. (ed.), *The Handbook of Mortgage-Backed Securities* (4th edition), Probus, Chicago, 1995.

Hayre, L. and Chang, H., "Effective and Empirical Durations of Mortgage Securities," *J. Fixed Income*, March 1997.

Huber, P., *Robust Statistical Procedures* (2nd edition), SIAM, Philadelphia, 1996; see Chapter VIII.

Mason, R., *2M (Keystart) Bond Analysis and an Introduction to Standard Mortgage Life*, Deutsche Morgan Grenfell (Sydney) research report, May 1994.

McConnell, J. and Singh, M., "Rational Prepayments and the Valuation of Collateralized Mortgage Obligations," *J. Finance*, July 1994.

Phoa, W., "Prepayment Analysis," in R. Mason (ed.), *Australian Mortgage-Backed Securities: August 1995 Guide*, Deutsche Morgan Grenfell (Sydney) research report, August 1995.

Sanyal, A., "Ammunition for ARMs: A Panel Data Approach to Prepayment Modeling," *J. Fixed Income*, December 1994.

Schwartz, E. and Torous, W., *An Empirical Investigation of Mortgage Prepayment and Default Decisions*, UCLA Anderson School of Management Working Paper #29–92 (sponsored by CMS), December 1992.

Chapter 6

Measures of Non Yield Curve Risk and Risk/Return

SETTING THE SCENE: THE CONCEPT OF OAS

Investors often attempt to outperform their benchmarks by holding bonds which will generate an excess return relative to Treasuries. Such bonds are usually riskier than Treasuries, and thus investors must ensure that the risk/return profile of the portfolio is satisfactory. There are three steps in this process:

1. Measure the "observable risk premium" which they can expect to earn from holding the bonds; this will be a function of the market price of the bond and the term structure model and prepayment model used to generate and value the bond's cashflows.
2. Identify and quantify the risks involved in holding the bond; this excludes risks which can be efficiently hedged, notably interest rate risk.
3. Determine whether the observable risk premium represents sufficient compensation for accepting these risks; a riskier bond should offer a higher risk premium.

In this chapter, we use option-adjusted spread as a measure of the "observable risk premium." We therefore start by discussing the widely misunderstood concept of OAS in a little more detail. The remainder of the chapter is more concrete, and concentrates on steps 2 and 3: identifying, quantifying and balancing risks.

Problems with the Concept of Option-Adjusted Spread

OAS is often loosely defined to be "the basis point risk premium of a bond versus Treasuries;" this risk premium is meant to be the compensation for the greater risks of holding the bond relative to holding an equivalent portfolio of non-callable Treasuries. Here "equivalent" means: having the same exposure to yield curve risk, i.e., to changes in the Treasury curve. Thus, OAS is compensation for risks other than yield curve risk; and this chapter shows how to identify and quantify these risks.

A more precise definition of the OAS of a bond, relative to a given term structure model, was given in Chapter 2. The bond's *option-adjusted spread* was the constant spread which must be added to the prevailing short rate to make the theoretical bond price (as calculated by the model) equal to the market price. In other words, *from the point of view of the model* it is the average excess return of the bond over the prevailing short rate.

Different models will calculate different option-adjusted spreads for the same bond. For example, consider a callable Treasury bond. Given the same initial volatility assumptions, a Gaussian model attaches a higher probability to extreme low interest rate scenarios than a lognormal model, and thus makes the call option seem more valuable. The Gaussian model will therefore compute a lower OAS for the bond than the lognormal model. For similar reasons, the Gaussian model will generally compute a lower OAS for a bond with an investor put option than the lognormal model.

Is there a "true OAS," independent of any model? Many investors believe that there is, and that one purpose of modeling is to calculate this "true OAS" as accurately as possible. But when examined more closely, the concept of OAS is more problematic than this naive assumption suggests.

For example, what is the OAS of an inflation-indexed Treasury bond? The intuition is not clear. Should it be zero, because it is a Treasury bond? Should it be slightly positive, because it is less liquid than an on-the-run Treasury? Should it be significantly negative, because it offers protection against inflation risk? Should it be significantly positive, because real yields are volatile and this risk is expensive or impossible to hedge because of the absence of liquid futures and repo markets? It is highly unlikely that all investors would answer the question in the same way. Thus, there is almost certainly no universally acceptable way of calculating the "OAS" of a TIPS.

Or consider low-grade corporate bonds and discount mortgage-backed securities. Both outperform when inflation is high: the former because corporate revenues available for debt service tend to rise with inflation, the latter because prepayments tend to accelerate when inflation is high, since rising house prices cause borrower loan-to-value ratios to fall. However, the impact of both of these effects is quite unpredictable. Should the OAS of corporate bonds and discount MBS reflect their estimated value as a partial inflation hedge, and thus a partial hedge against a rise in nominal interest rates driven by inflation expectations? One can see that similar issues arise as in the case of TIPS.

Focusing on corporate bonds a bit more closely: it is generally accepted that the OAS of a non-callable corporate bond is equal to the nominal spread to the Treasury curve. But it has often been noted that non-callable corporate spreads tend to compress when Treasury yields rise, causing corporate bonds to outperform Treasury bonds: see, for example, the recent paper of Duffee. Thus, if the OAS is meant to measure expected excess return versus Treasuries (assuming no credit losses) then it should be higher than the nominal spread. If one defines it to be equal to the nominal spread, one has effectively made the arbitrary decision to ignore the known but uncertain impact of interest rates on spreads.

For callable bonds, there is a further problem. Since corporate spreads tend to widen when Treasuries rally, the call option will not be exercised unless Treasury yields fall somewhat below the exercise yield predicted by an interest rate model which assumes a constant yield spread to the Treasury curve. Should the option pricing model be modified to link spreads to interest rate levels? This will change the computed OAS, and also seems to affect the interpretation of what the OAS means.

Spreads on mortgage-backed securities also appear to vary with interest rates: for example, the OAS on a current coupon passthrough is generally tighter than the OAS on a premium coupon. Thus if interest rates rally, the OAS on the current coupon will widen as it becomes a premium coupon — although the exact change in spreads is unpredictable. That is, changes in interest rates induce additional price effects stemming from the resulting changes in spreads. The interpretation of OAS as an excess return does not take this price effect into account, nor does the term structure model incorporate this effect when calculating theoretical hedges. Thus OAS is of questionable usefulness for forecasting MBS relative performance. (Cohler, Feldman and Lancaster have developed an alternative to OAS analysis for MBS — broadly related to some methods described later in this chapter — but they also point out that their improved methodology remains imperfect.)

To take an example not involving spread risk, there are a few CMO tranches with return profiles that are so volatile, so complex, and so obviously impossible to hedge, that many investors regard the concept of OAS as inapplicable or useless for these bonds, while others might disagree violently about what the OAS of one of these bonds was trying to measure.

To give a different kind of example, consider a bond backed by a pool of fixed-rate loans which may well experience interest rate sensitive prepayments, and suppose that (a) no prepayment data is available, and (b) market participants are known not to take interest rate sensitive prepayments into account when valuing the bond. If market pricing reflects a targeted return of 50 bp over Treasuries, then intuitively the OAS of the bond is not 50 bp, but something lower. In fact, there is no way of measuring the OAS without making some assumption about prepayments; and with no data, any assumption is arbitrary.

Finally, observe that if even if there were a universally accepted definition of OAS, it could have no overriding significance for all investors. For example, suppose each investor's basic goal was to maximize after-tax return on capital. Then each investor would in principle compute a "tax- and capital-adjusted OAS" for each bond, which would depend on the taxes and capital charges to which that investor was subject; and this would be the true measure of value for that investor.

For all these reasons, time spent on the abstract question of whether a given definition of OAS is "the right one" is probably time wasted. It is more useful for each investor to understand the precise assumptions behind a given OAS calculation, and to determine whether the calculation gives answers which are useful to the portfolio's specific investment objectives — for example, whether the OAS figures can sensibly be compared to help assess relative value between different securities. Generally speaking, OAS is a very useful measure, provided one understands its limitations.

Some Brief Technical Comments on OAS

(The following discussion may be skipped at a first reading.) Recall from Chapter 2 that the price of an option-embedded bond satisfies a partial differential equation which states that its income return plus its expected price return is equal to the short rate plus the OAS of the bond. For a one factor short rate model, the PDE is:

$$\text{cpn}(t) + \frac{dP}{dt} + \mu\frac{dP}{dr} + \frac{1}{2}\sigma^2\frac{d^2P}{dr^2} = (r_t + \text{OAS}) \cdot P$$

The price of a mortgage-backed security also satisfies this PDE, except one must also take into account the fact that principal repayment are regularly being received at par, and that the bond price may jump when principal is repaid. For example, if the price of a passthrough is $108 immediately before a principal repayment which is (expected to be) equal to 10% of face value, the price immediately after the principal repayment must (be expected to) jump to $110. This ensures that the total value of the investment is (expected to be) unaffected when the principal repayment is made: $108 = $10 + 0.9 × $110.

We deal with this by adding a so-called *jump condition* (see Wilmott et al.) to the PDE. If t is a principal repayment date and is the forecast percentage of principal repaid on that date — which may depend on the current and past level of interest rates — then:

$$P(t^-) = \text{prin} + (1 - \text{prin}) \cdot P(t^+)$$

Here t^- and t^+ refer to the instant immediately before the repayment of principal, and the instant immediately afterwards.

With this modification, the price of a mortgage-backed security satisfies the same PDE shown above. Alternatively, if one assumes that principal is being repaid continuously at the (potentially variable) rate π, so that the bond price does not exhibit discontinuous jumps, the bond price can be shown to satisfy a slightly modified PDE, where the term $\pi(1-P)$ is added to the left-hand side to reflect the impact on an investor's total return of principal repayments at par.

It is important to note that *the PDE cannot be used to price the bond*, since the bond's forecast principal repayment rate depends on the pool's prepayment rate and (for a CMO) the pool's prepayment history, and thus on the history of interest rates up to time t; this means that we cannot solve the PDE by working backwards in time, as we could for a callable bond. However, the fact that a mortgage-backed security's price satisfies the PDE does show that its OAS has the same basic interpretation as the OAS of a callable bond.

Other definitions of OAS have been proposed. For example, recall that OAS for a mortgage-backed security is computed by valuing it along a large number of random interest rate paths. Kopprasch has suggested that these paths could also incorporate random changes in volatility parameters or even prepayment model parameters. The resulting "OAS" then has a different interpretation: the calculation implicitly assumes that volatility and prepayment model parameters are additional stochastic factors whose dynamics can be described, that volatility risk and prepayment model risk can thus be hedged, and that this "OAS" therefore does not reflect a risk premium for volatility risk or prepayment model risk of the kind specified in the model: it only reflects a premium for illiquidity, credit risk and/or model risk not captured by simply varying the model parameters. One would expect Kopprasch's "OAS" to be significantly lower than the OAS calculated using fixed volatility and prepayment model parameters.

"Percentage Price Premium" is Sometimes a Useful Alternative to OAS

When trying to express the "risk premium" implied by a term structure (and prepayment) model, there is an alternative to using OAS: the difference between the model price — using the unadjusted short rate to discount all cashflows — and the market price can be regarded as a direct measure of the risk premium. For example, if the market price of a passthrough is $104 and the model price is $105 (assuming an OAS of zero, an investor who borrowed cash to purchase the bond, and hedged it with Treasury futures, would theoretically make a profit of $1 over time. Note that the rate at which this $1 is captured is uncertain, since it depends on the rate at which the bond prepays.

This suggests that we can define the *percentage price premium* to be $(P_{theor} - P_{mkt})/P_{mkt}$, where P_{mkt} is the market price of the bond and P_{theor} is the model price, based on a zero spread to the Treasury curve. This is the theoretical percentage return from the bond if it is funded and hedged as described above. Price premium is closely related to OAS, and suffers from many of the same problems of interpretation. However, it can be a useful measure of value for bond with very volatile or very short durations, for which the OAS calculation is unstable. For example, when comparing two CMO support tranches, or two very short-dated ABS tranches, it is generally more useful to look at price premium rather than OAS.

For corporate bonds, OAS is usually more useful. One can show that the OAS of a fixed rate corporate bond is equal to its price premium divided by its effective duration. If the price premium is regarded as a dollar premium for default risk — which is not the only interpretation — then the OAS can be interpreted as a basis point premium for default risk. Thus, if a portfolio of corporate bonds is expected to sustain default losses of 0.5% per annum, a portfolio OAS of 50 bp would seem to offer reasonable compensation; however, an OAS of 50 bp would correspond to different price premiums for different bonds. In this case, OAS is probably a more convenient basis for comparison than price premium. (The appendix to this chapter describes the theoretical relationship between default risk and corporate spreads. In practice, as we observe below, default risk does not fully explain option-adjusted spreads on corporate bonds.)

ADVANCED RISK MEASURES

Spread Risk and Spread Duration

Most fixed-income securities are priced relative to the Treasury curve, either on a spread basis (for non option-embedded bonds) or on an OAS basis (for option-embedded bonds and MBS). Provided the OAS calculations are performed within a consistent framework, this helps ensure consistency in pricing between different securities. Price changes affecting different market sectors or quality ratings tend to correspond to systematic changes in OAS within each sector or quality rating. Thus, it makes sense to develop risk measures which look at the sensitivity of bond or portfolio returns to changes in spreads, i.e., to changes in OAS.

The *spread duration* of a bond is defined to be its percentage price premium divided by its OAS — in other words, it is the "value of each basis point of option-adjusted spread." For example:

1. The spread duration of a *fixed rate corporate bond with no embedded options* is simply equal to its modified duration. This is because a 10 bp tightening in OAS has the same effect on the bond price as a 10 bp rally in Treasury yields.

2. The spread duration of a *fixed rate corporate bond with embedded options*, such as a callable corporate, is equal to its effective duration. Again, a 10 bp tightening in OAS has the same effect on bond value as a 10 bp rally in Treasury yields — its impact on the value of an embedded call or put option (i.e., on the likelihood that the option will be exercised) is the same.

3. The spread duration of a *floating rate corporate bond* (with no caps, floors or other embedded options) is equal to the modified duration of a fixed rate par bond with the same maturity. Note that this will be considerably higher than the bond's effective duration: a change in OAS affects returns to maturity, while a change in interest rates only affects returns to the next coupon reset.

4. The spread duration of a *mortgage-backed security* need not be equal to its effective duration. This is because a 10 bp widening in OAS need not have the same effect on bond value as a 10 bp rise in Treasury yields.

This last point requires some explanation. A rise in yields triggers a rise in prevailing mortgage rates, and thus slows down refinancings and alters the bond's expected cashflows. An OAS widening will only have the same effect on the bond's expected cashflows if it, too, triggers a corresponding rise in prevailing mortgage rates. In a perfectly competitive and efficient market this might be true.

In the real world, the link between MBS spreads and consumer lending rates appears to be much looser, because of the many intervening factors: e.g., flexibility in servicing margins and the fact that the value of servicing rights depends on expected prepayments, the ability of the agencies to influence pricing, the ability of lenders to shift their marketing focus between different mortgage products, and the fact that many lenders can warehouse loans on balance sheet before securitizing. It might be just as reasonable to assume that a change in OAS has no effect on mortgage rates, and thus no effect on the bond's cashflows; this does appear to be the case in the short term. The spread duration of an MBS is in fact somewhat ill-defined.

By contrast, corporate treasurers focus closely on changes in spreads, and the market for new corporate bond issues to refinance called debt is highly efficient; thus an OAS shift will affect the value of an embedded call option, which explains why spread duration is equal to effective duration for callable bonds (point 2). However, it is not clear whether the same argument applies to low grade corporate debt or municipal bonds, since these markets appear to be less efficient, and issuers are subject to greater financial constraints which may prevent them from refinancing debt even if it would otherwise be rational to exercise call options on outstanding bonds.

A useful application of spread duration is to calculate breakeven spread shifts. Investors who are attempting to outperform Treasury bonds by overweighting corporate and/or mortgage-backed securities often need to determine how much spreads can widen before the additional income from these higher-yielding securities will be offset by a negative price effect in comparison to Treasuries. This gives some indication of the risk of the strategy.

The following quick method of calculating breakeven spreads is quite accurate for holding periods of up to 12 months:

$$\text{breakeven spread shift} = \frac{\text{excess income}}{\text{spread duration}} = \frac{\text{holding period} \times \text{spread}}{\text{spread duration}}$$

For example, suppose a portfolio matches the duration of a benchmark portfolio of Treasury bonds, but has an OAS of 40 bp; and suppose the portfolio has a spread duration of 4. Over a 6-month holding period, the excess income return versus Treasuries is 0.20%; thus, if spreads widen by 0.20%/4 = 5 bp or more over that six months — that is, if the portfolio OAS widens beyond 45 bp — the portfolio will underperform Treasuries.

Although this rule of thumb is useful for quick calculations, it is not a replacement for detailed simulation: it does not take aging and detailed reinvestment assumptions into account. Detailed simulation is also required if more complex relationships between market factors are assumed.

Spread Risk and Credit Quality

Just as the effective duration of a portfolio measures its sensitivity to a parallel shift in the whole Treasury yield curve, the spread duration of a portfolio measures its sensitivity to a uniform shift in (option-adjusted) spreads across all quality ratings, sectors and maturities. In Chapter 1, we verified that duration was a useful measure of risk, by using principal component analysis to identify the various fundamental yield curve shifts that occur, and to verify that the dominant kind of yield curve shift was indeed a parallel shift across the whole curve.

Exhibit 6–1 shows the results of a principal component analysis of spread shifts on industrial bonds by quality rating. Here again, the dominant kind of shift is a nearly uniform change in spreads across all quality ratings. But this uniform shift explains only around 70% of the observed variation in spreads. The remaining principal components have quite high weightings. Note that the second most important kind of shift is a steepening in the credit curve by quality.

This suggests that if a portfolio contains bonds with a variety of quality ratings, its spread duration only gives us partial information about its spread risk. It may also be useful to measure the sensitivity of the portfolio to a more "typical" shift in spreads, in which lower quality spreads experience greater shifts. This would give us a measure of spread risk that discriminated between quality ratings. It would correspond to using some "typical" combination of the principal components shown in Exhibit 6–1.

To determine what a typical spread shift looks like, we can carry out a regression between observed spread shifts at different quality ratings. For example, Exhibit 6–2 plots weekly shifts in A-rated industrial spreads against weekly shifts in Aa-rated industrial spreads. Although there is a significant amount of noise, a regression suggests that a 10 bp shift in A-rated spreads is (on average) accompanied by a shift of slightly more than 8 bp in Aa-rated spreads.

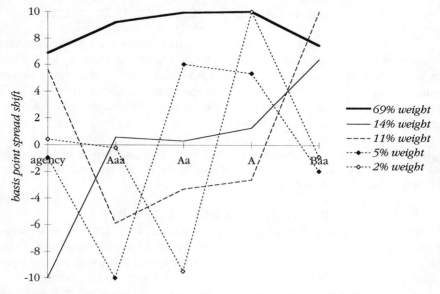

Exhibit 6–1: Principal Component Analysis of Spread Shifts versus Quality (1991-1997 Data)

Exhibit 6–2: Relationship between Spread Shifts for Aa- and A-Rated Industrials

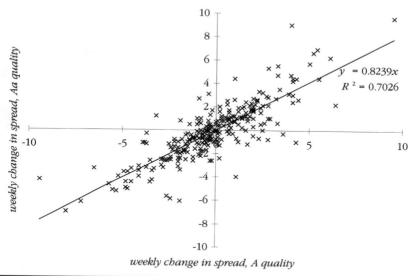

If we repeat this exercise for different quality ratings, the results suggest that a typical spread shift looks something like the one shown in Exhibit 6–3: a 10 bp shift in Baa spreads corresponds to a shift of just over 5 bp in Aaa spreads, and less than 2 bp in agency spreads. Note that the precise results are quite dependent on the dataset used, so that it is meaningless to attempt to be too precise.

Further refinement might be possible. For example, spread shifts tend not to be uniform across maturities; instead, spreads on longer bonds tend to be more volatile than spreads on shorter bonds. Unfortunately, it is very difficult to quantify this relationship reliably, if one wants results that apply equally to callable bonds, since it is hard to define how "long" a callable bond is: both its effective maturity and its effective duration vary widely under different interest rate scenarios.

On a more theoretical level, the OAS of a corporate bond is often regarded as the "market risk premium for default risk," and one might therefore imagine that spread risk could be subsumed under default risk. That is, spreads change because the market's expectations about future default probabilities changes, and thus one could derive a model of corporate spreads from a some stochastic model of default probabilities. This would give us a way to model the behavior of spreads across different quality ratings and maturities in a unified manner.

The appendix to this chapter describes a static model of default risk which, when used in conjunction with rating agency default statistics, can be used to determine theoretical spreads required as compensation for default risk. Even though this model is very simple, it can be used to derive some interesting conclusions.

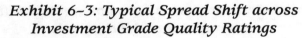

Exhibit 6–3: Typical Spread Shift across Investment Grade Quality Ratings

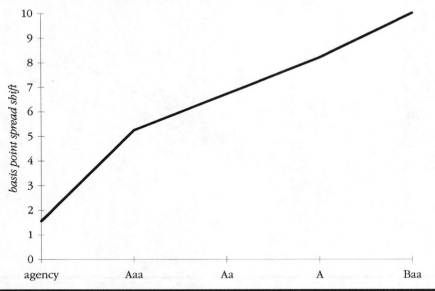

Unfortunately, Duffee has demonstrated that it is very difficult to construct a dynamic model of default probabilities which is consistent with actual corporate spreads as observed in the market. In particular, theoretically reasonable models imply that the term structure of spreads is very flat, while observed spreads usually rise with maturity. It seems that other factors affect corporate spreads, such as perceived liquidity, investor rating thresholds on bond holdings, or perhaps second-order uncertainty about the nature of default risk. Thus, when analyzing portfolio spread risk, it seems preferable to model spreads directly, rather than attempting to deriving them from default probabilities. Experience shows that this approach is very robust for investment grade bonds, where actual credit losses are extremely unlikely to occur.

Spread Risk and Treasury Yields

So far we have treated spread risk as if it were independent of interest rate risk. As mentioned earlier in the chapter, Treasury spreads on non-callable corporates have some correlation with outright Treasury yields: when yields rise, spreads tend to tighten, and vice versa. Note that the effect will not be apparent if one attempts to regress, say, single-A spreads against Treasury yield levels, for the simple reason that large spread shifts on specific bonds tend to coincide with changes in their credit quality: i.e., the single-A population is not closed, and its composition changes systematically with changes in yield levels.

Exhibit 6–4: Corporate Spread Shift for a 100 bp Fall in Treasury Yields (Due to Duffee)

	2–7 year maturity	7–15 year maturity	15–30 year maturity
Aaa	+9 bp	+6 bp	+8 bp
Aa	+10 bp	+11 bp	+17 bp
A	+10 bp	+12 bp	+23 bp
Baa	+23 bp	+18 bp	+36 bp

Source: Duffee

The effect must be measured on an issuer-by-issuer basis. Also, in analyzing the effect, it is sensible to look at the short end of the curve, because money market rates are most closely linked to the current state of the economy and thus the issuer's immediate earnings prospects — a primary focus for investors. Finally, the importance of this effect may depend on both the sector and credit rating of the issuer, and spreads might be sensitive to both the level and the slope of the Treasury curve.

Exhibit 6–4 shows the results of an empirical study of corporate bond spreads from 1985–1995 carried out by Duffee. He found no statistically significant differences between sectors, and only weak evidence that the slope of the yield curve was relevant. Interestingly, he also found that, while yield spreads are negatively correlated with stock returns (as expected), the inclusion of stock returns had no important effect on the explanatory power of the level of Treasury yields.

In most OAS calculations the relationship between outright yield levels and corporate spreads is ignored, so that the OAS of a non-callable bond is equal to its nominal spread to the Treasury curve (i.e., its yield spread to a cashflow-matched portfolio of Treasury STRIPS). However, an investor might want to take the effect into account when carrying out simulations. This can easily be done by combining results from different simulations carried out using different yield curve assumptions.

For example, suppose we want to analyze 12-month holding period returns on a portfolio of investment grade bonds, using a spread widening assumption: more precisely, we want to calculate portfolio returns on the assumption that Baa spreads widen by 20 bp. We also want assume that Treasury yields may vary (with an annual volatility of 75 bp p.a.), and we therefore need to look at a number of different scenarios to capture this interest rate uncertainty. We have already seen what kind of shift to use for higher quality ratings (Exhibit 6–3), and Exhibit 6–4 shows us how to adjust for the assumed level of Treasury yields in each scenario. Exhibit 6–5 show five suggested scenarios and their appropriate probabilities, the assumed Treasury curve shift in each scenario, and the assumed OAS shift in each scenario for each quality rating.

This example shows that even though the definition of OAS is arguably oversimplified, OAS-based simulation can be combined with more powerful simulation tools — here, the ability to carry out probability-weighted simulations — to analyze portfolio returns using more sophisticated assumptions.

Exhibit 6–5: OAS Simulation with Probability-Weighted Interest Rate Scenarios

Probability	Yield Shift	OAS Shift, Aaa	OAS Shift, Aa	OAS Shift, A	OAS Shift, Baa
6.25%	−150 bp	+22 bp	+33 bp	+39 bp	+59 bp
25.00%	−75 bp	+16 bp	+23 bp	+27 bp	+40 bp
37.50%	0 bp	+10 bp	+13 bp	+16 bp	**+20 bp**
25.00%	+75 bp	+4 bp	+3 bp	+5 bp	0 bp
6.25%	+150 bp	−2 bp	−7 bp	−7 bp	−29 bp

Estimating Volatility Risk:
Bond Markets versus Option Markets

Option-embedded bonds and mortgage-backed securities are subject to volatility risk: their value depends on the volatility assumptions used to price them. These assumptions cannot be chosen arbitrarily, but must be linked to market option implied volatilities; volatility risk is thus a kind of market risk. The link exists because the value of an embedded option must in theory be consistent with the value of options traded in the OTC derivatives market; if not, an arbitrage opportunity exists. For example, consider the following two portfolios, which are equivalent:

1. A non-callable 7.5% coupon bond maturing in 2006.
2. A 7.5% coupon bond maturing in 2006, callable at par on any coupon date from 2001; *plus* a swaption to receive a fixed semiannual coupon of 7.5% until 2006, in exchange for floating rate payments, exercisable on any bond coupon date from 2001. (Recall that a swaption is an option to enter into a swap at a predetermined swap rate; it is either a "payer" or "receiver" swaption, and may be European, American or exotic.)

The price of the non-callable bond must equal the price of the callable bond plus the price of the swaption; otherwise, an arbitrageur could buy (sell) the non-callable bond and sell (buy) the callable bond and the swaption. Now, if implied swaption volatilities rise, the price of the non-callable bond is unaffected but the price of the swaption rises; the price of the callable bond must therefore fall. That is, arbitrage-freeness creates the link between the corporate bond market and the OTC derivatives market. This link is not merely theoretical: any anomalies which arise will in fact be exploited — for example, by hedge funds or investment bank proprietary desks.

(An important caveat is that, because of market segmentation and inefficiency in OTC options markets, the link exists at the level of broad trends in volatility — day-to-day fluctuations in OTC option implieds will not be mirrored by corporate bond prices. Also, there are no liquid options markets for expiries beyond about 10 years, so that option-embedded bonds with long maturities tend to be less closely tied to OTC option markets.)

Exhibit 6–6: Examples of Vega

	Modified Duration	Effective Duration	Bond Price	Option Value	Vega
Du Pont	11.00	7.84	$101.51	$5.92	0.54
Equitable	8.28	2.25	$108.79	$17.18	0.13
Z PAC	8.45	5.88	$101.60	n/a	0.86

As we saw in Chapter 2, OTC implied volatilities have historically been extremely variable. Here is a practical example of how changes in implied volatility affect portfolio returns. In January 1997, the Lehman mortgage-backed securities index showed a return of 0.74%. A duration-matched portfolio of Treasuries would have returned only 0.35%. The best explanation for the return difference is that mortgages benefited from a fall in option implied volatilities. Volatilities fell for options on both short and long maturity instruments, and for options with both near and distant expiries.

To see how this kind of volatility shift affects returns on mortgages, consider a current coupon mortgage passthrough. If "short volatility" falls from 20% to 15%, the price of the bond will rise by $0.27. Conversely, if "long volatility" falls from 15% to 11%, the price of the bond will rise by $1.04. Historically, 4%–5% shifts in implied volatility within a single year have not been unusual. Thus, shifts in implied volatility are just as important to MBS investors as major trends in sector spreads.

The most straightforward measure of volatility risk is *vega*, which is defined to be the percentage change in a bond's price if the model volatilities are all shifted by 1%. Because it assumes a uniform shift in volatilities (for different underlying instruments and option expiries), vega measures volatility risk in the same way that effective duration measures yield curve risk, or that spread duration measures spread risk.

Vega tends to be greatest where embedded options are at-the-money, rather than deep out-of-the-money or deep in-the-money. The reason is that volatility has the greatest impact on securities for which it is most uncertain whether an option will be exercised. Thus, a current-coupon passthrough has more volatility risk than a discount or premium passthrough.

Here are some examples:

• a Du Pont 7.95% 1/15/23, callable on 1/15/2003;
• an Equitable Resources 9.90% 4/15/13, callable on 15/98; and
• a Z PAC tranche, FHLMC 1346–PN.

Exhibit 6-6 analyzes these bonds.

• The Du Pont bond is trading approximately $4.00 under its call strike. Since the exercise date is over 6 years away, there is a reasonable chance that the call will be exercised; and the volatility assumptions will obviously make a significant difference to the likelihood of exercise. Note that the

$5.92 value of the option to the issuer is, at the moment, purely time value — the option currently has zero intrinsic value.

- The Equitable Resources bond is trading approximately $4.60 over its call exercise price, and is thus extremely likely to be called; the option is in fact worth $17.18. A shift in volatility will make little difference to the probability of exercise and hence to the option value, so the vega is relatively low. The fact that the exercise date is sooner also means that the vega is lower: any change in volatility has an impact over a shorter period.
- The Z PAC tranche has a higher vega than either of the corporate bonds. Note that the collateral has a WAC of 8%, which at the time of writing was only a small premium; this is one reason why the vega is relatively high. Another is that any CMO tranche which has a leveraged exposure to prepayment risk will also have a leveraged exposure to volatility risk.

It is sometimes useful to express vega in "OAS equivalent" terms. Define the *basis point vega* of a bond to be its vega divided by its spread duration. For example, the Du Pont bond has a spread duration of 7.84, so its basis point vega is 54 bp. This means that a 1% rise in volatilities has the same effect on bond returns as a 6.9 bp widening in OAS. This is a useful way of relating the spread risk and volatility risk of an option-embedded bond. Clearly, for this bond, spread risk and volatility risk are of comparable importance.

Vega focuses on a uniform shift in volatilities; how reasonable is this? Exhibit 6–7 shows the results of a principal component analysis of daily changes in cap/floor implied volatility. As with yields and spreads, the most important shift in implied volatilities is indeed a roughly uniform shift.

Exhibit 6–7: Principal Component Analysis of Shifts in Cap/Floor Implied Volatility

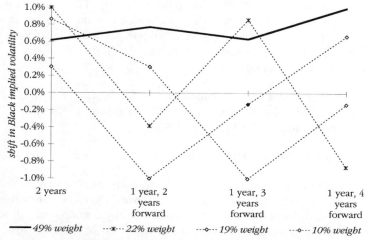

In this case, the dominant (uniform) shift appears to explain only around 50% of observed fluctuations in implied volatilities. This is partly because the relative illiquidity of the market means that OTC option implied volatilities are subject to many idiosyncratic shocks related to supply/demand imbalances, often cause by participants attempting to execute single, large deals. If we regard these disturbances as purely transitory, we can conclude that the relative importance of a uniform shift in volatility is understated by the analysis. This means that vega, as a risk measure, has as much validity as effective duration or spread duration.

However, it is clearly useful to be able to carry out more detailed volatility simulations — for example, to modify short and long volatilities separately. This is particularly useful when an investor is attempting to hedge out volatility risk by holding "offsetting" positions in option-embedded bonds: for example, MBS plus corporates with put options (which have a negative vega, since the option is in the investor's favor). If the mortgage-backed bonds are significantly shorter or longer than the corporates, the volatility hedge is imperfect; and this risk will not be detected if vega is the only measure of volatility risk being used.

Prepayment Model Valuation Risk

Prepayment model risk was discussed at length in Chapter 5. It takes two forms:

- *model drift* occurs when patterns of behavior change gradually over time, making prepayment models gradually less reliable — the process may be well underway before the impact on bondholders begins to be noticed; and
- *model shock* occurs when a more sudden and unexpected shift in borrower behavior takes place, leading to a radical shift in prepayment patterns and thus in MBS price behavior — this is generally caused by some external event, e.g., a change in Government policy.

Investors thus need to monitor prepayment model risk to determine which securities are vulnerable to model shocks, and to determine how model drift may affect forecast portfolio returns. For example, BondEdge quantifies model risk at the most precise possible level, by modifying the projected monthly prepayment rates (SMMs) along each Monte Carlo path. More specifically, it computes a measure of *prepayment model valuation risk* by scaling all SMMs up and down by 10%, and repricing the security along each path.

This can be done either for prepayments as a whole, or for refinancings and baseline prepayments separately — this is useful when an investor believes, for example, that a model will accurately capture future relocations but that it may be less good at predicting refinancing patterns. In some cases a pattern will emerge more clearly when refinancing uncertainty and uncertainty in baseline prepayments are disaggregated. Exhibit 6–8 shows how prepayment forecasts are modified to calculate prepayment model valuation risk.

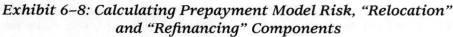

Exhibit 6–8: Calculating Prepayment Model Risk, "Relocation" and "Refinancing" Components

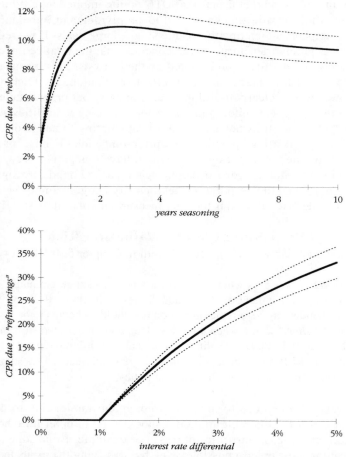

As an example of prepayment model valuation risk, consider the following CMO tranches:

• a Z tranche, class Z of FNMA 1992–137; and
• an accretion-directed tranche, class VD of FHLMC 1548.

The analysis is set out in Exhibit 6–9. The Z tranche has a prepayment uncertainty of −0.57. This means that if market participants revised their prepayment projections down by 10%, the market price of the bond will fall by 0.57%, causing significant underperformance; conversely, if forecasts are revised upwards, the market value of the bond will rise.

Exhibit 6–9: Prepayment Model Valuation Risk for Two CMO Tranches

	Price	Expected Average Life	Prepayment Uncertainty: Overall	Refinancing	Relocation
Z	$94.03	7 years	–0.57	–0.03	–0.54
AD	$96.83	11.75 years	0.11	0.08	0.03

Conversely, the AD tranche has a prepayment uncertainty of 0.11. This means that if prepayment forecasts are revised down by 10%, the value of the security will rise by 0.11%, and vice versa. Observe that:

- The Z tranche is much more vulnerable to model risk than the AD tranche. This is primarily because the Z tranche is vulnerable to extension risk while the AD tranche cannot extend; thus, if the model does not value extension risk accurately, the Z tranche will be affected more severely.
- Even though it is an inherently stable tranche type, the AD tranche is not completely protected from prepayment model risk, because it is still subject to some call risk.

Neither bond has much model risk arising from the refinancing component of the model, because a relatively low level of refinancings is forecast for the underlying (burned-out) collateral. The value of the Z tranche is much more sensitive to an incorrect specification of baseline prepayments such as relocations since this may affect extension risk severely.

As with vega, it is sometimes useful to express prepayment model valuation risk in terms of OAS rather than price: that is, to divide it by the bond's spread duration. For example, if the prepayment model valuation risk for a passthrough is 0.20 and it has a spread duration of 4, then a 10% shift in prepayment forecasts has the same impact on the value of the bond as a 5 bp shift in OAS.

The use of a 10% shift in prepayment forecasts is arbitrary, just as it was arbitrary to use a 100 bp shift in Treasury yields to calculate effective duration or a 1% shift in volatility to calculate vega. We saw in Chapter 5 that a reasonable band of uncertainty need not be ±10%, but depends on the collateral and the data available: for example, ±20% is reasonable for a pool of agency mortgages, while ±30% may be reasonable for some whole loan or home equity loan pools. In these cases the above prepayment model valuation risk measure should be multiplied by 2 or 3 to obtain a more realistic assessment of risk.

Prepayment Model Duration Risk

The effective duration of an MBS shows how its price should respond to a shift in interest rates. The actual price change will depend on market prepayment expectations; if these change, then observed durations will also change. Thus, if there is an upward revision to expectations of future housing turnover, the observed durations of discount passthroughs will fall. This introduces a further element of risk: investors cannot be sure about the precise durations of their MBS holdings, or about the precise interest rate exposure of their portfolios. This risk particularly affects investors who are attempting to track a bond index or other benchmark, as it introduces potential tracking error.

As with model valuation risk, the impact of possible changes in prepayment expectations can be modeled by changing the appropriate parameters in the prepayment model. A *standard prepayment model duration risk* measure can be calculated by scaling all prepayment forecasts up or down by 10% and seeing what effect this has on the computed effective duration. (As discussed above, in order to obtain a realistic measure of model risk, it is usually reasonable to look at a ±20% band of prepayment forecasts.)

To see what the potential impact of model duration risk is, suppose 25% of a portfolio consists of 8% mortgages with a model duration risk of 0.4, and suppose the portfolio effective duration is estimated at 4.0. Then the actual duration of the portfolio may realistically lie anywhere between 3.9 and 4.1, leading to a potential annual tracking error of ±0.16% (a two standard deviation band, based on a yield volatility of 80 bp p.a.).

The actual potential tracking error is somewhat greater, as a change in prepayment expectations affects not only portfolio duration but exposure along the yield curve. If revisions to prepayment expectations cause securities to be regarded as longer or shorter, this will tip the portfolio weighting towards the longer or shorter end of the yield curve. However, in most cases these effects are not significant compared to model duration risk.

Further examples of prepayment model valuation risk and prepayment model duration risk, and some applications, appear later in this chapter.

Just as duration does not fully capture yield curve risk and vega does not fully capture volatility risk, the risk measures described here do not fully capture prepayment model risk. Developing further measures of model risk, and determining how important they are in practice, is an important area of future research. Cohler, Feldman and Lancaster make some plausible suggestions, but point out that it would not be feasible to implement them using current technology. As with term structure modeling, we confront a trade-off between comprehensiveness and efficiency.

Zero Volatility Spread

OAS measures a bond's potential return versus Treasuries, calculated using a very large number of random interest rate paths. It is sometimes useful to compute a bond's return versus Treasuries under a single neutral scenario, where "neutral" means that interest rates follow the path predicted by the current forward curve. This is a measure of value which assumes that bond yields remain stable.

This relative return is called the bond's *zero-volatility spread* or *ZVO* versus the Treasury curve. It is computed in a completely static way, as follows:

1. Determine projected bond cashflows — including those arising from exercise of embedded options, or predicted mortgage prepayments — based on the current forward rates, and compute the yield of the bond based on these assumed cashflows.
2. Construct a portfolio of Treasury STRIPS which match these cashflows precisely, and compute the yield of this portfolio.
3. Subtract the STRIPS yield from the bond yield to obtain the ZVO.

The ZVO of a callable bond is generally significantly higher than the bond's OAS. In fact, it is clear that the ZVO equals the OAS calculated under the assumption that interest rate volatility is zero, so that future bond yields must equal their current forward yields. Hence the name.

The difference between the ZVO and the OAS is the time value of the embedded option, expressed in basis points. Recalling the classical Black-Scholes analysis, this time value may be regarded as *the theoretical cost of hedging the embedded option*. This information is useful when formulating portfolio strategy. If this time value is low, the embedded options are relatively unimportant and the investor is essentially earning a straight credit spread. If the time value is high, the investor is significantly short options, and may wish to hedge these options using futures, OTC derivatives or other physical securities.

As an example of ZVO, the Du Pont bond has an OAS of 46 bp and a ZVO of 75 bp. If an investor buys the bond and holds it unhedged, *and* bond yields evolve precisely as predicted by the forward curve, then the bond will out-perform Treasuries by 75 bp (the ZVO). Alternatively, an investor who hedges the call risk might expect outperformance of 46 bp (the OAS) under any interest rate scenario, not just the neutral scenario; the 29 bp difference is the theoretical cost of hedging over time. For example, an investor who owns the bond and hedges with bond futures to maintain a constant target duration would average 0.29% p.a. mark-to-market losses from rehedging (excluding transaction costs. This does not allow for the cost of hedge slippage due to maturity mismatches between the bond and the hedge instruments, or uncertainty in volatility.

Asset-backed securities often trade on the basis of ZVO: i.e., a fixed set of cashflows is assumed, and these are valued at a spread over the Treasury zero coupon curve equal to the quoted ZVO. Although this is harmless when used as a trading convention, it is crucial to remember that two asset-backed securities with the same average life and ZVO need not represent equivalent "value" to an inves-tor, if one is more interest rate sensitive than the other. When evaluating interest rate sensitive ABS (such as home equity loans) one should always calculate dynamic measures such as OAS as well as static measures like ZVO. One should not ignore interest rate linked prepayment risk just because of a dearth of data; it is better to make some assumption about interest rate sensitivity, no matter how tentative, than to ignore it entirely.

RELATIVE VALUE ANALYSIS FOR MORTGAGES

Examples of Risk Measures: FHLMC Passthroughs

Exhibit 6–10 illustrates all the risk measures which have been discussed in this chapter, for FHLMC 30-year TBA passthroughs, computed as at 1/31/1997 using the CMS term structure and prepayment models. In each case, as we move from discount to par to premium coupons, we observe a meaningful pattern. For example, vega rises, peaks at around the current coupon, and then falls — which is consistent with the observation that vega is highest for at-the-money options.

Risk Measures and Relative Value Analysis

There is no single, correct way to combine all the available risk measures into a comprehensive method for assessing relative value. Future MBS performance depends on homeowners' future behavior and on the market's changing views about homeowners' future behavior; neither can be fully captured by any mechanical system. Analytical tools and historical data, no matter how sophisticated, can never eliminate the subjective, psychological element.

With this *caveat*, it is interesting to see how one might go about constructing a method for relative value analysis using the risk measures discussed in this chapter. As our data set, we use the FHLMC passthroughs analyzed above, and we only look at a single day's data, 1/31/97. In practice, of course, one would look at historical data over a much longer period; however, looking at a single snapshot keeps things simple while illustrating the main ideas.

The results presented below are of course purely illustrative — in practice, each investor may combine these and other risk measures in different ways, and may make use of prepayment research from different sources to interpret them.

A little experimentation reveals the existence of two nearly linear relationships. The first is shown in Exhibit 6–11. In basis point terms, we can write:

$$\text{ZVO} \approx 320 \cdot (\text{duration risk}) - 20$$

Intuitively, ZVO measures expected return in a zero volatility environment, and this return should be higher for securities which introduce more potential tracking error into the portfolio. Note that there seems to be no *a priori* reason why the relationship should be linear. This is only a provisional assumption which is consistent with the data.

The second observed relationship, shown in Exhibit 6–12, could have been more easily predicted. Again, in basis point terms:

$$\text{ZVO} - \text{OAS} \approx 53 \cdot (-\text{convexity}) - 16$$

Intuitively, the difference between ZVO and OAS represents the theoretical cost of rehedging over time, and clearly this cost should be greater for securities with a greater negative convexity. Here it seems more likely *a priori* that the relationship should be linear.

Exhibit 6-10: OAS, ZVO and Risk Measures for FHLMC Passthroughs

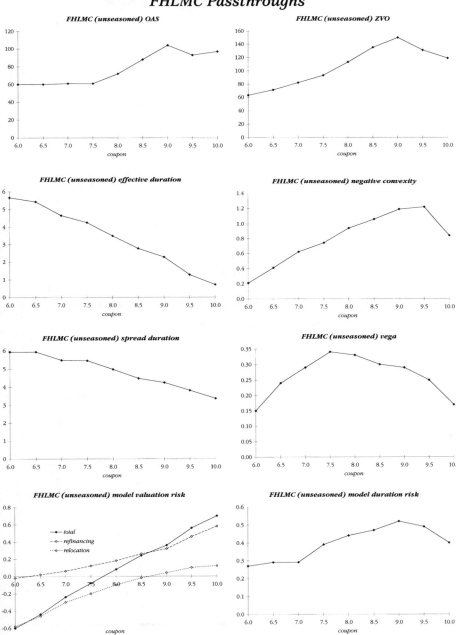

Exhibit 6–11: Static Spread to Treasuries (ZVO) versus
Prepayment Model Duration Risk

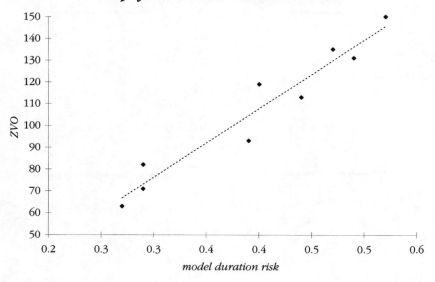

Exhibit 6–12: Theoretical Hedging Cost (ZVO minus OAS)
versus Negative Convexity

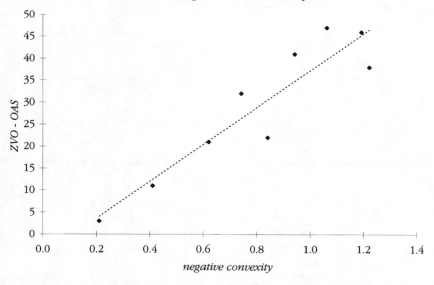

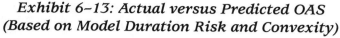

Exhibit 6–13: Actual versus Predicted OAS (Based on Model Duration Risk and Convexity)

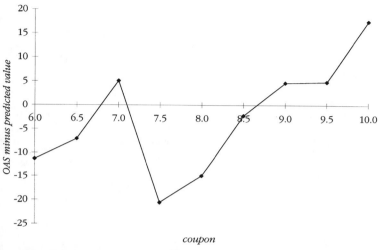

We can combine these two relationships into a simple linear formula which attempts to predict a security's OAS given only its negative convexity and model duration risk. Exhibit 6–13 compares the OAS predicted by this formula with the OAS actually observed.

This exhibit suggests that the market is making a distinction between discount coupons and premium coupons (the 7.5% coupon generic was valued at $100.18 on 1/31/1997). This distinction makes sense. With premium coupons, the primary concern is prepayment risk, and investors are worried about how well their models predict refinancings. With discount coupons, the primary concern is extension risk, and investors are worried about how well their models predict housing turnover, i.e., relocations.

Exhibit 6–14 shows that for premium (respectively, discount) coupons, there is an approximately linear relationship between the error in predicted OAS and the refinancing (respectively, relocation) component of model valuation risk.

We can use these relationships to derive a new (linear) formula for predicting OAS, which uses:

- model duration risk;
- negative convexity; and,
- model valuation risk, where we look at the refinancing component for premium mortgages, and the relocation component for discount mortgages.

Exhibit 6–15 shows the difference between the actual OAS of each passthrough and the OAS predicted by the new formula.

Exhibit 6–14: Error in Predicted OAS versus Model Valuation Risk

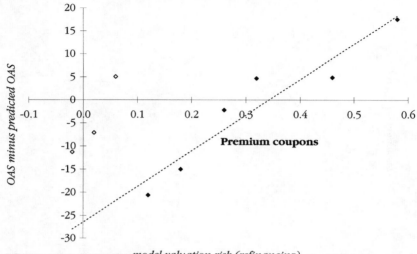

model valuation risk (refinancing)

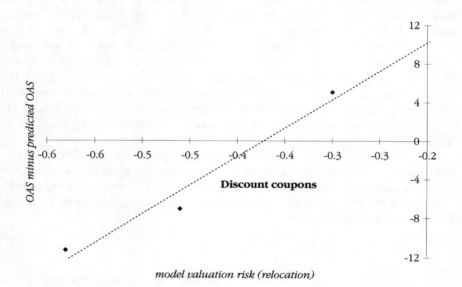

model valuation risk (relocation)

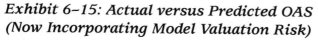

Exhibit 6–15: Actual versus Predicted OAS (Now Incorporating Model Valuation Risk)

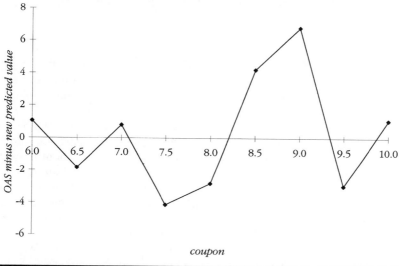

coupon

If we think of the formula as attempting to tell us the "fair OAS" of each security, then Exhibit 6–15 shows that most of the securities are close to fair value, but that:

- the 8.5% and 9% coupons both appear cheap relative to other coupons;
- the 7.5% coupon appears somewhat expensive.

Note that one would expect the 7.5% coupon to be expensive, as it was the current coupon and hence more liquid and in greater demand.

It should be emphasized again that the above analysis is just a simplified example. In practice, one would use a lengthy history and attempt to observe:

- How the fitted coefficients (which may be regarded as "prices of risk," estimated via regression) varied from day to day, and whether these fluctuations were meaningful or spurious.
- Whether cheap or expensive securities tend to revert to "fair value," and over what time scale.
- The performance of trading strategies based on the relative value analysis.

One might also attempt to incorporate more different risk factors — for example, by taking into account the greater spread risk of discount and premium coupons relative to the current coupon (this would make the 9.5% and 10% coupons look overvalued). One might also look more closely for non-linear relationships, although this approach would tend to make an analysis less stable.

The important point is that it is not enough simply to find various relationships by carrying out regressions between different variables. One must also verify that each proposed relationship is intuitively plausible. If it is, it is likely to continue to hold in the future; if not, it is probably an artifact of the specific data used, and cannot be relied upon.

Liquidity Risk and Theoretical Liquidity Premia

The previous analysis did not take relative liquidity into account. In practice, investors demand a premium for holding less liquid securities, such as high premium passthroughs, highly seasoned pools or volatile CMO tranches. The reason is that higher transactions costs translate into lower returns. Clearly, the size of the liquidity premium will depend on transaction costs and transaction frequency.

There are two possible assumptions one might make about transaction costs. On the one hand, one could (a) base the whole analysis on *observed* bid/offer spreads. In this case, one should then take into account the possibility of a "liquidity crisis" such as that which occurred in February 1994. This is the approach we will adopt. On the other hand, one could (b) carry out a theoretical analysis of the risks involved in making markets in mortgage-backed securities, and hence attempt to derive *theoretical* dealer bid/offer spreads for different securities. We will not adopt this approach, as it does not correspond to the way the market works.

Similarly, there are two possible assumptions one could make about transaction frequency. On the one hand, one could (a) assume a *passive* investment strategy, corresponding to an optimal consumption-investment problem. We will adopt this approach, for reasons explained below. On the other hand, one could (b) assume that the investor adopts an active strategy involving more frequent trading.

Assumption (b) might at first appear more realistic: most managers are not purely passive — they do take active yield curve and sector bets — and in any case the consumption-investment framework does not take fund inflows and outflows into account. However, note that the market liquidity premium will usually be determined by the most efficient market participants. For such participants:

- yield curve exposure can be modified at low cost using exchange-traded derivatives, i.e., without transacting MBS;
- to the extent that an active strategy can succeeds in timing sector exposure, it is reducing sector spread risk — that is, a successful sector strategy shifts portfolio risk from spread risk to liquidity risk and should therefore not assume an additional liquidity premium; and
- the impact of volatile investment inflows and especially redemptions can be mitigated via financing strategies, e.g., in the dollar roll market (see the next section).

Thus an efficient market participant need only trade MBS as often as suggested by an optimal portfolio consumption-investment approach, and we are justified in assuming a passive strategy for our analysis.

Exhibit 6-16: Theoretical Liquidity Premia for Various CMO Tranche Types

	Assumed Bid/Offer Spread	Liquidity Premium
Passthrough	1/16	2 bp
PAC/VADM	1/8	3 bp
TAC/PAC II	1/4	4.5 bp
SEQ	1/4	4.5 bp
FL	1/8	3 bp
Z	1/4	4.5 bp
IO/INV	1	11 bp
PO	1	11 bp
ARM	1/8	3 bp

Although definitive results on theoretical liquidity premia are still missing, there are some suggestive results for the case where transaction costs are proportional to the size of the transaction. Constantinides found that for transaction costs above 0.5% a return premium of approximately 0.14 times the transaction cost was required (this was an upper bound), while Shreve showed that if g is the transaction cost then provided g is small, the theoretical liquidity premium is $O(g^{2/3})$.

Using these results as a guide, Exhibit 6-16 shows theoretical liquidity premia for generic securities of various classes, based on assumed bid/offer spreads. These premia should form part of the OAS demanded by an investor.

Note that:

1. For securities less liquid than generic passthroughs or CMOs — e.g., passthroughs backed by non-standard agency or whole loan collateral, or unusually risky CMO tranches — bid/offer spreads, and the theoretical liquidity premium, will be correspondingly higher. Thus an assessment of the likely bid/offer spread on an unusual security must be carried out as part of relative value analysis.

2. It can be argued that Exhibit 6-16 probably understates "fair" liquidity premia, for the following reason. The analysis concludes that the fair liquidity premium does not rise in proportion to the bid/offer spread, because less liquid securities will be traded less often. However, for benchmarked investors, this less frequent trading will result in some index tracking error, and they will therefore require a small additional premium.

It remains to assess the impact of a "liquidity crisis," i.e., a situation where liquidity suddenly vanishes. This has occurred for relatively short periods when interest rates and prepayments have been volatile, making it extremely difficult for dealers to make markets without assuming unacceptable risk. Investors require an *additional* liquidity premium as compensation for the risk that this may happen.

In these crisis situations, dealers' reluctance to make markets will depend on:

• the premium/discount on the security;
• the negative convexity of the security;
• perceived volatility risk; and,
• perceived model valuation risk.

All these factors will contribute to determining the size of the additional liquidity premium on a specific security. Clearly, this will vary from bond to bond. However, the fact that a severe "liquidity crisis" occurs very infrequently — perhaps a few times a decade — means that this additional premium will be both small and difficult to determine precisely.

(Note that in an efficient market, there would be no liquidity crises, since the potential impact of prepayment model risk or model shock would have been anticipated and would be reflected in bid/offer spreads which were wider from the start. However, as noted in Chapter 5, bid/offer spreads in the US mortgage-backed securities market do not fully reflect model risk: they are "too tight," particularly for unseasoned passthroughs, thus making liquidity crises not only possible but inevitable when prepayment shocks occur. This "liquidity illusion" may be regarded as a form of cognitive dissonance, and it might be possible to quantify its potential economic impact: cf. the work of Akerlof and Dickens. However, this is a topic for future research.)

Finally there is an additional, more remote, form of liquidity risk: the risk that for certain classes of risky MBS, future regulatory changes will result in a contraction of the investor base. This would apply mainly to high premium passthroughs and certain medium risk CMO tranches. However, the additional return demanded for this risk is likely to be small.

What is the Purpose of Prepayment Research?

As we have seen, relative value analysis means analyzing the trade-off between value and risk. "Value" can be assessed using measures like OAS, percentage price premium or ZVO; "risk" can be assessed using the range of quantitative risk measures discussed above, together with research which suggests how those risk measures should be scaled.

Broker/dealers and many investors have devoted enormous resources to collecting and analyzing prepayment data in an effort to understand homeowners' prepayment behavior. *Relative value analysis, not prepayment forecasting, is the major purpose of detailed prepayment research.* That is, the true importance of detailed prepayment research — beyond that required to construct and maintain a prepayment model — is that:

• it gives investors insight into the different factors influencing prepayments;
• it helps them to quantify prepayment uncertainty and model risk in terms of a breakdown into factors;

- it allows them to test the plausibility of any relationships identified via an empirical analysis of market data;
- it enables them to relate prepayment risks to their own views on the domestic economy as a whole; and
- it allows them to make a more detailed assessment of relative value opportunities identified by a quantitative model.

For example, suppose an investor's quantitative relative value model suggests that 9.5% mortgages originated in 1994 are cheap. Why might this be so? One explanation is that the housing market declined from 1994 to 1996, leaving those borrowers unable to refinance as rates fell; they may now be eager to refinance as soon as an upturn in house prices makes this possible. Hence it is difficult to estimate the likelihood of future refinancings at an assumed interest rate level, since this depends on the state of the housing market. This also suggests that these mortgages may be subject to unusually high model valuation risk. Detailed prepayment research could be used to investigate this hypothesis.

Thus, it does not make sense to attempt to force all the results of one's prepayment research into the particular model one is using to analyze securities. By providing a means to assess relative value, detailed prepayment research does its most important job "outside" any prepayment model. This also means that investors cannot afford to ignore prepayment research and rely blindly on any model; they need to understand prepayment behavior at a detailed level in order to formulate meaningful MBS investment strategies.

APPENDIX: DEFAULT RISK AND DEFAULT SPREADS

Intuitively, the spread required on a bond to compensate investors for default risk is determined by the expected default loss from the bond; this assumes that investors can assess expected default risk (e.g., based on historical default and recovery rates), and that they can eliminate catastrophic default risk via diversification — either by holding diversified portfolios of risky bonds or by employing credit derivatives to diversify exposure. Under these assumptions, we present a simple static model which allows us to calculate what the *theoretical default spread* should be.

Let p_t be the probability that a bond will default in year t, conditional on its survival up to that year (i.e., p_t is the marginal default probability in year t), and let r be the expected recovery rate from the bond if it defaults. We assume that the marginal default probability may possibly change over time, but that the expected recovery rate remains constant. For example, rating agency statistics suggest that, broadly speaking:

- for Baa-rated bonds, $p_1 \approx 0.2\%$, p_t approaches 1%, and $r > 50\%$;
- for B-rated bonds, $p_1 \approx 15\%$, p_t approaches 2%–4%, and $r \approx 40\%$.

The probability that the bond survives to the beginning of year t is clearly

$$s_t = \prod_{\tau = 1}^{t-1} (1 - p_\tau)$$

and the (unconditional) probability that the bond will default in year t is $P_t = p_t s_t$. Note that if the bond matures in T years, there are $T+1$ possible scenarios: either it defaults in year 1, year 2, ... or year T, or it survives to maturity — this final scenario having probability

$$Q = s_{T+1} = 1 - \sum_{\tau = 1}^{T} P_\tau$$

Using the assumed recovery rate, it is straightforward to compute the bond cashflows under each of these scenarios.

For any given yield y, we can now compute the net present value of the bond cashflows under each of the $T+1$ scenarios: call these NPV_1, NPV_2, ..., NPV_T, NPV_{T+1}, where is the net present value of the bond's default-free cashflows. Let $P(y)$ be the probability-weighted average over all scenarios:

$$P(y) = \left(\sum_{t=1}^{T} P_y \cdot NPV_t \right) + Q \cdot NPV_{T+1}$$

Then $P(y)$ is the expected value of the NPV of the bond's cashflows; thus, the expected yield earned by purchasing the bond at price $P(y)$ and holding it to maturity is y. If we fix a desired yield y, say the constant maturity Treasury yield for the same maturity, then we can determine the coupon rate c for which $P(y) = \$100$. Because of the possibility of default, c will be greater than y; the *theoretical default spread* is defined to be $c - y$, expressed in basis points. In particular, if the probability of default is zero, then obviously $c = y$ and the theoretical default spread is zero.

Exhibit 6–17 shows that for a given maturity and recovery rate, if we assume a constant default probability, then the theoretical default spread is almost exactly proportional to the default probability. In general, as noted above, the expected default probability will not be constant over time. Exhibit 6–18 shows the theoretical default spreads for Baa rated bond of various maturities: note that, since the marginal default probability rises from 0.2% in the short term to 1% in the long term, longer bonds have higher annual default risk and thus a higher theoretical default spread. However, the required spread levels off for maturities of over 25 years, since by then the expected default probability has settled at 1%.

For junk bonds, we get the opposite result: since the marginal probability of default falls as we move into the future, the theoretical default spread on a long bond is lower than that on a short bond. This is because if the long bond survives the first few years, it will then be a less risky bond, but the investor will continue to earn the same spread.

Exhibit 6–17: Theoretical Default Spread on a 30-Year Bond (50% Recovery Rate)

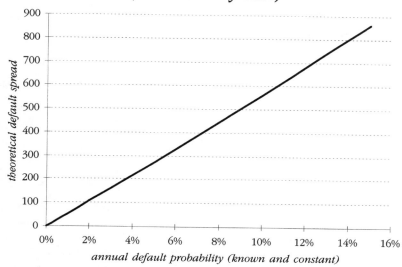

annual default probability (known and constant)

Exhibit 6–18: Theoretical Default Spread on a Baa Rated Bond, versus Maturity

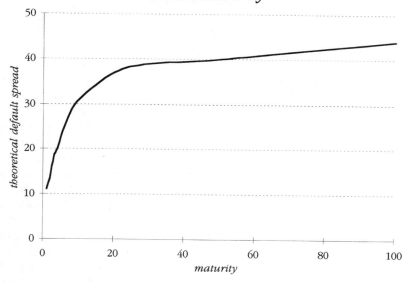

maturity

Exhibit 6–19: Theoretical Default Spread on a B Rated Bond, Uncertain Default Probability

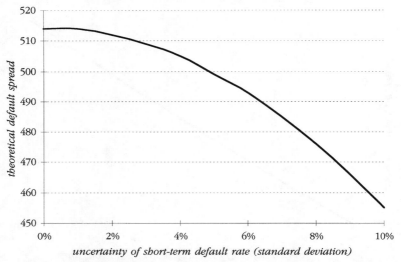

So far our calculations have assumed that the default probability is known. In fact, future default probabilities are themselves uncertain — and rating agency studies suggest that riskier bonds also have more uncertain default probabilities. For example, an investor might expect a 30-year Baa-rated bond to have a default probability somewhere between 0.5% and 1.5%, but might expect a 5-year B-rated bond to have a default probability of anywhere from 5% to 15%. What impact does uncertainty about default probabilities have?

We can estimate this by assuming some probability distribution for the default probability itself, and repeating the analysis using the range of possible default probabilities rather than a single, known default probability. One might expect to get the same theoretical default spreads. In fact, it turns out that there is a "convexity"-like effect: the greater the range of uncertainty about the future default probability, the lower the theoretical default spread. This effect is negligible for investment grade bonds, but very significant for junk bonds: it is illustrated in Exhibit 6–19.

At first, this phenomenon seems rather unintuitive. The explanation is that assuming lower default probabilities generates scenarios with higher cash-flows, and the scenarios generated by these low default probability assumptions have a correspondingly higher weight. This can be viewed as a convexity-like effect as follows. Recall that the convexity results of Chapter 4 follow from the fact that, when computing yields by taking an average across different interest rate scenarios, low interest rate scenarios have a higher weight. In the present context, we can think of the "default-adjusted interest rate" being earned under a given default assumption as being, broadly speaking, the coupon rate minus the loss rate (where the loss rate is the annual default probability times the recovery rate). Thus a low default probability assumption corresponds to a lower default-adjusted interest rate, and for similar reasons has a higher weight in determining the theoretical default spread than a high default probability assumption. Greater uncertainty about the default probability means that more extreme low and high default probability assumptions are being used, and the low assumptions tend to dominate the calculation, dragging down the theoretical default spread.

Now, what happens if we assume that there is some correlation between default probabilities and outright yields — that default is more likely in a lower yield (i.e., recessionary) scenario? The result depends on whether the default probability is assumed to rise or fall over time: see Exhibit 6–20. If the default probability falls as we move into the future — as it does for a junk bond — then the theoretical default spread is positively correlated with the yield level. If the default probability rises as we move into the future — as it does for an investment grade bond, or as it might for an infrastructure project (like a power station or telecommunications system) which is initially viable but may grow obsolescent — then the theoretical default spread is negatively correlated with the yield level.

There is thus a theoretical relationship between spread risk and interest rate risk. However, the theoretical impact on investment grade bonds is in fact negligible, so this result unfortunately does not explain the observations of Duffee, cited earlier, about the relationship between corporate spreads and Treasury yield levels.

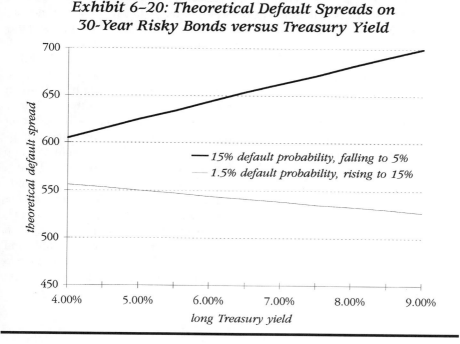

Exhibit 6–20: Theoretical Default Spreads on 30-Year Risky Bonds versus Treasury Yield

—— 15% default probability, falling to 5%
—— 1.5% default probability, rising to 15%

theoretical default spread

long Treasury yield

Exhibit 6–21: Duration of 30-Year Bond Subject to Default Risk (50% Recovery)

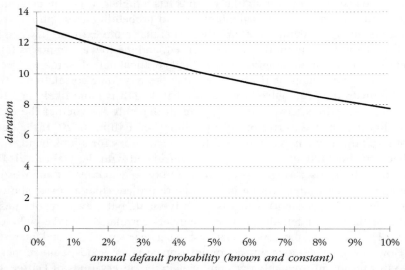

annual default probability (known and constant)

There is another relationship between default risk and interest rate risk. If two bonds have the same maturity but one has a higher probability of default, that bond is intuitively "shorter" since it is more likely to experience premature cashflows (in the event of default). Exhibit 6–21 shows that the theoretical duration of a bond does indeed fall as its assumed default probability rises.

Thus, an investor who owns bonds subject to default risk should, in theory, take default risk into account when computing portfolio duration. Again, the result is mainly relevant to junk bonds rather than investment grade bonds, which have annual default probabilities of 1% or less. However, note that the result may be relevant to insured bonds, if there is a possibility that default will trigger an immediate repayment of principal from the bond insurer rather than an assumption of the obligation to make interest and principal payments in the future.

The static model used to derive all of these results is simple and intuitive, and can easily be implemented on a spreadsheet; it is also easy to determine plausible parameters for the model using rating agency statistics. Although the dynamic models used to price credit derivatives are usually far more complex, most of the basic concepts are the same. This demonstrates how useful it is, when studying some market phenomenon, to begin with a model which is simple and tractable; even if it appears oversimplified, such a model can generally be used to identify and analyze the key issues, and often yields results which are surprisingly subtle.

Selected References

Akerlof, G. and Dickens, W., "The Economic Consequences of Cognitive Dissonance," *American Economic Review*, June 1982.

Cohler, G., Feldman, M. and Lancaster, B., "Price of Risk Constant (PORC): Going Beyond OAS," *J. Fixed Income*, March 1997.

Corporate Bond Defaults and Default Rates, Moody's Investor Services, updated annually.

Duffee, G., "Treasury Yields and Corporate Bond Yield Spreads: An Empirical Analysis," *Federal Reserve Board*, May 1996.

Duffee, G., "Estimating the Price of Default Risk," *Federal Reserve Board*, July 1996.

Geske, T. and Klinkhammer, G., "Advanced Risk Measures for Fixed Income Securities," in Fabozzi, F. (ed.), *Advances in Fixed Income Valuation, Modeling and Risk Management*, Frank J. Fabozzi Associates, New Hope, 1997.

Kopprasch, R., "Option-Adjusted Spread Analysis: Going Down the Wrong Path?" *Financial Analysts Journal*, May-June 1994.

Phoa, W., *Credit Ratings and Yield Spreads: The Theoretical Pricing of Default Risk*, Deutsche Morgan Grenfell (Sydney) research report, May 1994.

Shreve, S., "Liquidity Premium for Capital Asset Pricing with Transaction Costs," in Davis, M., Duffie, D., Fleming, W., Shreve, S. (eds.), *Mathematical Finance*, Springer, Heidelberg, 1995.

Wilmott, P., Dewynne, J. and Howison, S., *Option Pricing: Mathematical Models and Computation*, Oxford Financial Press, Oxford, 1993.

Chapter 7

Risk Measurement and Performance Attribution

CLASSIFYING RISK MEASUREMENT TOOLS

Most of this book has been about risk in the bond markets. From an investor's point of view, the central task of modeling is risk management. Security valuation is critical, but can be provided by independent pricing services. The most important application of valuation models is for computing durations and other risk measures, and for carrying out stress testing and other simulations. Note that risk measures are not just useful for risk measurement *per se*; they are also critical in the security selection process, since, as illustrated in Chapter 6, this process involves an assessment of *risk-adjusted* relative value.

A major problem that investors face is the proliferation of risk measurement tools. Increasing sophistication and competition between market participants has made it essential to continually develop new tools and enhance existing ones. But the sheer number of tools available makes it difficult to develop a risk management policy which is coherent as well as comprehensive.

This section attempts to clarify matters by proposing a simple-minded but useful classification of risk measures. This is based on two independent distinctions: between "top-level" and "detailed" measures, and between "objective" and "subjective" measures.

A *top-level* risk measure is concerned primarily with risk at the level of the firm or division. The intention here is to focus on the potential consequences (rather than the causes) of risk, and to express the potential impact of a set of complex, interacting risks in terms of a few simple numbers. The goal of top-level risk measures is to ensure the overall financial soundness of the firm, and to aggregate risks across the firm, determining when they offset or exacerbate each other. Value-at-risk is a prime example of a top-level risk measure.

By contrast, a *detailed* risk measure is used to monitor risk at a much lower level, e.g., an individual portfolio. It focuses on a specific cause of risk; thus, the idea is to break down risk into its detailed components, rather than to aggregate it. A detailed risk measures is primarily a portfolio management tool rather than a tool for higher level risk control, and it is usually only the qualitative conclusions that feed through to higher levels of management. Detailed risk measures include duration, slope duration, spread duration and vega.

Exhibit 7–1: Classification of Fixed Income Risk Measurement Tools

	Top-Level	Detailed
Objective	return confidence levels (VaR)	effective duration & convexity
	return confidence levels vs. index	yield curve slope risk
		key rate durations
		spread duration
		vega (volatility risk)
		prepayment model risk
	FFIEC	
	FLUX	performance attribution
	A. M. Best	compliance checking
Subjective	probability weighted returns	interest rate simulations
	scenario solvency testing	spread simulations
		volatility simulations
	Regulation 126	vector analysis (MBS)

Moving to the second distinction, an *objective* risk measure is one based on objective, market-determined probability distributions for market variables. For example, value-at-risk is an objective measure. Measures such as duration can also be viewed as objective risk measures, since duration measures portfolio exposure to an objectively identifiable risk: parallel risk (see Chapter 1). From an investor's point of view, tests imposed by regulatory bodies may also be viewed as objective risk measures.

By contrast, a *subjective* risk measure is based on an investor's informed, subjective judgment about which scenarios are relevant and what their probabilities are. Subjective risk measurement tools include scenario analysis (using a "likely" scenario), stress testing (using "worst case" scenarios) and the calculation of expected returns across a range of probability-weighted scenarios. These can all be extremely flexible risk management tools, but their usefulness depends on the quality of the investor's judgment.

To illustrate these distinctions, Exhibit 7–1 lists a selection of risk measurement tools (available in the CMS BondEdge product), showing how they may be classified as objective or subjective measures, and top-level or detailed measures.

It is useful to keep these distinctions in mind when developing a portfolio risk management policy. To give an oversimplified example, one could specify that:

- daily portfolio risk profiling focuses on detailed, objective measures;
- security selection (relative value) uses detailed, subjective measures;
- portfolio strategy (duration/sector bets) uses top-level, subjective measures;
- "upward" risk reporting uses top-level, objective measures.

Risk measurement and performance attribution are intimately linked. The same detailed analysis of market risks, and their interaction, that leads to the development of detailed risk measures also provides the foundation for developing performance attribution frameworks.

The role of performance attribution in the risk management process should not be forgotten. A reliable performance attribution system provides a good way of monitoring a risk management policy, because it allows the manager to compare, for a given period, the prospective assessment of various portfolio risks carried out at the start of the period with a retrospective analysis of their actual impact. Any serious discrepancy must point to a flaw in the risk control process. Thus, such systems are useful for more than just determining managers' compensation; they can add considerable value to risk assessment, and to improving risk management.

There are two common misconceptions about performance attribution. The first is that performance attribution means applying a battery of statistical tests to long time series of attribution results. The second is that there must be a single, "right" performance attribution framework; or, which is a weaker statement, that one must be able to decide whether one framework is better than another. The rest of this chapter consists of two independent essays which discuss these misconceptions in somewhat more detail.

INTERPRETING THE RESULTS OF PERFORMANCE ATTRIBUTION

"As a rough rule of thumb, you probably need at least twenty-five years of fund performance to distinguish at the 95% significance level whether a manager has above-average competence." [Richard Brealey]

A performance attribution system breaks down portfolio return into a set of underlying components. For example, the PART system in BondEdge breaks total return down into the following broad categories: income return, treasury curve effects, sector/quality spread changes and bond selection effects. (This is only an outline of the system; in fact, PART provides a much more detailed analysis within each of these categories, takes account of factors such as transaction costs and strategic effects — i.e., active versus passive returns — and provides comparisons with a specified performance benchmark.)

Performance attribution figures are often used to evaluate managers' performance, by determining whether a manager's yield curve, sector/quality or selection bets have paid off. A system which reports both portfolio-level and security-level return attributions will give an objective answer to this question.

For example, suppose a manager believes that the finance sector will outperform, and is particularly bullish on Chase Manhattan spreads; on this basis, she switches out of some existing Treasury holdings into the non-callable 6.5% 8/2005 issue. If performance attribution figures subsequently show a positive sector/quality effect and a positive selection effect for the portfolio relative to the index — and a security-level breakdown reveals that this was due to the purchase of the Chase security — then this establishes that the bet paid off.

The next question is: was the result due to the manager's skill, or merely to luck? There are two fundamentally different ways to tackle this question: one is *statistical* and one is based on *informed judgment*. For the reasons described below, CMS recommends the approach based on informed judgment.

The statistical method involves running rigorous statistical tests on performance attribution histories. This method has many advocates in the academic literature, particularly among statisticians. The advantage of the statistical method is that it is completely mechanical and objective: for example, standard methods can be used to produce Bayesian estimates showing the expected future return distribution (relative to the index) based on past performance figures.

The statistical method suffers from two major disadvantages. The first is that it ignores the fact that management styles change over time: they may change as a fund gets larger, as market conditions change, or simply as the manager becomes more experienced. A change in style will partly or totally invalidate the performance history. Furthermore, it is not apparent from the performance history alone whether there has indeed been a change in style.

The second disadvantage is that a very long history is required to obtain statistically significant results. For example, assuming that both index and manager returns were normally distributed with the same constant variance, and the manager appeared to be outperforming by about 0.5% per annum, around 6–7 years of data would be required before one could be 95% confident in making this assertion.

In practice, the situation is even worse than this analysis suggests. It is not safe to assume that return variances are constant; it is not safe to assume that index and manager returns have the same variance; and it is not even safe to assume that returns will be normally distributed. For example, a manager who is typically overweight mortgages or callable bonds will tend to have negatively skewed returns, while a manager who makes use of portfolio insurance or stop-loss strategies may have positively skewed returns. All these considerations mean that much more complicated statistical tests must be used, which in turn require much longer histories.

The difficulty is compounded when one is trying to evaluate, not simply relative returns, but risk-adjusted returns. Prudent decision-making is based on an assessment of risk/return; but to determine whether a particular management style has been a good risk/return trade-off, one needs to estimate, not just the return difference, but its whole distribution. This requires an unrealistically long performance history.

There is no way to evade this problem. In fact, apparently high levels of outperformance can be achieved with surprisingly low levels of forecasting ability: outperformance requires only a slight "edge," which can be economically significant even though it is statistically insignificant (Hodges cites some relevant studies here). Thus, a dogmatic statistical evaluation would tend to undervalue the performance of most managers — and market efficiency suggests that the few who could pass the statistical tests would already have left to set up their own hedge funds.

The other way to distinguish between skill and luck is to apply the informed judgment method. Thus, in the above example, one would ask why the Chase Manhattan bonds outperformed. If the manager justified her view in a strategy paper setting out an analysis of the finance sector and Chase in particular, and if the conclusions of that paper were borne out by subsequent news and events, one would conclude that the outperformance was due to skill. On the other hand, if Chase spreads had tightened due to an unanticipated takeover by a AAA rated bank, most of the outperformance was probably due to luck.

The disadvantage of the informed judgment method is that, unlike the statistical method, it has a large subjective component: it relies heavily on market knowledge and experience. It is also more time-consuming than merely running statistical tests.

The advantage of the informed judgment method is that it makes use of *all* relevant information — both quantitative and qualitative — rather than relying solely on total return time series. In particular, performance attribution figures are simply one input into the process. Thus, even a single quarter of performance attribution statistics can provide useful information, *if it is correctly interpreted*. A second advantage of the informed judgment method is that it can take account of changes in investment style.

Like successful trading, performance evaluation cannot be reduced to a mechanical process. Judgment is always critical. Indeed, an important part of the value added by an organized investment operation is the ability to monitor the performance of its investment managers in a meaningful way, and to take appropriate action. This process must combine a rigorous quantitative analysis of historical return data with a qualitative analysis of trading strategies and individual trading decisions.

"The implication of this is not that the plan sponsor should go on vacation for twenty-five years but that he should not focus exclusively on achieved returns while ignoring other information about a manager's competence and diligence." [Richard Brealey]

RELATING DIFFERENT FRAMEWORKS FOR PERFORMANCE ATTRIBUTION

By the close of trading on 1/3/97, the GNMA 7.5% coupon 30-year TBA had rallied 7/32 from the previous day's close. However, the 10-year Treasury note had only rallied 3/32; in fact, there was a uniform rally of about 2 bp across the Treasury curve. On the face of it, the shift in Treasury yields does not appear to explain the change in the price of the GNMA security. A portfolio manager interested in performance attribution or risk management would like an explanation for this price behavior, which was observed across all liquid agency passthroughs. From this point of view, some possible explanations include:

1. Option-adjusted spreads tightened. This corresponds to a decrease in the risk premium demanded by investors for the risks involved in holding the securities which cannot be efficiently hedged.
2. Implied volatilities fell. This would cause the theoretical value of the prepayment option against the investor to fall.
3. Prepayment expectations changed. The 7.5% GNMA is a discount security. Thus, when investors revise their prepayment speed forecasts upwards, the price of the security should rise.

Of course, a trader might seek a different kind of explanation, at a greater level of detail: for example, a change in OAS might be due to a general shift in demand towards non-Treasury securities, or increased demand for mortgage-backed securities generally, or investor optimism that prepayments would be stable.

Each explanation can be tested for plausibility. On 1/3/97, implied volatilities in the cap/floor market generally fell for high strikes at all tenors (although it generally rose for low strikes); although the link with MBS "implied volatilities" is not direct, this market behavior is consistent with explanation 2. Explanation 3 seems implausible: as the prices of both premium and discount securities rose, we would have to assume that investors revised their (implicit) prepayment forecasts in a complex way, expecting low rate mortgages to prepay more quickly but high rate mortgages to prepay more slowly; this would be an unusually sophisticated way for investors to revise their expectations. Finally, explanation 1 seems consistent: the presumed change in OAS varies quite smoothly between different coupons, from around 3–6 bp, except for the 9.5% GNMA where the required change in OAS would have been 12 bp. Thus, in this example, we might favor explanation 1 — or a combination of explanations 1 and 2.

However, it is important to note that there is usually no single "correct" explanation. This is not simply because the different explanations are not mutually exclusive, but because of an essential arbitrariness in their definitions. To elaborate:

• As explained in Chapter 6, there are different ways of computing OAS. Firstly, any OAS computation for an MBS must use some prepayment model. Secondly, the set of stochastic factors used to generate random scenarios may vary. For example, some OAS computations allow random fluctuations in implied volatility as well as in interest rates, so that the resulting OAS is based on the implicit assumption that volatility risk can be hedged efficiently.
• Implied volatilities can only be calculated from observed option prices using a term structure model, and results computed using different mod-

els may be difficult to compare. Furthermore, illiquidity and inefficiency in OTC option markets means that selecting the "relevant" implieds to focus on is a matter of individual judgment. Finally, the link between the "volatilities" needed to value 30-year passthroughs and the implied volatilities derived from caps/floors/swaptions with much shorter tenors can be problematic.

- The prepayment models used by market participants are not observable and may, in any case, vary widely. One can attempt to measure "implied" prepayment speed forecasts from observed MBS prices by fitting implied parameters to a predetermined model (see Chapter 5) — by analogy to the computation of implied volatilities — but as we noted, this often results in unrealistic prepayment speeds. The derived forecasts are also highly dependent on the choice of model and OAS assumptions. On the other hand, it is not possible to derive the underlying structure of a prepayment model from the price data alone, as the range of possibilities is too vast.

It is also critical to note that the definitions of OAS, implied volatility and "implied" prepayment expectations are all strongly coupled — no matter how these terms are defined. There is no strict logical priority. The difficulty stems from the fact that none of these terms correspond to directly observable quantities, like prices; rather, they arise in the course of attempts to understand changes in security prices. This explains why there can be a wide variation between different risk management systems or different performance attribution systems, in the key concepts they rely on and, especially, the precise way those concepts are defined and related.

The normal procedure is to adopt a specific framework — a set of precise definitions and relationships — and to attempt to defend it. However, it is useful to step back from the fray and make some methodological observations about what we are really trying to do when setting up a framework for risk management or performance attribution, and how this differs from the task of providing analytical support for trading.

Lévi-Strauss points out that in attempting to make sense of the world, science has two ways of proceeding. A *reductionist* approach tries to reduce complex phenomena to simpler ones on a lower level; a *structuralist* approach does not postulate a lower level, but tries to characterize the relationships between phenomena, by finding invariants and constructing a system around these invariants. Thus physics and physical chemistry are reductionist, while biology and linguistics tend to be structuralist.

The distinction between these two approaches is not always as clear as it is in these examples. In particular, modern fixed income investing is based on achieving a scientific understanding of bond market behavior; but here, certain lines of research can have both reductionist and structuralist interpretations.

As a simple example, consider pure interest rate risk. A common approach to understanding changes in Treasury bond prices is to carry out a principal component analysis of historical changes in Treasury yields, as described in Chapter 1. We recall that in most countries, the first two principal components turn out to be a nearly parallel shift in yields across the Treasury curve, and a change in yield curve slope; from there on, results vary.

A reductionist approach uses this evidence to draw conclusions about the underlying determinants of bond yields. For example, it may postulate that bond yields are determined by investor expectations regarding future interest rates, and that expectations are determined by economic fundamentals, so that a parallel shift results from changing expectations about future inflation or real growth rates, while a slope shift is caused by a reassessment of the link between current monetary policy and long-term inflation or growth. This approach is useful to traders who wish to relate their own economic views to what they observe in the markets.

A structuralist approach, by contrast, would treat the principal component analysis as identifying basic risk factors — e.g., parallel risk and slope risk — and would proceed, not by trying to find an economic explanation for these risk factors, but by using them as a basis for a framework which measures yield curve risk. That is, the analysis shows how to define "parallel duration" and "slope duration" measures (and so on) which, taken together, constitute a notion of the "yield curve risk profile" of a single bond or a portfolio of bonds.

Clearly these approaches are not mutually exclusive. The question is: when is it appropriate to look at things from a reductionist point of view, and when is it appropriate to adopt a structuralist viewpoint? It is worth pointing out that constructing a fully satisfactory reductionist account of bond market behavior, even if this were possible, would be a daunting task. On the one hand, it would require a detailed account of how market participants form economic expectations, as well as the role of "non-fundamental" supply/demand factors. On the other hand, explaining the dynamics of interest rates requires, strictly speaking, a model of trading activity at the level of individual agents. Although, e.g., diffusion models for stock prices can be explained in these terms (see, especially, the work of Föllmer and Schweizer) this field of research is still at a very early stage of development.

Also, insisting on a reductionist viewpoint can involve tackling some uncomfortable conceptual issues. For example, most practical approaches to modeling the dynamics of the term structure take the "short rate" to be a state variable. But, as pointed out in Chapter 1, the short rate cannot be identified with any actual money market yield, as these are too idiosyncratic; instead, it must be regarded as a limit of yields in some sense. A reductionist should be obliged to explain exactly what this means (a subtle and interesting question), while a structuralist might be content with the fact that this device helps us construct a system which is self-consistent and consistent with reality, without seeking a lower level explanation.

Bond trading — in particular, active fixed income management and security selection — requires a *dynamic*, *reductionist* approach while performance attribution and risk management policy require a *static*, *structuralist* approach.

On the one hand, trading requires maximum responsiveness to changes in the market or to new insights. Concepts must be continually tested and broken down, and relationships questioned and explained, and new insights integrated as quickly as possible. The ideal analytical trading support system is one that evolves literally from day to day, as traders develop and test new frameworks. The introduction of new security classes often stimulates additional refinements. For example, the issuance of inflation-indexed bonds can trigger the transformation:

Old   expected inflation + interest rate risk premium
+ assumed long term real yield
→ theoretical long bond yield

New   expected growth + expected current account deficit effect
+ real yield risk premium
→ theoretical long real yield
expected inflation + inflation risk premium
+ theoretical long real yield − adjustment for liquidity
→ theoretical long nominal yield

On the other hand, performance attribution obviously requires a framework which is stable across time: using the same concepts with the same definition and the same interrelationships; otherwise, it is meaningless to speak of a performance history. And it is not necessary to keep breaking concepts down into lower level components — e.g., to explicitly model the various determinants of OAS. It may even be counterproductive — e.g., markets may price risk differently at different times, leading to inconsistent explanations of OAS. Performance attribution should not explain performance in terms of the most detailed possible concepts, as these concepts and their relationships will change over time. To be useful as a management tool, performance attribution needs to be based on a consistent and stable framework — which, of course, also has to have a strong link to market practice and empirically observed reality.

Most of the same comments apply to risk management policy. A risk management system is also a management tool. It is useless if it is constantly in flux, and relies essentially on unobservable quantities which are continually being redefined or decomposed, and which may be hard to grasp intuitively because they are not directly derived from market practice. Nobody uses risk management systems like this to design compliance policies or to set trading limits.

Thus the concept of OAS is admissible in performance attribution, and it makes sense for a compliance policy to set portfolio limits on spread risk. This is because "OAS" is observed market terminology — e.g., the assertion that "corporate spreads tightened" is rarely a controversial or problematic statement. In fact, for non-option-embedded securities, OAS is directly observable; while for option-embedded bonds, it can be defined entirely rigorously *in the context of a specific model*.

The concept of prepayment model risk premium is not admissible in risk management *policy*, since it is not a standard market concept and, more importantly, there is no way to quantify it completely; this would involve considering every possible prepayment model, which is impossible. This does not mean that prepayment model risk is unimportant or cannot be measured: model risk is critical, and important components of it can be measured by fixing a model and examining the effect of changing the model parameters; indeed, this is a powerful way for *traders* to assess risk and risk-adjusted relative value. However, it is not appropriate to try to set formal portfolio limits for "model risk", because no way of quantifying it can be comprehensive: it is an essentially reductionist concept, which cannot be frozen into a single definition; descending to a lower (more detailed) level of prepayment analysis always reveals additional sources of model risk. Similarly, "change in model risk premium" should not be a component of a performance attribution system.

Note that static, structuralist approaches to modeling markets are not necessarily less valid or less reliable than dynamic, reductionist approaches. The point is simply that their purpose is different. A concern about the structuralist approach is that it seems to make meaningful comparisons impossible. If performance attribution frameworks are simply regarded as autonomous, internally consistent systems whose validity does not depend on some "lower level" of financial reality, how can we compare them?

In fact, there are ways to relate different systems without appealing to any common lower level description, by identifying parallel features of different systems: i.e., components and their relationships. To take the simplest possible example, we might have the following parallel relationships in two different performance attribution frameworks:

Framework A	OAS ↓	↔	(implied vol. constant)
Framework B	(OAS constant)	↔	implied vol. ↓

It is then possible to identify transformed or missing features in the different frameworks. Thus one can recognize the arbitrariness in any framework without sacrificing the ability to make meaningful comparisons.

Interestingly enough, similar (but much more complex) methods have been developed to compare the mythological beliefs about nature and society which are held by, for example, different South American native peoples. Once deciphered, these turn out to be detailed, systematic, structured bodies of practical knowledge derived from empirical experience. A risk management policy — or performance attribution system — may seem quite different from a corpus of native American myths; but both are ways of coping with a chaotic and dangerous outside world.

Selected References

Brealey, R., "Portfolio Theory versus Portfolio Practice," *J. Portfolio Management*, Summer 1990.

Fabozzi, F. and Fong, G., *Advanced Fixed Income Portfolio Management: The State of the Art*, Probus, Chicago, 1994; see chapter 12.

Föllmer, H., "Stock Price Fluctuation as a Diffusion in a Random Environment," in Howison, S., Kelly, F. and Wilmott, P., *Mathematical Models in Finance*, Chapman & Hall, London, 1995.

Hodges, S., "Dynamic Asset Allocation: Insights from Theory," in Howison, S., Kelly, F. and Wilmott, P. (eds.), *Mathematical Models in Finance*, Chapman & Hall, London, 1995.

Kahn, R., "Bond Performance Analysis: A Multi-factor Approach," *J. Portfolio Management*, Fall 1991.

Lehman Family of Indices, Lehman Brothers Fixed Income Research, July 1996.

Lévi-Strauss, C., *Structural Anthropology* (tr. Jacobson, C. and Schoepf, B.), Harmondsworth, 1963.

Lévi-Strauss, C., *Myth and Meaning*, University of Toronto Press, 1978.

INDEX